SOCIETY FOR NEW TESTAMENT STUDIES
MONOGRAPH SERIES

GENERAL EDITOR
MATTHEW BLACK, D.D., F.B.A.

ASSOCIATE EDITOR
R. McL. WILSON

29

SŌMA IN BIBLICAL THEOLOGY

SŌMA IN BIBLICAL THEOLOGY

WITH EMPHASIS ON
PAULINE ANTHROPOLOGY

ROBERT H. GUNDRY

Westmont College, Santa Barbara, California

CAMBRIDGE UNIVERSITY PRESS

CAMBRIDGE

LONDON · NEW YORK · MELBOURNE

Published by the Syndics of the Cambridge University Press
The Pitt Building, Trumpington Street, Cambridge CB2 1RP
Bentley House, 200 Euston Road, London NW1 2DB
32 East 57th Street, New York, NY 10022, USA
296 Beaconsfield Parade, Middle Park, Melbourne 3206, Australia

First published 1976

Printed in Great Britain
at the
University Printing House, Cambridge
(Euan Phillips, University Printer)

Library of Congress Cataloguing in Publication Data

Gundry, Robert Horton.
Sōma in biblical theology, with emphasis on Pauline anthropology.

(Monograph series – Society for New Testament Studies; 29)

Bibliography: p. 245

Includes index.

1. Man (Theology) – Biblical teaching. 2. Bible. N.T. Epistles of
Paul – Theology. 3. Sōma (The Greek word) I. Title. II. Series:
Studiorum Novi Testamenti Societas. Monograph series; 29.
BS2655.M3G78   233   75–22975
ISBN: 0 521 20788 6

To Marchant King

CONTENTS

vii

Contents

ACKNOWLEDGEMENTS

My thanks go to the Editorial Board of *Studiorum Novi Testamenti Societas*, especially to Professor Ernest Best, and to the Syndics of the Cambridge University Press for accepting the present work for publication in the Monograph Series of the society; to the staff of the press for the excellence of their work; to the readers of the typescript, including my colleague Dr Moises Silva, for their valuable suggestions; to my secretary Mrs Betty Bouslough for her nearly flawless typing of the manuscript; and to the administration and trustees of Westmont College for a sabbatical leave which enabled me to devote a large amount of time to the present work.

ROBERT H. GUNDRY

Westmont College
Santa Barbara, California
July 1975

ABBREVIATIONS

PSEUDEPIGRAPHICAL BOOKS

Adam and Eve	Books of Adam and Eve
II–III Apoc Bar	Syriac and Greek Apocalypse of Baruch
Apoc Mos	Apocalypse of Moses
As Mos	Assumption of Moses
I–II–III Enoch	Ethiopic, Slavonic, Hebrew Enoch
Ep Arist	Epistle of Aristeas
Jub	Jubilees
Mart Isa	Martyrdom of Isaiah
Odes Sol	Odes of Solomon
Pss Sol	Psalms of Solomon
Sib Or	Sibylline Oracles
T 12 Patr	Testaments of the Twelve Patriarchs
T Levi	Testament of Levi
T Benj	Testament of Benjamin, etc.

DEAD SEA SCROLLS AND RELATED TEXTS

CD	Cairo (Genizah text of the) Damascus (Document)
DSS	Dead Sea Scrolls
1QH	*Hôdāyôt* (Thanksgiving Hymns) from Qumran Cave 1
1QM	*Milḥāmāh* (War Scroll)
1QS	*Serek hayyaḥad* (Rule of the Community, Manual of Discipline)
1QSb	Appendix B (Blessings) to 1QS

PERIODICALS, REFERENCE WORKS, AND SERIALS

APOT	*Apocrypha and Pseudepigrapha of the Old Testament* (ed. R. H. Charles)
ATANT	Abhandlungen zur Theologie des Alten und Neuen Testaments
BA	*Biblical Archaeologist*
BDB	F. Brown, S. R. Driver, and C. A. Briggs, *Hebrew and English Lexicon of the Old Testament*
BibOr	Biblica et orientalia
BO	*Bibliotheca orientalis*
BWANT	Beiträge zur Wissenschaft vom Alten und Neuen Testament
BZ	*Biblische Zeitschrift*

List of Abbreviations

BZNW	Beihefte zur *ZNW*
CBQ	*Catholic Biblical Quarterly*
EvT	*Evangelische Theologie*
ExpT	*Expository Times*
FRLANT	Forschungen zur Religion und Literatur des Alten und Neuen Testaments
ICC	International Critical Commentary
Int	*Interpretation*
JBL	*Journal of Biblical Literature*
JBR	*Journal of Bible and Religion*
JTS	*Journal of Theological Studies*
LQ	*Lutheran Quarterly*
Meyer	H. A. W. Meyer, *Kritisch-exegetischer Kommentar über das Neue Testament*
NovT	*Novum Testamentum*
NTD	Das Neue Testament Deutsch
NTS	*New Testament Studies*
NTSMS	New Testament Studies Monograph Series
RGG	*Religion in Geschichte und Gegenwart*
RHPR	*Revue d'histoire et de philosophie religieuses*
RSR	*Recherches de science religieuse*
SBT	Studies in Biblical Theology
SJT	*Scottish Journal of Theology*
ST	*Studia theologica*
Str–B	H. Strack and P. Billerbeck, *Kommentar zum Neuen Testament*
StudOr	Studia orientalia
TDNT	*Theological Dictionary of the New Testament* (eds. G. Kittel and G. Friedrich)
TU	Texte und Untersuchungen
TZ	*Theologische Zeitschrift*
WMANT	Wissenschaftliche Monographien zum Alten und Neuen Testament
ZAW	*Zeitschrift für die alttestamentliche Wissenschaft*
ZNW	*Zeitschrift für die neutestamentliche Wissenschaft*

PAPYROLOGICAL PUBLICATIONS

P Enteux.	*Publications de la Société royale égyptienne de Papyrologie, Textes et Documents*, i, Ἐντεύξεις... (ed. O. Guéraud; Cairo, 1931–2)
P Hal.	Halle Papyri = *Dikaiomata: Auszüge aus alexandrinischen Gesetzen und Verordnungen in einem Papyrus des Philologischen Seminars der Universität Halle, mit einem Anhang...herausgegeben von der Graeca Halensis*...(Berlin, 1913)
P Lille	*Institut papyrologique de l'université de Lille: Papyrus grecs publiés sous la direction de Pierre Jouguet*...(Paris, 1907–28)

xi

P Mich. Zen.	*Zenon Papyri in the University of Michigan collection* (ed. C. C. Edgar; University of Michigan Studies, Humanistic Series 24; Ann Arbor, 1931)
P Petr.	*The Flinders Petrie Papyri*... (Parts I–II, ed. J. P. Mahaffy; Part III, ed. J. P. Mahaffy and J. G. Smyly; Royal Irish Academy, Cunningham Memoirs 8, 9, 11; Dublin, 1891–1905)
P Rev. Laws	B. P. Grenfell, *Revenue Laws of Ptolemy Philadelphus* (Oxford, 1896)
PSI	*Papiri greci e latini* (*Pubblicazioni della Società italiana per la ricerca dei papiri greci e latini in Egitto*; Firenze, 1912; cited by number of volume, papyrus, and line)

EPIGRAPHICAL PUBLICATIONS

Ditt.	*Orientis graeci inscriptiones selectae* (ed. W. Dittenberger; Leipzig, 1903–05)
IG I²	*Inscriptiones Graece*, Vol. I, editio minor (ed. F. Hiller von Gaertringen, 1924)

OTHER

Josephus, *AgAp*	*Against Apion*
Ant.	*Antiquities of the Jews*
JW	*Jewish War*
MT	Masoretic Text

PART I

FOR AND AGAINST
A HOLISTIC DEFINITION OF *SŌMA*

CHAPTER I

Sōma as the Whole Person: the Rise of a Definition

Because of his saying that God-talk is possible only through man-talk, theologians often charge Rudolf Bultmann with reducing theology to anthropology.[1] Yet some of his most stimulating work appears in his exposition of Biblical anthropology, especially the Pauline view of man. So it is generally agreed. We may take the first volume of the *Theology of the New Testament* by Bultmann as indicative of his interest and major contribution. There he devotes but thirty-two pages to 'The Message of Jesus', thirty pages to 'The Kerygma of the Earliest Church', and one hundred and twenty-one pages to 'The Kerygma of the Hellenistic Church Aside from Paul' – but (not counting three pages on 'The Historical Position of Paul') one hundred and sixty three pages to the Pauline doctrine of man. He even subsumes themes such as the righteousness of God, law, grace, faith, reconciliation, the Word, the Church, and the sacraments under the catch-word 'Man'.[2]

Bultmann begins his specific remarks on Pauline anthropology

[1] See E. Güttgemanns, *Der leidende Apostel und sein Herr*, FRLANT 90 (Göttingen, 1966) 199–206, and further references there. Güttgemanns agrees with Bultmann in principle, faults him for failure to carry out the obverse that every anthropological statement is also theological, or Christological, and proposes himself to carry out this missing line. In fairness to Bultmann, we should note that according to him the reverse is also true: man-talk is possible only through God-talk. For his denial that he has transformed theology into anthropology, see *The Theology of Rudolf Bultmann*, ed. C. W. Kegley (New York, 1966) 258. Cf. also S. M. Ogden, *The Reality of God and Other Essays* (New York, 1963) *passim*, and N. J. Young, *History and Existential Theology* (Philadelphia, 1969) 66–72.

[2] To be sure, the title of Chapter V, 'Man under Faith', formally subordinates anthropology; but the ensuing discussions show that the motifs listed above exist, not in their own right, but only in their existential relevance to man. H. Conzelmann has redressed his teacher's anthropological imbalance in his own *An Outline of the Theology of the New Testament* (New York, 1968) esp. 159–60. Nevertheless, Conzelmann largely takes over the special understanding of *sōma* questioned in the present study (*ibid.* 176–8).

3

with a discussion of *sōma*, usually translated 'body'.[1] Recognizing that the common (Bultmann says 'naive' and 'popular') meaning, 'the physical body', appears in a large number of instances,[2] he nevertheless regards them as theologically unimportant. He goes on to argue, however, that in a number of passages where the term is theologically significant Paul uses *sōma* in the sense of the human person as a whole: 'The most comprehensive term which Paul uses to characterize man's existence is *soma*, body'[3] and '*Man, his person as a whole*, can be denoted by *soma*.'[4] We can hardly overestimate the importance of this definition, for Bultmann gives pride of place to Pauline theology, interprets Pauline theology as anthropology, and makes *sōma* the key to that anthropology

For this view of *sōma*'s special meaning, Bultmann apparently has drawn upon his former teacher, J. Weiss. Expounding Paul's prohibition of immorality in I Corinthians 6, Weiss forsook the German idealistic understanding of *sōma* as bodily form and *sarx* as fleshly substance, noted that in some places *sōma* parallels the first personal pronoun, and concluded that *sōma* can denote the person as such without reference to the physical body.[5] Adopting this view in some of his early writings, Bultmann fully developed it in his *Theology of the New Testament*.[6]

---

[1] *Theology of the New Testament* (New York, 1951) 1: 192–203. Bultmann does not appear to commit the error of supposing a necessary correspondence between linguistics and concepts (against which see J. Barr, *The Semantics of Biblical Language* [London, 1961] 33–45 *et passim*), but rests his case on word-usage in the light of full statements.

[2] Rom 1: 24; 4: 19; 12: 4–5; I Cor 5: 3; 7: 34; 12: 12–26; II Cor 4: 10; 10: 10; Gal 6: 17; I Thes 5: 23.

[3] *Theology of the New Testament* 1: 192.

[4] *Ibid.* 195.

[5] *Der erste Korintherbrief*, Meyer 5, 9th ed. (Göttingen, 1910) 160–1. Actually, a similar understanding of *sōma* in I Corinthians 6 had already been proposed by W. M. L. De Wette, *Kurzgefasstes exegetisches Handbuch zum Neuen Testament*, 4th ed. (Leipzig, 1847) 2/1: 51, and T. T. Shore, 'The First Epistle of Paul the Apostle to the Corinthians', *A Bible Commentary for English Readers*, ed. C. J. Ellicott (London, 1903) 7: 305.

[6] 'Die Bedeutung der "dialektischen Theologie" für die neutestamentliche Wissenschaft', *Theologische Blätter* 7 (1928) 57–67; 'Paulus', *RGG* 4 (2nd ed., 1930) 1032–4. The German original of *Theology of the New Testament* appeared in 1948. Prior to Bultmann's writing, the view had also appeared in T. Schmidt, *Der Leib Christi* (Leipzig, 1919) 5–6, again in connection with I Corinthians 6.

4

The year after *Theology of the New Testament* appeared in English dress, J. A. T. Robinson's monograph *The Body: A Study in Pauline Theology*[1] made its appearance. Widely regarded as a paradigm in the upsurge of Biblical theological studies after World War II, the book has had a profound effect – along with Bultmann's *Theology of the New Testament* – on current understanding of Paul's use of *sōma*. Indeed, Robinson's work has been translated into French[2] and Italian.[3] Although he proceeds into Paul's ecclesiastical concept of the Body of Christ, Robinson begins by adopting and elaborating (with certain revisions to be noted later) Bultmann's holistic definition of *sōma*.

So influential has been the authority of Bultmann and so persuasive his and Robinson's discussions that it has become orthodoxy among NT theologians to say that in Pauline literature, and perhaps elsewhere as well, *sōma* frequently and characteristically refers to the whole person rather than especially, or exclusively, to the body. Sometimes the definition carries the qualification that *sōma* refers to the whole man by metonymy or under the aspect of his physical body. To what extent these qualifications may or may not undermine the purported distinctiveness of the usage remains to be seen. At other times the definition remains unqualified. The meaning of *sōma* may even be dematerialized completely.[4] The holistic definition has become so widely accepted that virtually all recent handbooks, dictionaries, and studies of Pauline theology take it for granted with little or no felt need for argumentative justification. W. D. Stacey writes of 'Bultmann's conclusive treatment of this point'.[5]

Typical of the more qualified statements is that of Bultmann's translator, K. Grobel, who explains that Paul does not materialistically equate man with his physical body but uses *sōma* by metonymy for the whole self.[6] 'Metonymy' may lead

---

[1] SBT 1/5 (London, 1952).

[2] *Le corps: Etude sur la théologie de S. Paul*, Parole et Tradition (Paris, 1966).

[3] *Il corpo: Studio sulla teologia di S. Paolo*, La Parola di Dio 3 (Turin, 1966).

[4] Weiss, *Der erste Korintherbrief*, 160–1. Weiss speaks of the 'Immaterialität' of an 'übermaterielle' *sōma*.

[5] *The Pauline View of Man* (London, 1956) 182.

[6] 'Σῶμα as "Self, Person" in the LXX', *Neutestamentliche Studien für Rudolf Bultmann*, BZNW 21 (1954) 52–9.

to confusion, however. Normally it has to do with the representation of one thing by another which is distinct though related. But Grobel does not appear to exclude the body from the whole man; at least the examples he draws from the LXX would not so indicate. 'Synecdoche', representation of the whole by a part, might more properly designate a usage of *sōma* for the entire person (unless the physical body is meant to be *excluded*).

But whichever term, metonymy or synecdoche, correctly designates the view of *sōma* here under discussion, the term presents a problem to the view it is meant to represent. For if by denying that Paul materialistically equates man with his physical body we mean that Paul does not limit man to his physical body, even a dualist would agree and, further, assent to a synecdochic use of *sōma*. And synecdoche would indicate that the comprehensive sense of *sōma* is only representative – i.e., figurative. But a figurative usage in which the body not only is itself but also represents the rest of a person – viz., his soul, or spirit – fails to satisfy the requirements of a holistic definition of *sōma*. Such a definition requires that *sōma* refer directly to the whole person rather than indirectly through one of his parts.

The same deficiency appears if we say that *sōma* refers to the whole man under the *aspect* of his physical body.[1] If we mean that *sōma* can actually *comprise* the whole man with the result that all that is man is *sōma* – not just represented by or contained in or projected through – but is in fact *sōma*, then we do indeed have a technical use of the term. We gain the impression, however, that in using the phrase 'under the aspect of the body' some writers (perhaps unconsciously) shy away from an absolute equation between *sōma* and the totality of the human person.

Other writers do not exhibit such caution. Under the slogan that man does not have *sōma* but is *sōma*, J. Schmid echoes Bultmann's statement that the term is Paul's most comprehensive for a human person.[2] In greater detail W. D. Stacey

---

[1] 'In Paul, σῶμα designates not only a part of a man, but the whole man in so far as he is seen under a particular aspect' (Conzelmann, *Theology of the New Testament*, 176).

[2] 'Anthropologie, Biblische A', *Lexikon für Theologie und Kirche*, ed. J. Höfer and K. Rahner, 2nd ed. (Freiburg, 1957) 1: 611.

treats *sōma* as the center of personal life both now and hereafter. Thus *sōma* is more completely identifiable with the
personality than *sarx, pneuma,* or *psychē,* which also can alternate with personal pronouns but refer to the whole person
only in a limited number of spheres. Man is *psychē* and *sarx*
in his bondage to sin and in his service to Christ, but not
in the resurrection. Man is *pneuma* in service to Christ and
in resurrection, but only in a narrow way in his bondage to
sin. Man is *sōma,* however, in all these spheres. Hence *sōma*
becomes for Stacey the comprehensive term for the human
personality.[1]

M. E. Dahl defines *sōma* as 'the totality of man from *every*
aspect'. Only when modifiers are added does the term refer to
the human totality under a single aspect or in a particular state.
Like Stacey, he contrasts the wide coverage of *sōma* with the
restricted meanings of *pneuma* – man as divinely endowed with
life, *sarx* – man as subject to weakness and hostile powers, and
psychē – man as elementally alive but capable of slipping back
into the Void.[2]

X. Léon-Dufour decries an understanding of *sōma* as an
assemblage of physical organs.[3] Since it means the whole person, *sōma* can be either spirit or flesh, according to L. Cerfaux.[4]
Perhaps A. M. Hunter goes farthest in his statement: 'For Paul
the body is the principle of identity which persists through all
changes of substance – "organism" or "person" would perhaps give his meaning. Now the body has a material means of
expression suited to this earthly sphere; hereafter God will
give it a new embodiment befitting the heavenly world – ...a
spirit-body.'[5] Notably, for Hunter the body *has* rather than
is a material means of expression, and in the resurrection the
body will be *given* rather than will *be* a mode of 'self-expression
and power to communicate with others' (phrases used in
Hunter's following paragraph).

[1] *The Pauline View of Man,* 190.
[2] *The Resurrection of the Body,* SBT 1/36 (London, 1962) 121–6.
[3] 'Corps', *Vocabulaire de théologie biblique,* ed. X. Léon-Dufour et al.
(Paris, 1962) 162.
[4] *Christ in the Theology of Saint Paul* (New York, 1959) 280.
[5] *The Gospel According to St Paul* (London, 1966) 55, cf. 57, and the earlier
form of this book, *Interpreting Paul's Gospel* (Philadelphia, 1954) 54–5,
133.

A list of other scholars who subscribe to a holistic definition of *sōma* might go on and on. Indeed, the definition is so widely assumed that such a list would not merit the space necessary for it. We need, however, to examine the evidence for treating *sōma* as the entire person.

CHAPTER 2

Sōma in Extra-Biblical Literature

In passages from extra-Biblical literature *sōma* often receives the translation 'person'. R. Hirzel cites a multitude of passages from the classics for such a meaning.[1] The translations in the Loeb editions of ancient Greek writings frequently have 'person' for *sōma*. The same is true of other translations. Liddell, Scott, and Jones devote a whole paragraph to references under the meaning 'a person, a human being'.[2] F. Preisigke and Moulton and Milligan concur with examples of the general sense 'person'.[3] So also do Bauer, Arndt, and Gingrich in their lexicon[4] and E. Schweizer in *TDNT*.[5] Do these references demonstrate an accepted usage which Paul may have borrowed and developed? The references demand examination. The wideness of the range of ancient Greek literature prevents exhaustive treatment, but representative examples will afford adequate ground for judgement. And that judgement should not be predetermined by the weighty authority of those who have assigned the definition 'person' to these references. Passages in the following discusssion come from the lexicographers just mentioned.[6]

[1] 'Die Person: Begriff und Name derselben im Altertum', *Sitzungsberichte der Bayerischen Akademie der Wissenschaften der philosophisch-philologischen und historischen Klasse* (1914) 10: 1–54. Hirzel is concerned to establish the early use of *sōma* for living persons as opposed to corpses. With that we have no quarrel except when it is added that *sōma* comprehends the *whole* of the living person.

[2] *A Greek–English Lexicon*, 9th ed. (Oxford, 1940) s.v. σῶμα (also in 'Addenda et Corrigenda').

[3] F. Preisigke, *Wörterbuch der griechischen Papyrusurkunden* (Berlin, 1927) s.v. σῶμα; J. H. Moulton and G. Milligan, *The Vocabulary of the Greek Testament* (Grand Rapids, Mich., 1949) s.v. σῶμα.

[4] W. Bauer, *A Greek–English Lexicon of the New Testament and Other Early Christian Literature*, translated, revised, and augmented by W. F. Arndt and F. W. Gingrich (Chicago, 1952) s.v. σῶμα 1b.

[5] 'σῶμα κτλ.', *TDNT* 7 (1971) 1026, 1028, 1030, 1032; but see 1048.

[6] In passing, we should note that an extra-Biblical use of *sōma* for the whole person would erode a supposed Hebraic base for the holistic definition

We may first of all dispose of those many instances where *sōma* refers to slaves. As in Rev 18: 13 and Septuagintal passages yet to be examined, this use of *sōma* emphasizes the thingness of slaves as property and working tools.[1] Wholeness of personality lies quite outside the scope of vision, in fact, runs contrary to it. By the same token, we should probably put *PSI* iv.359 and 366 (252–251 B.C.) into the same category, for there *to sōma* denotes a hired servant (*misthōtos*) who is delivered from hand to hand as an item of merchandise (in association with beasts of burden, cattle, and sacks of goods).

Closely related is Demosthenes' statement that *tois doulois to sōma tōn adikēmatōn hapantōn hypeuthynon esti*; i.e., slaves must suffer in their own bodies for all their misdeeds. By contrast freemen are usually able to satisfy the law by payment of fines (*eis chrēmata*). Androtion on the other hand has treacherously done vengeance *eis ta sōmata* ('against the bodies') of freemen (Demosthenes 22.55). The connotation of slavery, the parallel with *chrēmata*,[2] and the clear reference to physical punishment confirm the normal meaning of *sōma*.

Also closely related is a usage for prisoners. *P Petr.* ii.13 (3)[5] (258–253 B.C.) contains a warning that the wall of a prison may fall and kill some of the inmates (*diaphanēsai ti tōn sōmatōn*). Plato writes of a public prison close to the marketplace for the securing of the 'bodies' of the majority of criminals (i.e., average criminals; *Leg.* 908a). Physical confinement is in view; and, being prisoners, the criminals are looked upon – like slaves – as objects of manipulation. That, rather than personality, constitutes the stress in *sōma* when it stands for

by showing that Greeks, too, thought in this way. Consideration of Hebraic thinking follows below.

[1] Antithetically, Aeschines 2.5 speaks of a 'free body' with reference to a well-born Olynthian girl whom, according to Demosthenes' charge, Aeschines and others had abused by whipping at a drunken banquet. On the thingness of slaves under Roman law see Gaius *Institutes* I, cited and discussed by F. Lyall, 'Roman Law in the Writings of Paul – the Slave and the Freedman', *NTS* 17 (1970) 75. N.B.: standard translations of ancient texts have been followed in some measure; but because of frequent divergences for the sake of scholarly discussion in terms of more literal renderings, the present writer takes responsibility for the translations.

[2] To be sure, *sōma* and *chrēmata* contrast as *different* agencies of payment for wrongdoing, but both *are* such agencies with the result that in the larger picture they react on each other as parallels.

prisoners. Also, in the Petrie papyrus *sōma* is doubly suitable because of the threat of death (cf. II Mac 12: 26). As we shall repeatedly see, *sōma* appears not only for corpses but also for living bodies immediately threatened with death – i.e., corpses in the making. The emphasis again lies on thingness.

The same holds true for the use of *sōma* in the plural for troops. In Aeneas Tacticus 32.1 we read that enemies in battle are to be withstood *mēchanēmasin ē sōmasin* ('with engines or bodies [i.e. infantry]'). And the same writer gives instructions concerning the placement of troops (*sōmatōn*) in defense of a city (1.1). Sophocles writes about *ta polla sōmata* of an army in battle whose discipline through obedience to commanding officers keeps them from rout, defeat, and death (*Antigone* 676). Demosthenes speaks of the bodies that man the war-galleys (9.40) and refers to the expenditure of bodies and materials in battle (18.66). The same usage appears in Demosthenes 14.16–20; 18.20; Thucydides 1.85, 121, VI.12, VIII.65; and Chrysostom *De sacerdotio* 1.8. As before, the stress lies upon *sōmata* as objects of manipulation and tools of action. Along this line the parallels with 'engines (of warfare)' in a compound expression (Aeneas Tacticus 32.1) and with 'materials (*chrēmata*)' in very many passages are instructive. Furthermore, since the troops are spoken of as bodies *en masse*, personality is hardly the point. In Demosthenes 18.66 there is the added connotation of corpses, dead bodies on a battlefield – things. And in Sophocles *Antigone* 676 death at least threatens.

Sōma as used by Euripides in *Troades* 201 stands simply for 'corpse'. In Euripides *Andromache* 315, Menelaus threatens to kill the son of Andromache instead of Andromache's own body. Here again physical death is in view. Isocrates 4.156 speaks of physical conflict and the danger of war, and Aeschines 2.141 of the sparing of bodies from death. In Euripides *Hecuba* 301, Odysseus tells Hecuba he is ready to save her body, i.e., to save her from physical death. And in *Orestes* 1075, also by Euripides, Orestes says to Pylades, 'Give back your body to your father; do not die with me.' Dionysius Halicarnassensis writes of many bodies dying (*Antiquitates Romanae* 4.69), and Chrysostom speaks of Phinehas' killing two bodies with one stroke (*De sacerdotio* 1.9). So Thucydides speaks of men who are more willing to war with their bodies than with their wealth (I. 141) and of those who regard 'both their bodies and their wealth alike as transitory' (II.53). In all these passages physical death is either accomplished or threatening closely. Whole personhood lies quite outside the intended meaning of *sōma*. Rather, the actuality or possibility of becoming a *sōma* in its initial connotation – a dead thing, a corpse – receives stress.[1]

Xenophon writes about the devotees of Cyrus who because of his beneficence desired to entrust to him their possessions (*chrēmata*), cities (*poleis*), and their very own bodies (*sōmata*; *Anabasis* 1.9.12). He also quotes Cyrus as articulating the principle that to the conquerors belong the goods (*chrēmata*) and bodies (*sōmata*) in a captured city (*Cyropaedia* VII.5.73). The parallels with *chrēmata* in both instances and additionally with *poleis* in one instance show that *sōmata* does not connote whole personality but denotes people as things; and in *Cyropaedia* VII.5.73 *sōmata* also denotes them as slaves since the captured were enslaved. The same usage appears in Isocrates 9.63; Demosthenes 20.77; Polybius III.17.10, IV.75.2, XXI.39.9.

The emphasis on people as commodoties, or items, rather than persons appears again in *P Petr.* III.107, an account of fares and freights, where *sōma* in the plural repeatedly applies to passengers. Enumeration in terms of bodies also occurs in Wilcken's *Chrestomathie* 1.198(6), *P Lille* 27.17, and the papyrus quoted in Preisigke's *Sammelbuch* 5246(2). So again in *P Petr.* III.59(b)[2], a census paper in which males are called *sōmata arsenika*, and *P Rev. Laws* 50.9, where *kata sōma* means 'per individual' (cf. Gen 47: 12) and carries, additionally, the connotation of physical consumption or use of oil.[2] This distributive use appears

---

[1] This cancels out Hirzel's argument that the masculine gender of the relative pronoun *hoi* with reference to *sōmatōn* in Josephus, *JW* 7.8, 1 §265, points to a meaning 'person' for *sōma*. The context has to do with bodily injury and death. The masculine gender is *ad sensum*. Similarly, Pindar *Olympian* 9.34 refers to bodies in the process of becoming corpses (*thnaskontōn*); thus Hirzel's argument that *sōmata* must here mean 'persons' because Homer would have used *psychai* in such a passage falls short ('Die Person', 26–7).

[2] Except for the papyrus cited from Preisigke's *Sammelbuch*, a papyrus dating from the first century B.C., the papyri discussed in the above paragraph date from the third century B.C. Liddell, Scott, and Jones also cite *IG* I[2] 22.14. Although the relevant phrase (*hekastou tou sōmatos*) seems to have a kind of distributive sense ('per body') and may refer to slaves or

also in Aristotle *Oeconomica* II.ii.5, 20, 25 in connection with the assessment and payment of taxes. Conversely, Diodorus Siculus XIII.xiv.5 writes of the walls of a city being crowded with bodies – living people, but viewed *en masse* as physical objects filling physical space.

Aeschines 3.78 uses the phrase *ta philtata. . .sōmata* of children. Perhaps children, though beloved, were looked upon as objects of control, like slaves. But more to the point in this passage is the contrast Aeschines makes between children and non-kinsmen. Therefore his use of *sōmata* emphasizes the closeness of physical relationship between parent and offspring. So also Euripides *Orestes* 1075 (treated above) and *Alcestis* 636 ('Were you not, then, truly the father of my body?'), Sophocles *Electra* 1233 and *Oedipus Coloneus* 355, and Aeschines 3.78. And just as *sōma* is appropriate to the physical link between parent and child, it is also appropriate to citizenship by birth, as in Aeschines 1.77.

In Euripides *Helena* 66 7 the body stands opposite to reputation. Similarly, in *Helena* 587 Euripides makes Helen say, 'My name might be in many places, but not my body,' with reference to Herodotus' tradition that Helen never was in Troy. Isocrates 10.51 also uses *sōma* for Helen's physical presence.

Aeschines speaks about ambassadors whose bodies (*sōmata*) are in Athens rather than Macedonia even though their *names* are in the public archives (2.58). We meet the same contrast in Aeschines 1.193, 3.99. Euripides puts these words in the mouth of Orestes: 'My body is gone; but my name has not left me' – in other words, 'Though I die physically, my name lives on' (*Orestes* 390). In Sophocles *Electra* 1333 we read the statement, 'Your plans would have entered the palace [i.e., been reported, so that the enemy would have been forewarned and forearmed] before your bodies.' All these passages use *sōma* for the concreteness of physical presence as opposed to something intangible. (In Euripides *Orestes* 390 the connotation of a corpse also adheres to *sōma*.)

Similarly, Plato contrasts bodies with ideas, or forms (*Respublica* v.476A). And in *P Mich. Zen.* 70.12 (third century B.C.) *to sōma* twice occurs with reference to producing a

hired servants, the papyrus is so extremely fragmentary that no interpretation of *sōmatos* rests on a secure foundation.

defendant in court, as also in Aeschines 1.99, where the two connotations of *sōmata* as material evidence in court and as slaves combine. In *P Hal.* 1.117, 120 and in Ditt. 669.16 a man's presence in body stands over against merely written records concerning him. In Sophocles *Oedipus Coloneus* 266 *sōma* simply indicates physical presence without contrast. Although bodily presence may entail the presence of the whole person, that is not the point of the usage.

The phrase *ergazomenē hautē tō idiō sōmati* in *P Enteux.* 26.7 (third century B.C.) may mean 'working for her*self*, earning her own living',[1] but apparently has reference to physical sustenance; hence the holistic definition is poorly supported. The physical connotation is to be retained also in Herodotus 1.139, where the author states that the names of the Persians are like their bodies (*sōmasi*) and magnificence (*megaloprepeiē*). The pairing with *megaloprepeiē* probably points to physical appearance. And the comparison between name and body looks like another instance of the incorporeal over against the corporeal.

Euripides' use of the phrase *sōmata adika* in *Supplices* 223 refers solely to the union of bodies in marriage. *Leuka gēra sōmata* in Euripides *Hercules Furens* 909 (lyr.) is to be taken literally, 'bodies white with age', as is also his reference to the body prostrated with grief and fasting (*Medea* 23–4). On the other hand, physical fitness and beauty are in view in Aristotle *Rhetorica* I. v.6, 10–11, 14–15, and physical life, safety, and health in Thucydides 1.17, VI.9 (*bis*). It is hard to see anything but bodily torture in *P Lille* 29.23 (*hoi dikastai tēn basanon ek tōn sōmatōn poieisthōsan*), and Aeschines 1.31 has to do only with shameful treatment of the body through drunkenness and lewdness. Demosthenes' statement, 'My body was outraged' (21.7; see also 21.69, 106), refers to Meidias' physically striking Demosthenes in the face with clenched fist. Bodily harm or death (especially in connection with judicial sentences) appears in Sophocles *Oedipus Tyrannus* 642–3; Aeschines 2.6, 8, 184; 3.132, 210; Isaeus 3.62. A little different is Aristophanes, *Thesmophoriazusae* 895, where *sōma* appears in connection with abusive treatment which is not physical; however, Aristophanes simply makes the literal tossing of a carcass (*sōma*) by yelping dogs figurative for such abuse.

---

[1] So Liddell, Scott, and Jones, *A Greek–English Lexicon*, s.v. σῶμα.

We may fairly presume that the lexicographers have chosen the best examples known to them from ancient Greek literature to support the proposed meaning 'person' for *sōma*. Yet on examination in context it appears that *sōma* is not at all a comprehensive term. The term always points in a contrary direction – toward thingness in one or another capacity (as slaves, prisoners, troops, corpses, entries on a census list, and so on) or toward other specifically physical emphases (bodily presence, sustenance, procreation, and the like). We may excuse the lexicographers for giving 'person' as an equivalent for *sōma*, simply because in the cited passages 'body' would sound awkward in our language. But since context makes clear that *sōma* always focuses attention on the physical, we would make a mistake to appeal to these extra-Biblical passages in support of a holistic definition.

CHAPTER 3

Sōma in the LXX

We have already noted that the use of *sōmata* for slaves points to their use and abuse as physical objects. For this reason, occurrences of *sōma* for slaves in the LXX lose their force as pointers to the meaning 'whole person' (Tob 10: 10 B; II Mac 8: 11; Gen 34: 29). Nevertheless, K. Grobel, who has made the best attempt to find support for the holistic meaning in the LXX, derives special arguments from two passages, Gen 36: 6 and Bel 32.

In Gen 36: 6 *sōmata* stands for נפשות. (This is the only place in the LXX where *sōma* represents נפש in the sense of 'slave'.) Since נפש can mean 'person', Grobel concludes that its Greek translation here means the same.[1] In the absence of stronger evidence to the contrary, however, it is simpler to say that the Septuagintal translator has (correctly) interpreted the Hebrew as a reference to slaves and rendered with a good Greek idiom for slaves quite apart from any enlargement of the normal meaning of *sōma*. The term appears in a list, here between references to various members of the family and various material possessions. It is just that kind of context which suits the idiomatic Greek use of *sōma* for slaves as commodities.

According to the Theodotionic version of Bel 32, two *sōmata* and two sheep had daily been given to the seven lions in the den prior to Daniel's being cast in. *Sōmata* may mean 'dead bodies, carcasses', but Grobel attractively suggests that it refers to living slaves who were fed to the lions along with the sheep. The Septuagintal version has *tōn epithanatiōn sōmata dyo*; i.e., two bodies of those under sentence of death made up the daily diet of the seven lions. In this version does *sōmata* mean ' "person" pure and simple'?[2] Whichever version we choose to consider, the lions did not eat and digest whole personalities, but physical bodies. The proof-text therefore proves weak.

---

[1] 'Σῶμα as "Self, Person" in the LXX', *Neutestamentliche Studien für Rudolf Bultmann*, BZNW 21 (1954) 55.

[2] *Ibid.*

Searching for usages in the LXX other than the meaning 'slave' yet denoting the whole person, Grobel next cites the distributive expression *kata sōma* in Gen 47: 12 LXX: 'And Joseph was providing rations to his father and his brothers and to all his father's household *kata sōma* (for לְפִי הַטָּף, "according to the mouth of the children").' Admittedly, *sōma* could still mean 'body' because it is the body which is fed, just as 'mouth' in the English phrase 'so many mouths to feed' still denotes a real mouth. (The Hebrew phrase with 'mouth' in Gen 47: 12 is much closer at hand as an analogy, indeed, as a *Vorlage*.) But 'both expressions are clearly used by synecdoche for "person."'[1] In synecdoche, however, a part represents or stands for the whole; the synecdochic term does not itself bear the definition of the whole. Yet the latter needs to be proved in order to sustain a holistic meaning for *sōma*. Mere synecdoche does not suffice. And the objection still holds that simply physical bodies (and mouths) are fed in Gen 47: 12; therefore, *kata sōma* means 'according to body' in a distributive sense with reference to physical sustenance. And that is all.

In Gen 47: 18 the Egyptians lament to Joseph that as a result of the famine they have nothing left to sell for food except *to idion sōma kai hē gē hēmōn*. In the next verse *sōma* gives way to the first personal pronoun and in verse 23 to the second personal pronoun. Grobel regards *sōma* as the whole self, especially on account of the alternation with the personal pronouns.[2] We may discount the argumentative force of that alternation, however, because *sōma* determines the purview of parallel personal pronouns rather than vice versa. In the present passage *sōma* appears in association with money, possessions, cattle, and land – i.e., in the same sense of a physical commodity which appears in the usage for slaves. Indeed, in the next verse the Egyptians offer themselves for sale as slaves (*paides*) to Pharaoh (see v. 21, too). Also, the Hebrew text has גְּוִיָּה, 'body'. Since that word most frequently refers to a corpse, it points away from personality and toward corporeity. From every standpoint, then, the stress lies on physicality alone.

The same situation obtains in Neh 9: 36–7 LXX, where Ezra complains in prayer that 'we are slaves (*douloi*)', and foreign overlords eat off the land and exercise authority 'over

[1] *Ibid.*   [2] *Ibid.*

our *sōmata* and among our cattle'. Again the associations with slavery, land, and cattle emphasize the connotation of *sōma* as a physical object. And again the Hebrew substratum גויה tends in the same direction.

According to Tob 11: 15 א, Tobias praises God *en holō tō sōmati autou*. Grobel translates, 'with all his being, with his whole self'.[1] But because of the weeping and falling on each other's necks that is described in the context as the physical expression of joy, we do better to take this phrase as also indicating the physical accompaniment of exultant praise. Besides, more than a little doubt accompanies the reading *sōmati*. Rahlfs adopts Fritzsche's emendation *stomati*. That makes more natural sense with *eulogōn* ('praising') unless we think the *holō* somewhat awkward with *stomati*. In the similar and neighboring passage Tob 13: 7,[2] Codex Vaticanus has *en holō sōmati* and Codices Sinaiticus and Alexandrinus have *en holō stomati* with *exomologēsasthe autō* and in parallel with *eulogēsate kyrion* and *hypsōsate ton basilea tōn aiōnōn*. We might reason that *sōmati* is the more difficult reading and therefore original. But if the word really did bear the meaning 'person' and unless the scribe did not know that meaning, the reading *sōmati* would not have been difficult. Indeed, the presence of *holō* would have made *stomati* more difficult. Only if *sōma* did *not* mean 'person' to the scribe is *sōmati* the more difficult reading. But it could have arisen from *stomati* by simple error of sight and sound since the two forms look and sound fairly alike, just as easily as vice versa. If it is that kind of an error, *sōmati* adds nothing to our discussion.

Grobel thinks that the error worked in the opposite direction, from *sōmati* to *stomati*, as presumably in Judg 14: 8, where *en tō stomati* stands for בגוית ('in the body').[3] Perhaps so, but in Judg 14: 8 the Septuagintal translator(s) may have thought that it is easier to conceive Samson's reaching for honey into the mouth of the lion's carcass than into the torso. On the whole, *stomati* seems to have a stronger case in Tob because of the association with oral praise. Even granting that *sōmati* was the original reading rather than a simple mistake, in both verses

---

[1] *Ibid.* 57.
[2] Following Rahlfs' numbering. Grobel has 13: 6.
[3] 'Σῶμα as "Self, Person" in the LXX', 57.

we need to see only the physical expression which accompanied joy and praise in the ancient near eastern culture.

Another set of Septuagintal passages affords ground for discussion. In I (III) Kgs 14: 9 A, Neh 9: 26, and Ezek 23: 35 the LXX renders the Hebrew phrase 'behind (your, their) back (גו)' with the phrase 'behind (your, their) *somatos*', which Grobel translates 'behind your*self*'.[1] We should note, however, that since *sōma* represents גו in all its occurrences in the Hebrew OT – viz., these three passages – the translators of the LXX apparently took גו as equivalent to גויה (both words come from the root גוה) and therefore as meaning 'body'.[2] Perhaps they were correct. Interestingly, modern scholars disagree over the meaning of the related word גֵּוָה. Some take the meaning 'back'. Others take the meaning 'body' in line with the LXX.[3] Thus *sōma* for גו is a translation, not a personalizing interpretation; and the expression 'to cast behind the body [or 'back', if we disagree with the translators of the LXX]' is a simple metaphor based on a physical action. *Sōma* does not then gain the meaning 'person'.

In Sir 51: 2 5 *to sōma mou* alternates with the first personal pronoun as the object of *lytroō* in the thanksgiving of Jesus the son of Sirach for deliverance. But the nature of the deliverance was physical: rescue from a plot against his life by false accusations to the king. The alternation between *sōma* and the first personal pronoun therefore proves nothing in favor of the meaning 'person'.

The same is to be said concerning the parallelism of *anthrōpon*, *to sōma autou*, *tēs psychēs autou*, and *auton* in Job 33: 17–18. The statements have to do with deliverance from physical death:

---

[1] *Ibid.*

[2] The related גֵו rarely receives direct translation in the LXX, not even in Isa 38: 17, where Grobel appeals to the personal nature of the pronoun in the LXX's *opisō mou* for the Hebrew phrase אַחֲרֵי גֵוֶךָ. But the Hebrew has 'Thou has cast all my sins behind *thy* back' and the LXX, 'Thou hast cast behind *me* all my sins'. Grobel has failed to detect that the Septuagintal translator took the Masoretic אַחֲרֵי as אַחֲרַי ('behind me') and simply dropped גֵוֶךָ. Or maybe גֵוֶךָ did not even appear in his Hebrew text. Because the LXX of Prov 10: 13 gives an extremely loose translation of the Hebrew, Grobel's saying that *anēr* stands for and personalizes גֵו lacks justification.

[3] See the Hebrew lexicons.

'...to turn man from unrighteousness. And he [the Almighty] has rescued his body from falling (*to sōma autou apo ptōmatos* – with overtones of a corpse). And he has spared his life (*psychēs*) from death, so that he has not fallen in war.' The succeeding verses speak in contrast of illness on a bed, benumbed bones, inability to eat food, emaciation – and finally of the restoration of the body and bones. All is physical.

Grobel suggests that in Wis 1: 4 *psychēn* (line 1) and *sōmati* (line 2) are completely synonymous: 'Because wisdom will not enter a deceitful soul, nor dwell in a body enslaved to sin.'[1] But a strong Hellenistic strain runs through Wisdom, and elsewhere the body and soul stand opposite each other. See especially 9: 15, 'For a perishable body weighs down the soul, and this earthly tent burdens the thoughtful mind', and 8: 19–20, 'A good soul fell to my lot; or rather, being good, I entered an undefiled body.' Therefore 'pure synonymism' in 1: 4 is highly improbable. As counterparts, *sōma* and *psychē* together comprise the whole person, but do not each refer to the whole person.

The same may be true of Prov 11: 17 LXX: 'A merciful man does good to his (own) soul, but the merciless utterly destroys his body.' With a Hellenistic bent, the Septuagintal translator probably looked upon 'soul' and 'body' as complementary rather than synonymous. Besides, *sōma* is a mere attempt to render שאר ('flesh') quite apart from a connotation of personality; and the verb *exollyei* ('utterly destroys, completely kills', much stronger than the Hebrew counterpart עכר, 'disturbs, hurts') favors the simple physical definition of *sōma*, for only to that sense does *exollyei* relate very well.

Because Prov 25: 20 LXX 'seems clear by itself in its use of *sōma* as "person"', Grobel translates, 'As vinegar is harmful to a sore, so passion [πάθος], attacking a person [σώματι], grieves the "heart".'[2] But 'passion' is hardly the correct translation of *pathos* here. In connection with *sōmati* and the metaphors of harm (see also v. 20*a*), *pathos* surely refers to physical calamity, specifically, to illness. The statement *kardian lypei* then indicates that physical illness affects the inner man, too. There is a complementary relationship between the body and the heart, but not an identity.

---

[1] 'Σῶμα as "Self, Person" in the LXX', 57.   [2] *Ibid.*

To bolster his interpretation of the verse, Grobel cites the alternate proverb in verse 20*a*, 'As a moth in a garment and a worm to wood, so a man's [*andros*] grief [*lypē*] harms his heart', and reasons that the substitution of *andros* for *sōmati* demonstrates the meaning 'person' for *sōmati*.[1] But again there is a mistranslation. The metaphors of harm, the probable meaning of the alternate term *pathos* ('illness') in association with *sōmati*, and the slight contrast with the heart all favor our understanding *lypē* as the physical pain of illness. Thus *lypē andros* simply denotes the pain a man suffers when his body falls ill; and as in the previous form of the proverb, that physical pain adversely affects the heart, i.e., the inner man of feelings, emotions, thoughts.[2]

Another piece of evidence adduced from the LXX appears in Job 36: 28*b*: 'At all these things is not your understanding astonished (*existatai*, literally, 'standing outside'), is not your heart (*kardia*) estranged (*diallassetai*) from your body (*apo sōmatos* – Grobel: "from your self")?'[3] Having no equivalent in the Hebrew, the passage comes from the Septuagintal translator and may therefore be expected to reflect his Hellenistic pattern of thought. It does. It reflects the Greek idea of *ekstasis* ('ecstasy'), in which under stress of astonishment, terror, anger, and the like the mind or soul leaves the body to stand outside while a strong feeling or divine frenzy takes control of the body.[4] So here the *dianoia* and *kardia* separate from the *sōmatos*, which must then be taken in its physical sense as the dwelling place of the mind.

In Dan 3: 95 Nebuchadnezzar praises God that Shadrach, Meshach, and Abednego have given over *ta sōmata autōn* to be burned lest *they* ('not their bodies but they, themselves', suggests Grobel) should serve and worship another god. But the third personal pronominal endings of the two verbs *latreusōsi* and *proskynēsōsi* surely refer back to Shadrach, Meshach, and Abednego. Only if those endings referred to *ta sōmata autōn* would the holistic definition gain support; but that expression

---

[1] *Ibid.* 57–8.
[2] Cf. Grobel's admission of the contrast between pain of body and joy of soul in II Mac 6: 30 and many passages in IV Mac (*ibid.* 55, n. 6).
[3] *Ibid.* 58.
[4] See A. Oepke, 'ἔκστασις, ἐξίστημι', *TDNT* 2 (1964) 449–54, with copious references.

simply means the bodies that belonged to the three young men, not their 'personalities'. The fire threatened to burn their physical bodies, not their personalities. The parallelism of 'body', 'hair', and 'coats' in the preceding verse confirms this. G. Dalman's statement that the Aramaic word גשם, which underlies the Greek here, became an 'Umschreibung von "selbst" '[1] therefore lacks relevance because of the Danielic context, which allows only a physical connotation.

Jesus ben Sira's exhortation that fathers carefully guard their daughters' bodies (*sōmati*, collective singular; Sir 7: 24) might refer to a guarding of their daughters' persons. But that is doubtful because of ben Sira's low conception of women. For that reason the use of *sōmati* here may fall into the same category as its use for slaves to denote them as commodities. Alternatively and perhaps more likely, ben Sira exhorts fathers to guard their daughters from sexual immorality or molestation (see 42: 9–10; 26: 10–12). Either way, *sōmati* retains its exclusively physical connotation.

C. R. Smith adduces another Septuagintal passage, II Mac 12: 26: 'Then Judas...slaughtered twenty-five thousand people [literally, "twenty-five thousands of bodies"].'[2] But *sōma* here reverts to its earlier (and continuing) connotation of a corpse. The slain were not already corpses, but they are so designated from the standpoint of the author *post factum*. The numeration of the dead also suits *sōmatōn* as bodies to be counted (cf. the use for slaves). Personality is not in view.

Lev 14: 9 comes under consideration as evidence for a holistic meaning of *sōma*: 'he shall wash his body with water'. But this verse and many others like it, particularly in Lev, fail to carry weight. It is true that the reflexive personal pronoun could be substituted for *sōma*.[3] The passage has to do, however, only with physical actions performed on physical objects – shaving one's head, beard, and eyebrows, washing one's clothes and body.

Finally, J. A. T. Robinson draws a general argument from the twenty-one instances in the LXX where *sōma* translates בשׂר.

---

[1] *Aramäisch-neuhebräisches Wörterbuch*, s.v., quoted by Grobel. See further below, 'Excursus on the Meaning of גוף, גופא, גשם, and גשמא in Rabbinical Literature', pp. 94–6.

[2] *The Bible Doctrine of Man* (London, 1951) 80.

[3] This is the argument of E. Best, *One Body in Christ* (London, 1955) 215.

Since the Hebrew word represents 'the whole life-substance of men or beasts as organised in corporeal form', *sōma* takes on the same meaning.[1] But בשר in the OT displays a variety of meanings – the substance of which the body is composed, the body itself, the penis (euphemistically), one's kindred, mankind (sometimes in contrast to God), animals, all living creatures. Therefore, the specific context becomes decisive in our determining what coloration *sōma* may take on when it translates בשר. The foregoing discussion has shown that in the LXX – *whatever the underlying Hebrew*, בשר or another word – *sōma* refers to the physical body alone. And a mere look at Hatch and Redpath's *Concordance to the Septuagint* will immediately show that *sōma* translates בשר only when the Hebrew word denotes the physical body alone. The majority of instances occur in the Levitical laws of cleanliness (such as the verse discussed in the preceding paragraph).[2]

We conclude that the LXX offers no convincing support for a definition of *sōma* as the whole person.

[1] *The Body. A Study in Pauline Theology*, SBT 1/5 (London, 1952) 13, and the whole surrounding section.

[2] See further J. Barr, *The Semantics of Biblical Language* (London, 1961) 35–7, esp. 37, n. 2, 217–18 on 'illegitimate identity transfer', and below, p. 118.

CHAPTER 4

Sōma in the NT Outside Pauline Literature

Although the writings of Paul provide most of the evidence adduced to support the meaning 'whole person' for *sōma*, references to other passages in the NT have not been lacking. The statements in Matt 5: 29–30 are cited:[1]

If your right eye causes you to sin, pluck it out and throw it away; it is better that you lose one of your members than that your whole body be thrown into hell. And if your right hand causes you to sin, cut it off and throw it away; it is better that you lose one of your members than that your whole body go into hell.

But although the whole person may go to hell, that is more than the logion states. The terms 'eye', 'hand', and 'members' reinforce the purely physical connotation which *sōma* normally carries. Especially is this so in that these terms denote parts of the body in contrast to the whole of the body.

The parallel passages Matt 6: 22–3 and Luke 11: 34–6 receive similar citation in support of *sōma* as the whole person.[2] We quote the Lukan version:

Your eye is the lamp of your body; when your eye is sound, your whole body is full of light; but when it is not sound, your body is full of darkness. Therefore be careful lest the light in you be darkness. If then your whole body is full of light, having no part dark, it will be wholly bright, as when a lamp with its rays gives you light.

Two times the personal pronoun 'you' alternates with *sōma*. But as we shall repeatedly see in other passages, the pronoun does not broaden the meaning of *sōma* when the meaning of the passage as a whole is taken into account. Here, as in the passage just discussed, the term 'eye' and the contrast between it as a physical organ which is but part of the physical body and the

---

[1] B. Reicke, 'Body and Soul in the New Testament', *ST* (1965) 205; E. Käsemann, *Leib und Leib Christi*, Beiträge zur historischen Theologie 9 (Tübingen, 1933) 95.

[2] Käsemann, *Leib und Leib Christi*, 95.

whole of that body conjoin to reinforce the exclusively physical connotation of *sōma*. It may well be that the logion is metaphorical, or even parabolic.[1] Even so, it rests on the ancient notion that the eye radiates brightness from within the body; hence *sōma* retains its physical orientation.[2]

In Matt 6: 25 (= Luke 12: 22–3) *psychē* parallels *sōma*: 'Therefore I tell you, do not be anxious about your life (*psychē*), what you shall eat or what you shall drink, nor about your body (*sōmati*), what you shall put on. Is not life (*psychē*) more than food, and the body (*sōma*) more than clothing?'[3] However, *psychē* stands here, not for the 'soul', but for physical life with special reference to food and drink. Thus, by parallelism *sōma* stands, not for the whole person, but for the physical body with special reference to clothing. There is no need for a larger meaning in *sōma*.

The Words of Institution, 'This is my *sōma*', are sometimes taken to mean more than the physical body: 'This is my whole person' (I Cor 11: 24; Mark 14: 22; Matt 26: 26; Luke 22: 19).[4] Alternatively, the two statements 'This is my *sōma*' and 'This is my *haima*' add up to the expression 'flesh and blood' as a reference to the whole man.[5] But J. Jeremias has shown that 'This is my body/flesh' and 'This is my blood' refer to the two component parts of the body which are separated when a sacrificial animal is killed.[6] Thus, in the Words of Institution emphasis lies on the violence of Jesus' physical death as a sacrifice. Of course, the whole man is involved in the death of the physical body. But in themselves the flesh/body and blood – violently separated in sacrifice – refer solely to the physical aspect of death, from which the involvement of the whole man may only be inferred.

[1] Cf. C. H. Dodd, *Historical Tradition in the Fourth Gospel* (Cambridge, 1963) 367, n. 4.

[2] Cf. R. H. Smith, 'The Household Lamps of Palestine in New Testament Times', *BA* 29 (1966) 10–11.

[3] Best appeals to the parallel. *One Body in Christ* (London, 1955) 216.

[4] So R. A. Ward, *Royal Theology* (London, 1964) 153.

[5] So Käsemann, *Leib*, 95. For 'flesh and blood', see Matt 16: 17 and Str–B 1: 730–1.

[6] *The Eucharistic Words of Jesus*, 2nd ed. (London, 1966) 221–2. On *sōma* as an equivalent for 'flesh' in Hebrew or Aramaic, cf. John 6: 51c and Jeremias' discussion (198–201).

Some have thought that *sōma* includes the whole person in Jas 3: 2–3, 6:[1]

and if any one makes no mistakes in what he says he is a perfect man, able to bridle the whole body also. If we put bits into the mouths of horses that they may obey us, we guide their whole bodies...The tongue is an unrighteous world among our members, staining the whole body.

We may first of all observe that in its second appearance in this passage *sōma* refers to the bodies of horses and therefore does not carry the meaning 'person'. Since the bodies of horses make a point of illustration for the two other appearances of *sōma*, the normal physical sense proves preferable also for them. In fact, inspection of the text shows that nothing more than the physical sense is necessary to an adequate understanding. In the third appearance the 'whole body' consists of the tongue and other members. In the first appearance the whole body is capable of being controlled in its desires and functions by the man who is able to control its most unruly member, the tongue. Both times the entire physique is in view. Any further meaning for *sōma* would be extraneous.

Käsemann compares Mark 5: 29 with the foregoing passage as a further example of *sōma* for the whole man:[2] 'And immediately the hemorrhage ceased; and she felt in her body that she was healed of her disease.' The Greek *tō sōmati* may be taken as a prepositionless locative or as a dative of reference. Käsemann presumably wants 'in her body' to mean 'in her (whole) self', or 'with respect to her body' to mean 'with respect to her whole personality'. But the malady is presented as solely physical. So also is the healing.

A final example comes from Rev 18: 13: '...cattle and sheep, horses and chariots, and slaves [literally, "bodies"], i.e. (*kai*), human souls [literally, "the souls/lives/persons of men"]'.[3] We might at least debate whether the RSV correctly treats the last *kai* in the list as epexegetical, with the result that *psychas anthrōpōn* becomes appositional to and therefore definitive of *sōmatōn*. The preceding appearances of *kai* in this long list are not epexegetical but continuative. Moreover, the unexpected

---

[1] Reicke, 'Body and Soul', 205; Käsemann, *Leib*, 95.
[2] Käsemann, *Leib*, 95.　　　[3] Cf. Best, *One Body*, 216.

shift from the genitive to the accusative tends to separate the two expressions. Thus, the traffic in slaves specifically and that in human beings generally may be related but not equivalent.

On the other hand, *psychas anthrōpōn* probably echoes the Septuagintal version of Ezek 27: 13, where the Hebrew has בנפש אדם and refers to slavery (see also Gen 12: 5). The compound expression in Rev 18: 13, then, may bear a single reference to slavery; but the use of *sōma* would reflect Greek idiom and the use of *psychē* (for נפש in the sense of 'person') would reflect Hebrew idiom.[1] In itself, however, such an 'intercultural hendiadys' would display only a difference of idiom rather than the meaning 'person' for *sōma*. For the translator of the Septuagintal passage did not translate נפש with *sōma*; and the apocalyptist did not replace *psychē* with *sōma* but simply put *sōma* alongside as the proper Greek idiom.

More to the point is the use itself of *sōma* in the plural for slaves. We cannot deny the usage, well-known elsewhere in Greek literature. But to draw the conclusion that it confirms the broad meaning 'person' is to miss the very point of the usage. Why are slaves called 'bodies'? Precisely because they are *not* treated as persons, but as articles of merchandise – like 'cattle and sheep, horses and chariots' and the numerous other items in this list (but unquoted above) – i.e., as physical bodies *alone*. What superficially looks like proof of a larger meaning, 'person', turns out on close inspection to support the ordinary meaning of *sōma*.

Grobel admits the possibility that 'in origin soma for "slave" may have been an intentionally contemptuous degradation of a person to the level of a thing'. But to keep the usage as a witness to *sōma* in the sense of 'person' he notes that 'however much a slave might consent to being used as a thing, he nevertheless remained a person and might become disturbingly personal to his master'.[2] The slave 'remained a person', yes, but that is irrelevant until we have evidence showing that personality is the point of *sōma* when used for slaves. And we need evidence that the capability of slaves to become 'disturbingly personal' to their masters contributes to the connota-

---

[1] Grobel, 'Σῶμα as "Self, Person" in the LXX', *Neutestamentliche Studien für Rudolf Bultmann*, BZNW 21 (1954) 55–6.

[2] *Ibid.* 56.

tion of *sōma*. We may detect an equivocation, moreover, on the term 'personal', which in connection with 'disturbingly' means 'annoying' rather than 'characteristic of a rational being'. We shall therefore rest with the observation that slaves are *sōmata* in Greek idiom because of their common treatment as solely physical entities.

CHAPTER 5

The Alternation of *Sōma* with Personal Pronouns in Pauline Literature

J. Weiss thinks that Paul developed the meaning 'personality' for *sōma de novo* and admits lack of evidence for such a usage elsewhere in Greek literature.[1] Whether or not agreeing with Weiss, Bultmann contents himself with exegetical arguments from the writings of Paul. Such arguments commonly begin with Pauline passages where the word stands parallel to a personal pronoun or can be replaced by a personal pronoun. We first consider Rom 6: 12–14, 16*a*:

Let not sin therefore reign in your mortal body to make you obey its passions. Do not yield your members to sin as instruments of wickedness, but yield yourselves to God as men who have been brought from death to life, and your members to God as instruments of righteousness. For sin will have no dominion over you, since you are not under law but under grace...Do you not know that if you yield yourselves...

In the parallel statements 'Let not sin therefore reign in your mortal *body*' and 'For sin will have no dominion over *you*', *sōmati*, 'body', and *hymōn*, 'you', appear to be interchangeable. Moreover, in the parallel phrases 'yield your members' and 'yield yourselves', *melē*, 'members', as a synonym for *sōma* twice alternates with *heautous*, 'yourselves' (cf. v. 19). The conclusion drawn is that *sōma* must have as broad a meaning as the personal pronouns – and therefore include the whole person.

The hidden presupposition in this line of reasoning is that the personal pronouns expand the usual meaning of *sōma*, limited to the physical body. For the presupposition no proof is offered. We may ask why the reverse understanding – viz., that *sōma* delimits the personal pronouns to man as physical body – is not equally possible. In the parallel statements 'She slapped his face' and 'She slapped him', 'face' and the

---

[1] *Der erste Korintherbrief*, Meyer 5, 9th ed. (Göttingen, 1910) 161, with the possible exception of the *sōma athanaton* in Poimandres (Reitzenstein, 342ff.).

29

personal pronoun 'him' interchange. But their interchangeability does not imply that 'face' has here become
a technical term for the whole man. As a matter of fact, the
statement 'She slapped his face' means that she slapped *only*
his face, not other parts of his physique as well, let alone the
'inner man'. It is true that in his face the whole man is involved – but not comprehended. It does not clarify the picture
to say that the whole man is viewed 'under the aspect of' his
face. Insofar as the face represents the whole man, that is true.
To say so without qualification, however, tends to blur the picture by putting the emphasis on unitary wholeness where the
emphasis belongs on a representative part of the man. We are
dealing with a *part* for the whole. And its being a part *for* the
whole does not imply that the part *is* the whole or has become
a technical term for it. Similar examples could be multiplied
almost endlessly. Cf. the alternation of the personal pronoun
with the terms 'mind' and 'heart' in Isa 10: 7 and John 16: 6,
20, and even with the term 'foot' in Job 23: 11.

The *reductio ad absurdum* is obvious. It simply reads too much
into a common figure of speech to say that every time a partitive term concerning the make-up of human beings alternates
with a personal pronoun, a holistic meaning for the partitive
term is newly born. In themselves, personal pronouns can hardly
bear the weight of redefining *sōma* or any other words with
which they stand in parallel. And to take refuge in an 'aspectual' usage is to recognize the synecdoche which eviscerates
the alleged new meaning. For the alleged new meaning requires identification with the whole person, not mere representation of the whole person.

Considerations other than mere alternation with personal
pronouns therefore become determinative. In the passage
before us (Rom 6: 12–14, 16*a*), the preposition *en* with *sōmati*
favors the usual understanding, 'body'. The parallel term *melē*
has physical connotations which are hard to mistake. The metaphor *hopla* ('instruments, weapons, tools') also points to the
physical body as the medium of action in the material world.
And the phrase 'from the heart' in verse 17 shows that Paul
distinguishes the inner and outer aspects[1] of man's being in his

---

[1] Since, as we have seen, appeal to aspectual usage amounts to a relin-
quishment of a technically holistic meaning, we may feel free to use the

parenesis. The occurrence of *akatharsia* ('uncleanness', especially with reference to sexual immorality) in connection with *melē* (v. 19), the illustrative contrast between marriage and adultery (7: 3), the breaking of the marital bond through the decease of one's mate (7: 1–2), and the contrast between 'members' (a surrogate for 'body') and 'mind' (7: 23) – all these phenomena tinge the entire passage with a strongly physical coloration. We have no need to enlarge the meaning of *sōma* here. Paul writes quite straightforwardly about the Christian's responsibility to put his physical body into the service of righteousness. Of course, incorporeal features of man's constitution belong in the larger picture of Christian sanctification, but *sōma* does not indicate them.

We confront similar situations in other Pauline passages to which appeal is made for broadening the meaning of *sōma* to include the whole person:

> ...always carrying in the body the death of Jesus, so that the life of Jesus may also be manifested in our body. For while we live we are always being given up to death for Jesus' sake, so that the life of Jesus may be manifested in our mortal flesh. So death is at work in us, but life in you (II Cor 4: 10–12).

In the progression 'body...our body...our mortal flesh... us', we may suppose that the final item – the personal pronoun 'us' – enlarges the meaning of the preceding expressions with the result that they include the whole person.[1] But again, the possibility that 'body' and, in this passage, 'flesh' may restrict the reference of the personal pronoun needs consideration. And again, elements in the context favor restriction rather than expansion. Although we may detect overtones of eternal

term 'aspect' in a way which leaves open the possibility of duality. This does not imply a radical dualism in which the body becomes unnecessary to the true 'I'. Rather, *sōma* may refer to the physical aspect of man distinguishable and separable from the spirit, or soul, but representative of the whole living person because the living person is a unity of body and spirit/soul. Similarly, synecdoche may characterize the use of 'spirit' and 'soul'. The monistic view fails to distinguish the two parts as separable; the dualistic view fails to hold them together as properly belonging to each other and as separated only unnaturally. (For 'body' and 'spirit/soul', synonyms may be substituted.) See below, pp. 83–5.

[1] J. A. T. Robinson, *The Body. A Study in Pauline Theology*, SBT 1/5 (London, 1952) 29.

life, the contrast between physical death and physical life constitutes the underlying theme of the passage. Paul is alluding to recent persecution which hc has suffered – 'persecuted, but not forsaken; struck down, but not destroyed' (v. 9). Although Paul refers to its psychological effect, the persecution clearly was physical – thus the two references to *sōma* and the one reference to 'mortal flesh'. A number of factors in the surroundings of these verses make it difficult to construe 'flesh' and 'body' in any sense other than the purely physical:

(1) the unmistakably physical character of the persecution in Paul's first mention of it in this epistle (1 : 8–10: 'we despaired of life itself...the sentence of death...so deadly a peril', with contrasting hope of resurrection);

(2) in the immediate context the figure of 'earthen vessels' (4: 7), which most naturally defines 'body' in a physical sense in the following passage, to which verses 10–12 belong;

(3) the contrast between the outer man and the inner man in 4: 16;

(4) the figure of the 'earthly tent we live in' which can be 'destroyed' with consequent nakedness (the figure has changed to clothing) – again a pointer[1] to physicality; and

(5) the further contrast between being 'at home in the body' and 'away from the body' (5: 6, 8–9).
We conclude that Paul does not depart from the normal, restricted meaning of *sōma* in 4: 10–12.

Ephesians 5: 28–9 also comes into view: 'Even so husbands should love their wives as their own *bodies*. He who loves his wife loves *himself*. For no man ever hates his own *flesh*' (cf. v. 33; italics supplied).[2] The demands of the interchange between *sōma* and the reflexive personal pronoun are met in that the physical body constitutes an essential part of man's being. The noun 'bodies' limits the reference of the pronoun 'himself'. That ought to be clear from the parallel use of *sarx* in an unmistakably physical (and morally neutral) sense, as the con-

---

[1] Exegetical problems abound in II Corinthians 5. Some suggest that nakedness does not mean bodilessness but shame, others that Paul here abandons belief in physical resurrection. See below, pp. 149–54. Those questions apart, the phraseology of the passage leaves no doubt concerning the corporeal nature of the *present* body and therefore casts light backward on *sōma* as it should be understood in 4: 10–12.

[2] See Robinson, *The Body*, 19, 28–9.

nections with feeding (*ektrephei*), keeping warm (*thalpei*), and coitus (*kai esontai hoi dyo eis sarka mian*) substantiate. Therefore, it is superfluous to read more than the physical sense of *sōma* out of the passage.[1]

[1] See further F. Neugebauer, 'Die hermeneutischen Voraussetzungen Rudolf Bultmanns in ihrem Verhältnis zur Paulinischen Theologie', *Kerygma und Dogma* 5 (1969) 295–6 and his *In Christus* (Göttingen, 1961) 52–3, n. 45, against facile argumentation from the interchange of *sōma* and personal pronouns. Neugebauer notes that Paul's interchanging *pistis* and *agapē* does not identify them.

CHAPTER 6

Sōma elsewhere in Pauline Literature

We have exhausted those Pauline passages where alternation of *sōma* and personal pronouns might be thought to enlarge the meaning of *sōma*. Further passages need attention, however, passages in which for other reasons *sōma* possibly refers to the whole person. In them a personal pronoun, though absent, would have fit in place of *sōma* and can easily be substituted.

I Cor 7: 4 falls into this category: 'For the wife does not rule over her own body, but the husband does; likewise the husband does not rule over his own body, but the wife does.' We can hardly overlook the physical reference here in view of Paul's discussion of conjugal rights, but we might think that 'the *soma* is not a something that outwardly clings to a man's real *self* (to his soul, for instance), but belongs to its very essence...*soma* can be translated simply "I" (or whatever personal pronoun fits the context)'.[1] But there is no justification for the leap from the essentiality of the *sōma* to a supposed comprehensiveness of *sōma* as '*Man, his person as a whole*'[2] – certainly no justification in the solely sexual orientation of I Cor 7: 1–9 ('not to touch a woman...the temptation to immorality...conjugal rights ...Do not refuse one another...come together again...lack of self-control...exercise self-control...aflame with passion').

For the same reason, an appeal to Rom 1: 24 fails. There is nothing more than sexual immorality implied in the phrase, 'to the dishonoring of their bodies among themselves'. Since the *sōma* is part of the self, the dishonoring of it entails the dishonoring of the self. But *sōma* does not thereby become the whole self.

In Rom 12: 1 Paul writes, 'I appeal to you therefore, brethren, by the mercies of God, to present your bodies as a living sacrifice.' Again, the personal pronoun might be substituted for *sōmata*, and we might conclude that *sōma* refers to man's

---

[1] Bultmann, *Theology of the New Testament* (New York, 1951) 1: 194; see also 196.　　　[2] *Ibid.* 195 (Bultmann's italics).

person as a whole.[1] In addition, the spirituality of the service (*tēn logikēn latreian*) done through our *sōmata* might require a larger than physical meaning for *sōmata*.[2]

But in this verse, the term 'bodies' is much more pointed than a generalizing definition will allow. Paul uses *sōmata* precisely because he wishes to stress the sanctification of that part of our being which is the place and means of concrete activity in the world: '...freilich nicht nur in der Innerlichkeit blosser Gesinnung oder Bereitschaft, sondern im Gehorsam bestimmter Tat, also leibhaftig'.[3] Disparagement of the body in the Hellenistic world necessitated such an emphasis by Paul. Substitution of the reflexive personal pronoun reduces the emphasis and leaves a wrong impression concerning the meaning of *sōma*. Of course, the offering to God of the physical vehicle of life in the world implies also an inner consecration to God. But that implication should not lead to confusion of the *sōma* with the inner man.

When Paul wishes to refer to the inner man, he has appropriate vocabulary at his disposal. In fact, in verse 2 he exhorts to renewal of the mind. Thus, in the pair of verses 'bodies' and 'mind' stand distinct from each other but in complementary fashion: 'present your bodies' – the outer part of your constitution, the physical means of your activity in the material environment; 'be transformed by the renewal of your mind' – the inner part of your constitution where thinking, feeling, and willing take place.[4] The former stresses practicality and

---

[1] Calvin and many other older commentators saw a larger meaning in *sōmata* in Rom 12: 1; but it is doubtful that they inferred more than synecdoche.

[2] E. Käsemann, 'Gottesdienst im Alltag der Welt (zu Rm 12)', *Judentum, Urchristentum, Kirche. Festschrift für Joachim Jeremias*, ed. W. Eltester, 2nd ed., BZNW 26 (Berlin, 1964) 167–8.

[3] P. Althaus, *Der Brief an die Römer*, NTD 6 (Göttingen, 1949) 106.

[4] See Rom 7: 22–3 for the equivalence of the 'mind' and the 'inner man'. R. Jewett denies that in Rom 12: 2 the mind is an ontological part of man. It is rather 'a constellation of thoughts and assumptions' because 'the gospel does not make one more intelligent' (*Paul's Anthropological Terms*, Arbeiten zur Geschichte des antiken Judentums und des Urchristentums 10 [Leiden, 1971] 385–6). It is not a question of more or less intelligence, however, but of a redirected intelligence. The definition of *nous* is too large a question to be discussed here, but the contrast with *sōma* favors an ontological meaning so long as *sōma* itself is ontological (see below, pp. 184 ff.).

service; the latter emphasizes motivation and patterns of thought.

In Rom 12: 1 the *sōma* is not merely capable of redemption, but is Paul's precise term for a human life dedicated to God.[1] But elsewhere Paul uses *sōma* for a human life enslaved to sin (Rom 1: 24; 6: 6; 7: 24; 8: 10, 13; cf. Col 3: 5). In other words, *sōma* is capable of dedication to God *or* to evil; in itself the term fails to carry its own hermeneutic. We might think the rest of Romans 12 shows that *sōma* means the whole man because the Pauline exhortations deal with mental and emotional as well as physical items.[2] Verses 1–2 do indeed overarch the entire chapter. But *nous* stands alongside *sōma* in these verses. What follows therefore does not necessarily define *sōma*; i.e., the mental and emotional may go back to the mind in verse 2 rather than to the body in verse 1. And even though *sōma* were the sole point of reference, we should bear in mind that the body may be the instrument of the mind and emotions without being equated with them.

It is also worth noting that *sōma* bears a clearly physical sense in verse 4: 'For as in one body we have many members.' Bultmann cites this verse (and the following, where *sōma* becomes an ecclesiastical figure) as an example of the naive popular usage.[3] The proximity of verse 4 to verse 1 should make us hesitate to see different meanings in the two verses without compelling reasons.

We conclude that in Rom 12: 1 Paul singles out the physical body for consecration to God, and in Rom 12: 2 singles out the mind for divine renewal. Neither term alone comprehends man's being. Together they do. This is not to suggest that Paul frequently uses *sōma* and *nous* as formal terms for a dichotomous anthropology. Other terms come into play elsewhere. In this passage, however, the two terms – taken together, not separately – embrace the human constitution.

I Cor 9: 26 offers another possible piece of evidence for the holistic definition of *sōma*: 'but I pommel my body and subdue it, lest after preaching to others I myself should be disqualified'. Again we might substitute the reflexive personal pronoun

---

[1] A point made by W. D. Stacey (*The Pauline View of Man* [London, 1956] 186) in favor of the holistic definition.

[2] *Ibid.*   [3] Bultmann, *Theology of the New Testament* 1: 193.

and conclude that *sōma* refers to the whole person. But the context suggests that nothing more than the physical side of man comes into focus. Paul's statement follows on the heels of a discussion of meat dedicated to idols and food and drink due to preachers of the gospel and immediately precedes a discussion of idolatrous banquets and associated immorality. The athletic metaphors in 9: 24–7, particularly that of boxing, undergird the solely physical connotation of *sōma*.

With reference to I Cor 13: 3, 'and if I deliver my body to be burned', we need only ask whether the *whole* self can be burned, i.e., whether the inner man, or *nous*, is as combustible as the *sōma*. Or if we follow the reading 'so that I may boast', the parallelism between 'my body' and 'my goods' (*ta hyparchonta mou* in the earlier part of the verse) still favors a purely physical understanding of *sōma*. Certainly nothing requires any more than that.

In Phil 1: 20, Paul writes, 'as it is my eager expectation and hope that I shall not be at all ashamed, but that with full courage now as always Christ will be honored in my body, whether by life or by death'. *Sōma* here means 'individual and personal presence in the world of men and events'.[1] That kind of presence, however, is specifically physical, as Paul's talk about 'life in the flesh' in contrast to departure to be with Christ via physical death makes plain (vv. 19–26). 'Flesh' and 'body' interchange as in I Cor 6: 15–16. 'Christ will be honored' whatever the immediate fate of the body. Paul is thinking about his physical destiny in relation to his trial and the possibilities of execution and release. *Sōma* therefore does not signify the whole 'I' of Paul, but only that part of him more immediately affected by the outcome of his trial and through which he bears witness to the visible world around him. To 'remain in the flesh' is to continue alive in the body for the purpose of 'fruitful labor'. 'To depart' is to die bodily death. 'To be with Christ' is to be absent from the body (cf. II Cor 5: 7–9). No room is left for a holistic meaning of *sōma*, for then one could never depart and be away from it.

Rom 8: 11 also appears in lists of passages where *sōma* has the force of a reflexive personal pronoun: 'he who raised Christ

[1] R. A. Spivey and D. M. Smith, *Anatomy of the New Testament* (New York, 1969) 310–11.

Jesus from the dead will give life to your mortal bodies also through his Spirit which dwells in you'. 'Give life to your mortal bodies' means 'give life to *you*'. That is true insofar as bodies are a real part of human beings. But there is no necessity to understand Paul as saying more than the usual translation implies, and factors in the context militate against a reference to the whole person in the term 'bodies'. In the absence of good evidence to the contrary, we should probably assume that Paul retains his Pharisaical notion concerning the nature of resurrection as a raising of the physical body, improved though it be.[1] And the repeated mentions in verses 9–11 of the dwelling of Christ and his Spirit within the believer favor our understanding the *sōma* as the physical abode of the Spirit who guides and energizes the believer's actions worked out through the instrument of the body.

We might argue, however, that the use of *sōma* in the preceding verse requires a meaning larger than physical: 'And if Christ be in you, the body is dead because of sin; but the Spirit is life because of righteousness' (Rom 8: 10 AV).[2] 'Body' is a periphrasis for 'the flesh' mentioned in surrounding verses. Throughout this part of the passage 'flesh' bears its pejorative sense as the source of lawless desire and action and does not denote the materiality of man except by way of the background that sin expresses itself through the physical body (cf. v. 9, 'But you are not in the flesh' – certainly not written to ghosts!). If then 'body' is equivalent to 'flesh' *in that sense*, it cannot be physical. It must refer to the whole self of the believer, already reckoned dead by God and to be reckoned dead to sin on the part of the believer (cf. 6: 2–11; 7: 1–6).

Several parallel passages may seem to support this interpre-

---

[1] See below, pp. 162 ff., on I Corinthians 15. Concerning the Pharisaical view, see W. D. Davies, *Paul and Rabbinic Judaism* (London, 1962) 298–303. This is not to overlook the rabbinical debates over the constitution of the resurrected body. The evidence which Davies adduces for a spiritual view of the resurrected body in some Pharisaical circles seems unconvincing (*ibid.* 306–8). Physicality is far from denied in the literature cited; it is rather glorified. To say that Paul refers to a future possibility in this present life rather than in the eschatological future (C. F. Evans, *Resurrection and the New Testament*, SBT 2/12 [London, 1970] 168) hardly meets the demands of the expression 'will give life to your mortal bodies'.

[2] Here the AV comes closer to the Greek text than does the RSV.

tation.[1] The first is Rom 8: 12–13: 'So then, brethren, we are debtors, not to the flesh, to live according to the flesh – for if you live according to the flesh you will die, but if by the Spirit you put to death the deeds of the body [v.l. 'flesh' – D G latt Ir^lat Tert] you will live.' Here it might be thought that 'body' is a simple variation for 'flesh'. But the equation is not at all necessary. The deeds of the body have their immediate source in the *sōma*, but their ultimate source in the *sarx*, which dominates the *sōma* and is thereby distinguishable from it.

Thus, 'put to death the deeds of the body' means 'put to death the deeds worked out through the body under the influence of the flesh'. For the body as the instrument, or outward organ, of sin, we may note Rom 6: 13, 19; II Cor 5: 10; and for the body as the place where sin materially manifests itself, Rom 7: 5, 23 (cf. I Cor 6: 20).[2] 'Body' then retains its usual sense and no shift in its meaning occurs between verses 10–11 and verses 12–13. Moreover, the parallel between 'the body is dead' and 'put to death the deeds of the body' breaks down in that it is the *deeds* of the body, not the body itself, which are to be put to death. The reason for the difference is that the Holy Spirit dwells within the body and will raise it at the resurrection. Hence, only its deeds done under the influence of the 'flesh' become the object of mortification.

Another parallel passage confronts us in Rom 6: 6: 'We know that our old self (*anthrōpos*) was crucified with him so that the sinful body (*to sōma tēs hamartias*) might be destroyed, and we might no longer be enslaved to sin.' But 'the body of sin' is not equivalent to 'flesh'. It is the body which sin, or the flesh, dominates, as in Rom 8: 12–13. We may compare the phrase 'law of sin' (7: 23, 25; 8: 2), which does not mean that the law is inherently sinful (see 7: 7–20) but that empirically it incites to sin.[3]

---

[1] A. Sand, *Der Begriff 'Fleisch' in den paulinischen Hauptbriefen*, Biblische Untersuchungen 2 (Regensburg, 1967) 204–8.

[2] See further W. P. Dickson, *St. Paul's Use of the Terms Flesh and Spirit* (Glasgow, 1883) 260–2, 313–15.

[3] See H. H. Wendt, *Die Begriffe Fleisch und Geist im biblischen Sprachgebrauch* (Gotha, 1878) 114, 182ff., who explains *tēs hamartias* as a genitive of possession. Wendt draws the parallel to 'flesh of sin' (8: 3) rather than, as here, 'body of sin' (6: 6).

We meet yet another parallel passage in Rom 7: 24: 'Who will deliver me from this body of death?' But here the body of death is not 'flesh' in the sense of sin itself; it is the physical body destined to die because within its members dwells the law of sin and death. In 7: 4–8: 3 'flesh' bears a more physical and less pejorative connotation than in 8: 4–13; for in 7: 4–8: 3 sin dwells within the flesh and the flesh weakly submits to it. On both counts the flesh as a physical entity with 'members' is distinguishable from sin. But because of the tyranny of sin over the flesh, in 8: 4–13 flesh comes to stand for the sin which has so completely dominated the concrete physical life of the person as to become practically one with it.

Still another parallel passage might seem to demonstrate an equivalence between *sōma* and *sarx* in a hamartiological sense: 'And those who belong to Christ Jesus have crucified the flesh with its passions and desires' (Gal 5: 24). *Sōma* does not appear here; but the crucifixion of the flesh parallels and interprets the deadness of the body in Rom 8: 10. 'Flesh' certainly has its hamartiological sense in Gal 5: 24. However, unless other passages indicate that *sōma* can bear the same sense, the supposed parallel with and interpretation of Rom 8: 10 breaks down. We shall need to treat the two verses, already separated widely in the Biblical text, as separate in meaning.

A similar argument for the equation of 'body' and 'flesh' in the sense of evil might be drawn from the parallel between the *epithymia* (or -*ai*) *sarkos* in Gal 5: 16–17, 24 and the *epithymiai somatos* (indicated by *autou*) in Rom 6: 12. However, the *autou* is textually doubtful. The main witnesses for *autou* are ℵ A B C* *al* vg sy^p. *Autē* is read by P46 D G it Ir Tert. We might think that *autē* was original, and that *autou* arose because *sōmati* was nearer than *hamartia* and/or because a copyist with ascetical notions felt that lusts belong to the body. But if we are to accept *autou*, the verse does not need to mean any more than that sin utilizes bodily desires to gain a bridgehead in its attack upon men. The fact that Paul attaches the qualifier 'mortal' to 'body' in Rom 6: 12 militates against an equivalence with 'flesh' as sin. Moreover, sin is '*in* your mortal body' but should be driven *out* so as not to rule there; thus, we can hardly equate sin (represented by 'flesh') and *sōma*.

The only passage yet to be considered for the view that

sōma can mean 'flesh' in the hamartiological sense is Col 2: 11: 'In him also you were circumcised with a circumcision made without hands, by putting off the body of flesh in the circumcision of Christ.' The line of reasoning might run as follows: since the Colossian Christians still lived in their physical bodies, the body which had been stripped off them must have been the flesh in an immaterial and pejorative sense (cf. 3: 9).[1] But that line of reasoning too easily assumes that the body of flesh which is stripped off belongs to Christians. The flow of thought in the passage favors a reference to the physical death of Christ, for the phrase 'in the circumcision of Christ' immediately follows and defines the phrase 'by putting off the body of flesh'. And 'the circumcision of Christ' probably refers to the crucifixion, especially in view of the allusions to Christ's burial and resurrection in the following verse (see also v. 15). Of course, the believer's union with Christ in his death carries implications for the mortifying of the 'flesh' in a hamartiological sense. But Col 2: 11 refers immediately to the physical death of Christ.

Confirmation of this understanding comes from Col 1: 22, where the phrase 'body of flesh' appears with an indubitably physical meaning: 'he has now reconciled [you] in his body of flesh by his death'. See also Rom 7: 4; I Pet 2: 24; 4: 1; and the good discussion by C. F. D. Moule, *The Epistles of Paul the Apostle to the Colossians and to Philemon*.[2] Moule does not need to labor, however, under the absence of *autou* in 2: 11; for *Christou* with the appositional phrase *en tē peritomē* makes clear whose body of flesh is stripped off in circumcision. This obviates the need for saying that 'conceivably the identification of the baptized with Christ is regarded as so close as to render a specifying pronoun out of place'. The addition of *tēs sarkos* to *tou sōmatos* may counteract a docetic element in the Colossian heresy (cf. v. 9), may serve to distinguish this body from the ecclesiastical body, the Church, in verse 19 (and possibly v. 17), and/or may act as a 'lead' into the hamartiological use of *sarx* in the following verses (cf. the progression from the physical to the pejorative in Rom 7–8). Or the phrase 'his body of flesh'

[1] J. A. T. Robinson, *The Body*. A Study in Pauline Theology, SBT 1/5 (London, 1952) 30–1.

[2] Cambridge Greek Testament Commentary (Cambridge, 1958) 94–6.

as a whole contrasts the complete circumcision of Christ in death with the cutting off of a small piece of flesh in ordinary circumcision.

There remains the possibility that no special emphasis inheres in the phrase 'body of flesh', for it appears in 1QpHab 9: 2; 4QpNah 2: 6; and the Greek text of Sir 23: 17 in a simple physical sense. We may also note that the next uses of *sōma* in Col 2 are physical: as that which is physically substantial *sōma* contrasts with 'shadow' in verse 17; the *sōma* has a head, joints, and ligaments in verse 19; and 'severity to the body' in verse 23 means ascetic denial of physical appetites and needs.[1]

[Note: As that which is physically substantial *sōma* contrasts with 'shadow' in Col 2: 17 whether or not Paul here uses *sōma* for the Church. It is not certain that the contrast with 'shadow' necessitates our saying the body is non-human (Robinson, *The Body*, 27, n. 1). In writing that this is Paul's only use of *sōma* in a non-human sense, has Robinson overlooked I Cor 15: 40–1? See further Best, *One Body*, 220, with references. Best thinks Paul may have known and here adopted the Greek philosophical usage of *sōma* in the contrast between appearance and reality. Regarding the antithesis between *skia* ('shadow') and *sōma* as very awkward, I. A. Moir suggests repunctuating with a stop after *mellontōn* with the result that *to de sōma tou Christou* goes with the following *mēdeis hymas katabrabeuetō*... (' *The Bible Societies' Greek New Testament*, edited by Kurt Aland, Matthew Black, Bruce M. Metzger and Allen Wikgren', *NTS* 14 [1967] 142). That result is no less, and probably more, awkward in its word order. Does Moir want to take *to...sōma* as an accusative of general reference? If so, there is the difficulty that the motif of

---

[1] Since *ta melē* sometimes means *to sōma*, we might think that in Col 3: 5 the definition of *ta melē* by 'immorality, impurity, passion, evil desire, and covetousness, which is idolatry' – all to be 'put to death' – indirectly displays a hamartiological and non-physical meaning for *sōma* identical to that of *sarx* (cf. C. A. A. Scott, *Christianity according to St Paul* [Cambridge, 1927] 208; Robinson, *The Body*, 30). But since these members are 'upon the earth', whereas believers belong to the 'things above' by virtue of death and resurrection/exaltation with Christ (vv. 1–4), we should probably treat 'the members' as a figurative expression for sins which constitute the earthly 'old man' (v. 9) and not as a synonym for *sōma*. Unjustifiably, N. Turner suggests that *ta melē* may be vocative with reference either to the believer's own individual body or to believers as members of the Body of Christ, with the result that *ta epi tēs gēs* alone becomes the direct object further defined by the list of sins (*Grammatical Insights into the New Testament* [Edinburgh, 1965] 104–5).

the ecclesiastical Body of Christ is not picked up till a number of phrases later (v. 19). Or does he wish to take *to...sōma* as a direct object in apposition to *hymas*? If that, why the intervention of *mēdeis*? Although in the usual punctuation the condensed nature of the phrase *to de sōma tou Christou* may seem awkward, it is due to and explicable by the parallelism with *ha estin skia tōn mellontōn.*]

We conclude that elsewhere Paul never uses *sōma* as a synonym for *sarx* in a hamartiological sense; therefore no evidence for a non-physical definition of *sōma* in Rom 8: 10 is to be drawn from the parallel passages. But is that verse an exception?

We should note first of all that even though an equivalence between *sōma* and *sarx* in Rom 8: 10 were demonstrable, that still would not demonstrate the holistic definition, 'person', for *sōma*. For *sarx* in its hamartiological sense does not refer to the whole man, but partitively to the sinful proclivity *within* man. This becomes clear in the description of the inner struggle between sin and the I/inner man/mind (7: 7–25). It becomes clear also in the use of the phrases '*in* the flesh' and '*according to* the flesh', which become nonsensical if the 'flesh' is already the whole man.

Furthermore, if the dead body of verse 10 is the seat of sin (i.e., the 'flesh'), it would need casting off rather than the quickening which is indicated in verse 11.[1] That, in fact, is the fatal flaw in those interpretations which see the death of the body as 'flesh' reckoned dead by God and/or the believer. God will not make alive (*zōopoiēsei*) the sinful proclivity! Yet whatever it is, this dead body is destined for quickening. We can surmount the problem only by supposing a radical break between verses 10 and 11, with the result that the dead body of verse 10 is the sinful self, the 'flesh', but the mortal body of verse 11 something else destined to be made alive. But a break between verses 10 and 11 is unsupported by other evidence and is prohibited by the carrying over from verse 10 into verse 11 of *pneuma, en hymin, zōē* (*zōopoieō*), and *sōma* in connection with death (*nekros* and *thnētos*). Therefore the use of *sōma* in the two verses is almost certainly identical. And the evidence works backwards from verse 11 to verse 10: the mortal body to be made alive in verse 11 identifies the dead body of verse 10.

---

[1] E. Best, *One Body in Christ* (London, 1955) 218.

The 'quickening' of the mortal body has not yet received definition. We naturally think of bodily resurrection yet to come. But the physical body is not now dead. Yet the body of verse 10 *is* dead. Therefore, should we take *sōma* in the holistic sense of 'I' and interpret the statements of verse 10 in terms of Gal 2: 20: 'I [= "the body"] have been crucified [= "is dead"] with Christ; it is no longer I who live, but Christ [= "the Spirit"] who lives [= "is life"] in me'? The self has died and now lives again by virtue of the indwelling Christ.[1] But here is the rub: in Gal 2: 20 the life is *present*, in Rom 8: 11 *future*. And although the preceding verse in Romans contains a reference to life with an implied present tense, that life is associated with *pneuma* as opposed to *sōma*. Consequently, we should have to restrict the interpretation in terms of Gal 2: 20 to Rom 8: 10 and open a gulf between the *sōma* already dead in that verse and the mortal *sōma* yet to be made alive in verse 11. We have just seen the illegitimacy of that procedure because of the unity of vocabulary and motifs in the two verses.

By all odds it is easiest to see a reference to the future resurrection of the body in verse 11.[2] The parallels with I Cor 15 are strong and multiple: the common use of *sōma*; the common use of *thnētos;* the common use of *nekros*; the common use of *egeirō* and *zōopoieō*; the common association of *pneuma* with the resurrection; and the common basing of all this on the resurrec-

---

[1] *Ibid.*

[2] Contra H. Grass, *Ostergeschehen und Osterberichte*, 2nd ed. (Göttingen, 1962) 165–6, who in dependence on Lietzmann interprets Rom 8: 11 in terms of an awakening to the life of righteousness here and now, and thus, by contrast, *thnēta sōmata* as men given over to the power of sin and death. Grass argues that elsewhere Paul makes the resurrection God's work whereas here it is the Spirit's work. Moreover, the Spirit elsewhere in Pauline literature provokes believers to righteous living in the present; and the passage following Rom 8: 11 is uneschatological. In answer, though the following context does contain statements about righteous living in the here and now, it is highly eschatological. Paul presses eschatology into the service of parenesis. The expression *mellete apothnēskein* in v. 13 shows that the death in question is future. The contrast in v. 18 between *ta pathēmata tou nyn kairou* and *tēn mellousan doxan apokalyphthēnai eis hēmas*, the use of *apekdechomai* in vv. 19 and 23, the future tense of *eleutherōthēsetai* in v. 21, and the general thought of creation's coming redemption – including that of the body of believers – require an eschatological understanding. A careful reading of v. 11 will show that, as usual, Paul makes resurrection the work of God; the Spirit is only mediate.

tion of Jesus. I Cor 15 indisputably has to do with the death of the present physical body and the future resurrection. The common ground in terms and motifs with Rom 8: 11 therefore requires references to physical death and future resurrection there, too. (We may again recall the future tense of *zōopoiēsei* in Rom 8: 11.) The unity of terms and motifs between Rom 8: 10 and 11 then requires references to physical death and future resurrection in verse 10 as well as verse 11.

Thus, 'the body is dead' means that the body is 'mortal', as good as dead, under the sentence of death (so v. 11 and 6: 12; cf. 7: 25, 'this body of death'). 'Mortal' in verse 11 then interprets 'dead' in verse 10. Perhaps 'dead' is more vivid and pointed, especially as a contrast to 'life', with stress on factuality instead of mere quality. More probably, Paul simply patterns verse 10 somewhat after the statements in verse 6, 'the mind of the flesh is death, but the mind of the Spirit is life and peace', and so avoids using 'mortal' twice in adjoining sentences. The parallel is inexact since 'dead' is an adjective. But an exact parallel to verse 6 'the body is *death* [noun]' would have sounded harsh.

'Because of sin' then refers to the sin of Adam which brought death (5: 12–21). The bodies of Christians are proleptically dead and will actually die in the future, not because of their sins as individuals but because of involvement in the general judgement on the human species as such. Alternatively, 'because of sin' refers to God's condemnation of sin through the mission of Christ. Possibly Paul had both ideas in mind and meant the preposition *dia* in the sense of 'through' despite the following accusatives.

'But the Spirit is life.' He himself is proleptic of resurrection and eternal life in spite of the prospect of physical death. To this part of the verse the introductory clause 'But if Christ is in you' belongs: not 'if Christ is in you the body is dead', but 'if Christ is in you the Spirit is life'. The sense of the second clause is therefore concessive: 'But if Christ is in you, *although* (*men*) the body is dead because of sin, yet (*de*) the Spirit is life.'[1]

---

[1] Cf. Liddell, Scott, and Jones, *A Greek–English Lexicon*, 9th ed. (Oxford, 1940) s.v. μέν, on the opposition and possible subordination of one clause to another in the *men*...*de* construction, and Rom 6: 17 for a concessive clause (but without *men*) followed by a clause introduced with *de*.

Pneuma refers to the Holy Spirit throughout the passage, as is evident especially in verses 9 ('the Spirit of God...the Spirit of Christ') and 11 ('the Spirit of him who raised Jesus...his Spirit which dwells in you'). It is therefore illegitimate to interpret verse 10 in terms of life in the human spirit of the believer, as opposed to the mortality of his physical body. The Pauline antidote to physical mortality is not life in the human spirit, but life in the Holy Spirit, who vitalizes the human body and spirit alike.

How can the body as 'dead' be reconciled with the body as 'mortal' and so not yet dead but still producing 'deeds'? The answer lies in the antithetic parallelism with the clause 'the Spirit is life'. As already noted, the Spirit is proleptic life or, in Paul's term, the 'first fruits' (v. 23). By assuring us of our sonship to God as Father, the Spirit keeps us from fear of suffering and death (vv. 11–39). If then the Spirit is proleptic life, the parallelism requires that the body be proleptically rather than actually dead – hence 'mortal' and still capable of doing 'deeds'. The prolepsis of both the deadness of the body and the life of the Spirit illustrates the well-known eschatological tension of the believer's position 'between the times', the already and the not-yet of the kingdom of God.

'Because of righteousness' refers to justification or to righteous living. The background of 5: 12–21 favors the former, the proximity of 8: 4 the latter. Again, Paul may have both ideas in mind.

The general thought of confidence in the face of death in Rom 8: 10–11 is carried through the rest of the chapter and receives particularly succinct expression in verses 22–3: 'We know that the whole creation has been groaning in travail together until now; and not only the creation, but we ourselves, who have the first fruits of the Spirit, groan inwardly as we wait for adoption as sons, the redemption of our body.' We might play with the possibility that *sōmatos* is a genitive of separation: 'we wait for...the redemption *from* our body' just as the 'wretched man' in 7: 24 longs for deliverance 'from this body of death'. But 7: 24 has *ek* for 'from'; and despite the groaning, the mood in ch. 8 is not nearly so wretched as that in ch. 7. Moreover, the believer's hope for *tēn apolytrōsin tou sōmatos* is part of the hope of the whole creation for liberation from its bondage to decay (vv. 18–21). This hope on the part of the whole creation can hardly consist in liberation from materiality. It is rather hope for liberation of its materiality from decay. So also the believer's hope does not consist in liberation from the physical body, but in liberation of that body (objective genitive) from decay.

Taking the genitive as objective, we might reason that *sōmatos* means the whole man because a man is not redeemed apart from his body (cf. I Cor 15: 35–58).[1] A man is not redeemed apart from his body, it is true, but that does not require a holistic meaning for *sōma*. For to say that the physical body will experience redemption is not to deny that the rest of man's being will also experience redemption. The motif of decay in the physical creation, of which our bodies are a part, limits the purview of the passage. It is more natural, then, to see the redemption of the body as a reference to physical resurrection in conjunction with the renovation[2] of all creation at the Parousia. Although the whole man is the object of redemption, Paul here looks at the physical side.

II Cor 5: 10 belongs on the list of passages where we might think that *sōma* acts as a personal pronoun and therefore refers to the whole person: 'For we must all appear before the judgement seat of Christ, so that each one may receive good or evil, according to what he has done in the body (*ta dia tou sōmatos*).' 'This has no other meaning than "according to his own deeds" – i.e., according to what he has done *not with his body*, but with *himself*, what he has made of *himself*.'[3] There is a proper recognition here that the *sōma* and the man belong together, that the *sōma* is the man himself. But *sōma* is not the whole man. The observation that here *sōma* is the 'tool of action'[4] (*dia tou sōmatos*) leads to the conclusion that *sōma* refers only to that physical part of man through which he acts in the concrete world. Such a conclusion is not only natural within the verse

[1] Best, *One Body*, 218.

[2] Grass attempts to make out of 8: 18–23 a wholly new creation rather than a renovation (*Ostergeschehen und Osterberichte*, 167–71). However, the hope of creation in its present state requires continuity with the future state. Such continuity contradicts replacement and demands renovation.

[3] Bultmann, *Theology of the New Testament* 1: 196–7 (italics supplied).

[4] *Ibid.* 196.

itself, but necessary because of the immediately preceding statements: 'we know that while we are at home in the body we are away from the Lord...and we would rather be away from the body and at home with the Lord. So whether we are at home or away, we make it our aim to please him' (vv. 6–9).[1]

The statement in II Cor 10: 10 'his bodily presence (*hē...
parousia tou sōmatos*) is weak' has been taken as a reference to 'the external presence of the whole man'.[2] But *tou sōmatos* emphasizes 'external presence' *rather than* the whole man. In other words, without negating the presence of the whole man, *sōma* specifies visible and tangible presence in the physical body and lets the presence of the rest of the man follow only by inference. The emphasis on outward physicality becomes clear also in context: 'face to face' (v. 1) and 'Look at what is before your eyes' (v. 7). Cf. 5: 12. Therefore, to define *sōma* in terms of the whole personality is to miss the very point of its use here.

We might also view the phrase 'absent in body' as a reference to the external absence of the whole man (I Cor 5: 3; cf. Col 2: 5; I Thes 2: 17). However, the antithesis 'present in spirit' in that verse shows that Paul did *not* have in mind the absence of the whole man.[3] Though together making up a human being, *sōma* and *pneuma* here stand in a certain contrast. Thus *sōma* retains its purely physical connotation over against *pneuma*.

We cannot evade the force of this contrast by asserting that the context indicates Paul's presence with the Corinthians through the Holy Spirit, 'in whose δύναμις every Christian, despite geographical distance, is ὡς παρών in the συναγωγή of

---

[1] These statements receive no consideration in Bultmann's treatment of *sōma* as the whole man in v. 10, but elsewhere Bultmann recognizes in them the exclusively corporeal meaning of *sōma*: they are 'very close to Hellenistic-Gnostic dualism', but not identical because of the 'indirect polemic against a Gnosticism which teaches that the naked self soars aloft free of any body' (*ibid.* 201–2). Stacey writes that the 'deeds done in the body' are done 'on this limited, physical plane' (*The Pauline View of Man*, 184). But the very use of the term 'physical' shows that he has not successfully interpreted *sōma* in a holistic fashion; and '*in* [or *through*] the body' is more pointed and particular than 'on this...plane'.

[2] Robinson, *The Body*, 27. So also Best, *One Body*, 217; E. Käsemann, *Leib und Leib Christi*, Beiträge zur historischen Theologie 9 (Tübingen, 1933) 119.

[3] This is true whatever the difficulty may be in discovering *how* Paul thought of his spirit as present with the Corinthians.

the faithful'.[1] For *dynamis* appears in verse 4 in connection with 'our Lord Jesus' rather than with *pneuma,* and it is difficult to find in the context any indication that *every* Christian is quasi-present with all gatherings of believers in other places. The text indicates only that Paul will be present in spirit on a special occasion in order to exercise apostolic authority in the power and name of the Lord Jesus. Furthermore, the possessive pronoun in the phrase '*my* spirit' in verse 4 ill suits an allusion to the Holy Spirit in verse 3 (cf. Rom 1: 9; 8: 16; I Cor 14: 14; 16: 18; II Cor 2: 13; 7: 13; Gal 6: 18; II Tim 4: 22; Phlm 25). The Holy Spirit always appears as God's or Christ's Spirit. Paul refers to his own human spirit. Thus the contrast with *pneuma* makes *sōma* exclusively physical. This remains true even though, against the personal pronoun, we should strain to see an overtone of the Holy Spirit. So long as the human spirit comes into view at all, *sōma* is exclusively physical because of the contrast.

We might try another way of avoiding the force of the contrast between *sōma* and *pneuma.* The *sōma* may become 'of flesh' or 'of spirit' as either dominates it. 'Thus body comes to be an equivalent for what we call personality', with the result that 'absent in body' means 'absent in person'.[2] But by the same token, 'present in spirit' ought to mean 'present in person'; yet Paul could not simultaneously have been both present and absent in person. The only recourse is to take seriously the partitive implication of the contrast between absence in body and presence in spirit.

In several more passages *sōma* has been thought to refer to the whole self.[3] But we might wonder how Gal 6: 17 entered the list: 'I bear on (*en*) my body the marks (*stigmata*) of Jesus.' *Stigmata* carries an uncompromisingly physical connotation, here with probable reference to wounds and scars, and makes unnecessary a larger meaning for *sōma.* Any watering down of the impotence of 'his [Abraham's] own body, which was as good as dead because he was about a hundred years old' (Rom 4: 19) simply to '*his* impotence' – as though the impo-

---

[1] Robinson, *The Body,* 27, n. 3.

[2] J. Moffatt, *The First Epistle of Paul to the Corinthians,* The Moffatt New Testament Commentary (London, 1938) 69, 71–3.

[3] For the following, see Best, *One Body,* 217, n. 1.

tence had to do with the whole person, not simply the body – obscures the particular point that because of old age Abraham had found himself no longer able to procreate physically. Parallel to the impotence of Abraham's body is 'barrenness of Sarah's *womb*' – hardly a holistic reference. 'The deeds of the body' in Rom 8: 13 cannot be other than the deeds of the person himself, we must agree. But the proper conclusion is that the physical body belongs to the man as an integral part of him, not that it comprises the whole man. The *sōma* is simply that part of man in and through which he performs concrete actions. Finally, according to Phil 3: 21, Christ 'will change our lowly body to be like his glorious body'. The whole being is to be refashioned, not just the body as an outward shell. That may be true, but it is more than Paul writes here. His words need indicate no more than physical resurrection. Moreover, we do not have to view the physical body as 'just' an 'outward shell'. The *sōma* is in fact the body – no more, but no less either – and from the Pauline vantage point that is good and vital to the human constitution.

Word-statistics show a sudden rise in the frequency of *sōma* in I and II Corinthians and Romans. The denigration of the body at Corinth provides the reason. We might suppose that Paul counters by stressing the *sōma* as man in the wholeness of his existence.[1] Our survey of the pertinent passages throughout Pauline literature has shown, rather, that Paul counters by stressing *sōma* as the physical requisite to a whole existence. Within the Pauline passages themselves convincing indications of the definition 'whole person' fail, and numerous indications of the normal meaning of *sōma* appear.

The *sōma* denotes the physical body, roughly synonymous with 'flesh' in the neutral sense. It forms that part of man in and through which he lives and acts in the world. It becomes the base of operations for sin in the unbeliever, for the Holy Spirit in the believer. Barring prior occurrence of the Parousia, the *sōma* will die. That is the lingering effect of sin even in the believer. But it will also be resurrected. That is its ultimate end, a major proof of its worth and necessity to wholeness of human being, and the reason for its sanctification now.

[1] E. Schweizer, 'The Church as the Missionary Body of Christ', *NTS* 8 (1961) 4–5.

CHAPTER 7

Sōma in I Cor 6: 12–20

Yet another possible indication of a holistic sense of *sōma* appears in a pair of parallel statements rather widely separated: 'Do you not know that your bodies are members of Christ?' (I Cor 6: 15a); 'Now you are the body of Christ and individually members of it' (I Cor 12: 27). In the one, 'bodies' are members of Christ; in the other, 'you' are members. 'Bodies' and 'you' alternate with the result that 'bodies' takes on the meaning 'your whole persons'. Or so we might think.[1]

The personal pronoun 'you' is not limited to man's physical aspect in the statement 'Now you are the body of Christ'. The whole person belongs to Christ's Body. ('The exact force of 'the Body of Christ' does not affect the point made here.) But we need to ask, does the general statement of Paul concerning the whole person's membership in Christ's Body preclude his making a more specific statement elsewhere that a *part* of man's constitution belongs to Christ? It it possible that in a context quite different from that of the discussion concerning spiritual gifts, Paul may have limited his field of vision to the membership of the believer's physical body in Christ without ruling out the membership of the entire person of the believer? The answer lies in a close and lengthy look at the much-analyzed passage, I Cor 6: 12–20:

'All things are lawful for me', but not all things are helpful. 'All things are lawful for me', but I will not be enslaved by anything. 'Food is meant for the stomach and the stomach for food' – and God will destroy both one and the other. The body is not meant for immorality, but for the Lord, and the Lord for the body. And God raised the Lord and will also raise us up by his power. Do you not know that your bodies are members of Christ? Shall I therefore take the members of Christ and make them members of a prostitute? Never! Do you not know that he who joins himself to a prostitute

---

[1] With Bultmann, *Theology of the New Testament* (New York, 1951) 1: 194–5; J. A. T. Robinson, *The Body. A Study in Pauline Theology*, SBT 1/5 (London, 1952) 29.

becomes one body with her? For, as it is written, 'The two shall become one flesh'. But he who is united to the Lord becomes one spirit with him. Shun immorality. Every other sin which a man commits is outside (*ektos*) the body; but the immoral man sins against (*eis*) his own body. Do you not know that your body is a temple of the Holy Spirit within you, which you have from God? You are not your own; you were bought with a price. So glorify God in your body.

Digestion and Somatic Sexuality (Vv. 12–13b)

We might reason that Paul lays emphasis on the all-embracing character of sexual union. That union involves the whole personality, not just two purely material entities: 'Digestion usually goes on without touching my ego at all. Sexuality, on the contrary, always involves my body, i.e., the whole of my existence.'[1] In writing thus, Paul was refuting the libertine or proto-gnostic view that sexual unions, like the eating of food, were merely physical and therefore morally indifferent. Since *sōma* occurs repeatedly throughout the passage, Paul's argumentative emphasis demands a meaning for *sōma* which includes the whole person. Anything less would have played into the hands of the libertines against whom Paul was debating.[2]

Support for this interpretation may derive from Paul's distinction between the body and the stomach ((*hē koilia*) in verse 13. There, the association of the stomach with food[3] and the destruction[4] coming upon the stomach with its food both

---

[1] E. Schweizer, *The Church as the Body of Christ* (Richmond, 1964) 34. Schweizer unwittingly relinquishes his argument, however, by immediately writing that if the innermost self is *not* involved in sexual life, that in itself shows perversion. So it does. But the deduction that sexual-somatic union binds together *whole* persons (therefore *sōma* = whole person) depends on the *invariable*, not just usual or willed, wholeness of that relationship.

[2] So J. Weiss, *Der erste Korintherbrief*, Meyer 5, 9th ed. (Göttingen, 1910) 160–1, and many others after him.

[3] We do not know whether the association of the stomach with food is Paul's own or one initially made in a libertine, or proto-gnostic, slogan quoted by Paul: 'Food is meant for the stomach and the stomach for food.' If the latter, Paul accepts the association, but changes the direction of reasoning away from moral indifference of bodily functions and toward moral behavior in bodily relationships.

[4] Not necessarily total annihilation. The verb is *katargeō*. Cf. M. E. Dahl, *The Resurrection of the Body*, SBT 1/36 (London, 1962) 118.

seem to place the stomach in a purely materialistic sphere. The fact that the body stands in contrast to the stomach therefore casts a more than materialistic aura over the meaning of *sōma*. Perhaps the association of the body with the Lord and the destined resurrection of the body do the same.

Further support may derive from the appearance of the personal pronoun 'us' in verse 14 after the twin appearances of 'body' in verse 13, as though the pronoun broadens the meaning of *sōma*. But foregoing analyses have shown the faultiness of making the personal pronoun determine the meaning of *sōma*. Further, the contextual usage of *sōma* determines the nuance of the personal pronoun. Here, however, the presence of the personal pronoun may seem surprising, and therefore determinative; for we should have expected Paul to write, 'God...will also raise *our bodies*.' Instead, he writes, 'God... will also raise *us*' (v. 14).

Before delving further into the passage, we must pause to take stock of the considerations so far adduced. Certainly the passage shows that *sōma*, like *sarx*, refers to what man is, not just what he has. In other words, *sōma* is essential to man's true and full being. But it is a long jump to the conclusion that 'σῶμα is the nearest equivalent to our word "personality".'[1] For *sōma* might be essential to the true and full being of man without referring to the totality of his person.

Nor can we bridge the logical gap by asserting that he who joins his *sōma* to a harlot has more than superficial relationship with her.[2] Is it more than superficial? To be sure, the union produces one body, or flesh (vv. 15–16). But to what extent? Coitus with a prostitute is casual, occasional, momentary, and non-indicative of any larger union. On the other hand, union with Christ is fundamental, constant, and all-embracing – as is also marriage. Therein lies the reason that sexual union within marriage does not take away virtue and consequently does not contradict union with Christ. The very superficiality of fornication with a harlot makes that relationship spurious and interruptive of both Christian life and marriage.

If we deduce a holistic meaning for *sōma*, we find ourselves hard pressed to give an adequate reason why somatic union in marriage should not contravene union with Christ just as

---

[1] Robinson, *The Body*, 28.   [2] *Ibid.*

somatic union with a harlot does.[1] The problem remains acute so long as it is a comprehensiveness in somatic union with another human being which contradicts union with Christ. But if it is the superficiality of somatic union with a harlot which contradicts union with Christ, no base remains from which to reason to a holistic sense of *sōma*. In and by itself, somatic union between two human beings is not comprehensive; *sōma* refers in such statements to physical union alone.

We move to the distinction between stomach and body. Whatever the contrast, it has nothing to do with the material in contrast to the more-than-material. Rather, it lies between 'food' and 'Lord' and between destruction and resurrection: 'the stomach for food...The body...for the Lord', and 'God will destroy...God...will also raise us up.' The destruction of the stomach and its food need only mean that God 'will (at the Parousia) cause such a change to take place in the bodily constitution of man and in the world of sense generally, that neither the organs of digestion as such, nor the meats as such, will then be existent'[2] (cf. I Cor 15: 44, 51; Mark 12: 25 and parallels). In other words, Paul simply teaches that the physical constitution of the resurrected body will be different from that of the mortal body. Consequently, temporary physical appetites – whether for food or for sexual gratification – of the present body ought not to govern the Christian. He should rather govern them according to the Holy Spirit (cf. vv. 17–20). Nothing implies a larger meaning for *sōma*.

Alternatively, we may find it preferable to think that Paul does not contrast the stomach and the body nearly so radically

[1] The reason is, writes R. Jewett, that in fornication a man enters the evil sphere, whereas marriage is in the sphere of Christ (*Paul's Anthropological Terms* [Leiden, 1971] 269–70). This truism only restates the question. *Why* is the one evil and the other not – in terms of the larger definition of *sōma*? Admitting the logical difficulty, C. T. Craig comments that Paul's line of argument proves too much, viz., that contrary to I Corinthians 7 marriage, too, breaks union with Christ ('The First Epistle to the Corinthians', *The Interpreter's Bible* 10 [Nashville, 1953] 74). Only the wider definition of *sōma* necessitates an assumption of illogic in Paul's reasoning.

[2] H. A. W. Meyer, *Critical and Exegetical Handbook to the Epistles to the Corinthians* (New York, 1884) 139; cf. A. Robertson and A. Plummer, *A Critical and Exegetical Commentary on the First Epistle of St Paul to the Corinthians*, ICC, 2nd ed. (Edinburgh, 1914) 123; J. A. Schep, *The Nature of the Resurrection Body* (Grand Rapids, 1964) 95–6.

as is usually thought, and perhaps not at all. After the statements that food and the body are for each other and that God will destroy both, Paul writes, 'However, the body is not meant for immorality, but for the Lord, and the Lord for the body' (v. 13). The stomach here represents part of the present body either because Paul utilizes for his own ends a Corinthian slogan in which the term is mentioned or because he anticipates his impending discussion of 'meats'. The initial adversative *de* may well mean that *despite* the physical nature and ultimate destruction of the present body, it *nevertheless* is meant for the Lord rather than for immorality. Thus we have, not a contrast, but a parallel between the stomach and the body. Paul makes the stomach stand for the whole physique. Of course, the destruction of the present corruptible body does not preclude the Pauline doctrine of bodily resurrection (see I Cor 15). In fact, Paul immediately refers to the resurrection in verse 14. But he does not purpose to contrast stomach and body by denying resurrection to the one and affirming it for the other. He rather wants to indicate that by means of resurrection God will counteract the destruction of the stomach, which *ipso facto* entails the death of the body.

First, in favor of this interpretation, it ought to be apparent that the destruction of the stomach implies dissolution of the present physical body, of which the stomach is a necessary part. The reference to resurrection more naturally points, therefore, to a counteraction of the death of the physical body, stomach included, than to a contrast in this respect between stomach and body.

Secondly, the understanding in which the two stand in contrast implies that although the use of the *sōma* is morally significant, the use of the stomach is not. And if *sōma* has a somewhat immaterial connotation over against the crassly materialistic stomach, Paul is made to rest the difference between moral significance and indifference on the distinction between the immaterial and material. Few will recognize Paul in such a distinction. Although he allows the eating of meat sacrificed to idols, his exhortation to avoid damaging the weak brother by irresponsible use of Christian freedom (I Cor 8: 1 – 9: 27; 10: 23 – 11: 1), his prohibition of participation in idolatrous banquets (I Cor 10: 1–22), and his attack on glut-

3-2

tony at the Lord's table (I Cor 11: 20-2, 27-34) all indicate that for him the stomach and food are not morally indifferent. That the stomach and food are meant for each other and will finally be destroyed does not imply that they are inconsequential. Rather (*de*) the body, to which the stomach belongs, is meant for the Lord as shown by its destined resurrection, of which Christ's own resurrection is the guarantee.

Thirdly, the organs of reproduction will perish at death along with the organ of digestion. A contrast between the perishability of *part* of the body and the imperishability of the body *as such* would not meet the problem of immorality in which yet another kind of perishable organ comes into view. The Corinthians could still say, 'The sexual organs will perish, too!' Paul wants, not an unconvincing contrast, but a forthright denial that the mortal body in any of its parts is unimportant.

Fourthly, almost exactly the same complex of ideas appears in Rom 6: 1-14, only without the synecdoche of the stomach for the body which some have mistaken for a contrast. Many interpretive questions attach to the passage in Romans, but certain leading ideas are clear enough to be generally acknowledged. In writing about the death of the body of sin, Paul uses the very verb *katargeō* which he uses in I Cor 6: 13 for dissolution of the stomach (Rom 6: 6-7). He immediately introduces a statement about the reversal of death by means of resurrection and offers the guarantee of Christ's resurrection (Rom 6: 8-10). And all this he puts forward as an argument for good behavior. The parallelisms in the sequence of ideas and in the hortatory point are all the more remarkable in that they appear despite dissimilarities between the two passages in other respects: I Corinthians lacks the baptismal background of Romans 6, and Romans 6 lacks orientation toward the specific problem of immorality. That in Romans 6 Paul writes about the death of the body in terms of the verb *katargeō* and about resurrection favors, therefore, the view that in I Corinthians 6 he also writes about the death of the body in terms of that verb (as used with 'stomach') – and about resurrection.

Short Excursus on Rom 6: 6a

It may be questioned that Paul refers to the future death of the physical body in writing, 'We know that our old self (*anthrōpos*) was crucified with him so that the sinful body (*to sōma tēs hamartias*) might be destroyed (*katargēthē*)' (Rom 6: 6a), in view of the following clauses: 'and we might no longer be enslaved to sin. For he who has died is freed from sin. But if we have died with Christ...' (Rom 6: 6b–8a, cf. 2–5). We must certainly agree that Paul stresses as an accomplished fact the historical death, with Christ, of the believer in terms of baptism. The pastness of the believer's coming alive with Christ does not receive similarly explicit statement. (Perhaps Paul did not want to give a handle to those who would deny future resurrection.)[1]

Nevertheless, the repeated exhortation to consider oneself 'alive to God in Christ Jesus' (v. 11) 'as men who have been brought from death to life' (v. 13) 'so that as Christ was raised from the dead by the glory of the Father, we too might walk in newness of life' (v. 4) – that exhortation implies the historicalness of the believer's resurrection with Christ.[2] But the expectation of future resurrection is not cancelled. 'We believe' – in the statement 'we believe that we shall also live with him' (v. 8) – demands a true future for the verb *synzēsomen* and probably also for *esometha* (v. 5: *alla kai tēs anastaseōs*), against a merely logical future. By the same token, the expectation of future death is not cancelled by the historicalness of union with Christ in his death. Hence (to paraphrase v. 6) past crucifixion with Christ with its present moral imperative looks forward to the future dissolution of the present physical body, which has been dominated by sin.[3] Past, present, and future interpenetrate one another. The point to be emphasized here, however, is

[1] Cf. R. C. Tannehill, *Dying and Rising with Christ*, BZNW 32 (Berlin, 1967) 10–14; R. Schnackenburg, *Baptism in the Thought of St. Paul* (New York, 1964) 55–61; J. M. Robinson, 'Kerygma and History in the New Testament', *The Bible in Modern Scholarship*, ed. J. P. Hyatt (Nashville, 1965) 122.

[2] Cf. D. M. Stanley, 'Response to James M. Robinson's "Kerygma and History in the New Testament"' in *The Bible in Modern Scholarship*, 151–5.

[3] Similarly, in Rom 8: 3 'the flesh of sin' is the weakness of natural instincts exploited by sin which dwells within. Only in 8: 4–13 does 'flesh', through association with sin, come practically to mean sin. See below, pp. 137–40.

that the past and the present of death do not annul its future any more than in the strictly parallel case of the resurrection. Thus, the similarity to I Cor 6: 13–14 remains intact with the resultant implication that the stomach is not to be set over against the body.

In line with this understanding, A. Schlatter also argues that for Paul new life in Christ quite literally demands a new body. Baptism promises such a body since in baptism believers belong to the resurrected Christ. They cannot live eternally in the kingdom of the Resurrected One with mortal bodies. Just as Christ's mortal body had to give way to an immortal one, so also the believer's 'body of sin'.[1] *To sōma tēs hamartias* therefore does not refer to an abstract mass of sin, to the system of sinful desires, to Sin personified as a sphere of power in the old Aeon, or to the sinful personality, but concretely to the physical body which has been dominated by sin,[2] is doomed to destruction, and will receive resurrection.

Does Paul come close to gnosticism in rooting sin in the body and in making redemption consist in the destruction of the body?[3] It would be more accurate to say that Paul *associates* sin with the body and makes redemption consist in the *resurrection*, in new form, of the old body necessarily destroyed because of the weakness of its natural instincts and consequent vulnerability to sin. This hardly comes close to gnosticism, especially with the addition of the Pauline doctrine of the present indwelling and sanctification of the body by the Holy Spirit in anticipation of the resurrection.

To our consideration of the relationship between the stomach and the body in I Cor 6: 13, we should add the suggestion that the clause 'and God will destroy both one and the other' belongs to a slogan of the libertines, or proto-gnostics, and/or appeared in a letter from the Corinthians.[4] These additional

---

[1] A. Schlatter, *Gottes Gerechtigkeit. Ein Kommentar zum Römerbrief*, 4th ed. (Stuttgart, 1965) 206–7.

[2] Cf. vv. 12, 16; and 8: 3 (*sarx hamartias*).

[3] So Jewett, *Paul's Anthropological Terms*, 291–2; cf. Bultmann, *Theology of the New Testament* 1: 199–200.

[4] *Pace* the argument of Güttgemanns (*Der leidende Apostel und sein Herr*, FRLANT 90 [Göttingen, 1966] 229) that the statement cannot form part of such a slogan because it presupposes an un-gnostic belief in a future

words would then draw out more explicitly the implication of moral indifference behind the first part of the slogan 'Food is meant for the stomach and the stomach for food.' In other words, 'Since the stomach and food will perish with the body and there is no future resurrection [cf. I Cor 15: 12*b*], it does not matter what or how or where we eat.' Similar indifference governed attitudes toward sexual morality: 'Since sexual organs will perish with the body and there is no future resurrection, it does not matter how or with whom we satisfy our sexual appetites.'[1]

The extension of the supposed slogan does not at all shift our understanding of *sōma*, however; for as in the foregoing interpretation, Paul still takes the stomach as representative of the whole physical body in order to discuss the problem of immorality. Although in the divine economy the stomach and food *are* meant for each other, one's body and prostitutes are not meant for each other.

The Body vis-à-vis the Lord and the Resurrection (Vv. 13c–14)

We need not think that the association of the body with the Lord and the destined resurrection of the body extend the meaning of *sōma* beyond the physical. Why should not the Lord be associated with a simply physical entity, the body, especially when it stands in a unitary relationship with the intangible 'inner man'? Thus far in Paul we have found no reasons to oppose or to confuse the material and the immaterial in man. The doctrine of creation eliminates any reticence to bring a material organism into relationship with the divine. Paul's reference to the resurrection reinforces the physical

eschatological judgement. Physical death itself may be the destruction to which reference is made. That would hardly be un-gnostic. Besides, Gnostics could and did have a futurist eschatology (M. L. Peel, 'Gnostic Eschatology and the New Testament', *NovT* 12 [1970] 155–62; cf. his *The Epistle to Rheginos*, The New Testament Library [Philadelphia, 1969] *passim*). Güttgemanns is correct, however, in arguing that the statement in v. 13*b* does not imply a background of gnostic asceticism (as Wikenhauser and Schmithals think), for the context has to do with libertinism.

[1] Cf. J. Schniewind, *Nachgelassene Reden und Aufsätze*, ed. E. Kähler, Theologische Bibliothek Töpelmann 1 (Berlin, 1952) 128, who suggests that *sōma* and *koilia* were paralleled in Corinth.

connotation of *sōma*. Otherwise the Corinthians would not have entertained their objections to the doctrine, objections with which Paul must deal in ch. 15, to say nothing of the physicalness of resurrection in Paul's own Jewish, Pharisaical heritage.[1]

As for the personal pronoun where we might have expected *sōmata* in verse 14 – 'And God...will also raise *us* up by his power' – Paul has already used *sōma* twice in verse 13 (and will use it again in v. 15). Stylistically he hesitates to use the word again so quickly and unnecessarily. In fact, from the standpoint of style the parallelism within verse 14 between 'God raised the Lord' and 'God...will also raise us' makes the personal pronoun a more appropriate mate to the personal title 'Lord' than *sōmata* would have been. The three appearances of *sōma* before and after verse 14 should determine the nuance of the pronoun 'us' rather than vice versa.

'Members of Christ' (*V. 15*)

We may now proceed to Paul's writing 'Your bodies are members of Christ' (v. 15), a statement which has led L. Cerfaux to conclude that the physical bodies of believers are very realistically united to the singular physical (*not* collective mystical) body of Christ.[2] To his credit, Cerfaux has recognized the physical connotation of the *sōmata* of believers and has detected in the phrase 'members of Christ' an anticipation of 'the body of Christ' in ch. 12.[3] We ought not to argue against

---

[1] Generally, even those who trace development in Paul's thinking from a literal to a spiritual view of resurrection in II Corinthians 5 recognize that in I Corinthians Paul still thinks rather literally. I. T. Beckwith notes, however, the improbability of a change from the strong and clear convictions in I Corinthians 15 to a view in II Corinthians 5 fundamentally different, and that within only a few months. Also, Paul gives expression to the 'earlier' doctrines of the resurrection and Parousia in letters written after II Corinthians 5 – see the statements in Rom 13: 11–12 and Phil 3: 20; 4: 5 [but the possibility of an early date for Philippians weakens the latter two references] – and perhaps in II Corinthians itself (4: 14; *The Apocalypse of John* [Grand Rapids, 1967, reprint of 1919 ed.] 91–2). For more on II Corinthians 5, see below, pp. 149–57.

[2] *The Church in the Theology of St Paul* (New York, 1959) 279–82.

[3] So also J. C. Hurd, Jnr, *The Origin of I Corinthians* (New York, 1965) 88; cf. U. Luz, 'Zum Aufbau von Röm. 1–8', *TZ* 25 (1969) 170, who shows that such anticipations are a regular feature of Paul's style.

Cerfaux that verse 17 'But he who is united to the Lord becomes one spirit with him' dematerializes the meaning of verse 15, in contrast to the fleshly and corporeal meaning of verse 16 (regarding union with a prostitute).[1] One might just as validly say that verse 15 materializes the meaning of *pneuma* in verse 17. More to the point, what could be the nature of a union between the physical bodies of Christ and of believers? A satisfactory answer seems lacking. The conclusion to be drawn, however, is not that *sōma* has a more-than-physical meaning when used anthropologically, but that *melos* here and *sōma* in ch. 12 have a figurative meaning when used ecclesiastically. The figure rests, however, on a strictly physical definition of *melos* (and in ch. 12, *sōma*). Verse 15*a* simply anticipates the figure of the Church as Christ's Body.

Quite apart from the larger issue of the nature of the Body of Christ which lies behind the phrase 'members of Christ' in verse 15, Paul's question does not imply that 'bodies' means 'whole persons'. It is of course true that the whole person of a believer belongs to Christ. But for that very reason the physiological side of his constitution, as well as the intangible, belongs to Christ.[2] And in the context of an injunction against sexual immorality Paul serves his purpose better by a pointed reference to man's physique than by a general reference to the totality of man's being. Thus, 'Do you not know that your bodies are members of Christ? Shall I therefore take [the ERV properly adds 'away' for *aras*] the members of Christ and make them members of a prostitute? Never!'[3]

[1] Cf. F. Mussner, *Christus das All und die Kirche* (Trier, 1955) 119–20.

[2] Cf. H. L. Goudge: 'The union of the Christian with Christ is a union of Christ with his whole personality, not with his soul or spirit alone. The body has its share in this union; Christ, as it were, is the informing spirit which directs it' (*The First Epistle to the Corinthians*, Westminster Commentaries [London, 1903] 48).

[3] It should be mentioned that Héring accepts the poorly attested *ara* and *poiēsomen* because of the plural of the first person elsewhere and because of the (wrong) assumption that *Christou* must awkwardly indicate separation with *aras* (*The First Epistle of Saint Paul to the Corinthians* [London, 1962] 43). But the singular of the first person occurs in v. 12, and *Christou* is possessive; the thought of separation lies in *aras* alone. Also, see Jewett, *Paul's Anthropological Terms*, 282–4, for a demonstration that *ouk oidate* does not imply previous teaching about the Body of Christ.

'One Body/Flesh' (V. 16)

Paul goes on to ask why the Corinthians do not recognize that the man who joins himself to a prostitute becomes one body with her, and adduces the OT proof-text 'The two shall become one flesh' (Gen 2: 24). The term 'flesh' in the quotation stands as a synonym for 'body' in the preceding clause. The parallelism and especially the introduction of the quotation with the conjunction *gar* confirm the equivalence: ...*ho kollōmenos tē pornē hen sōma estin; Esontai gar, phēsin, hoi dyo eis sarka mian.* So also does the interchange of 'body' and 'flesh' in a similar discussion of marital relationship in Eph 5: 22–33. (Of course, 'body' and 'flesh' are not always synonymous.)

Although the pejorative connotation of 'flesh' elsewhere may suit the general topic of immorality under discussion in I Corinthians 6,[1] the specific use of 'flesh' in the quotation and in its parallelism with *sōma* is not derogatory. In other words, only insofar as the context has to do with an illicit sexual union does a bad connotation adhere; this is not an instance of the type where 'flesh' *as such* denotes man as weak, transitory, and even evil. Neither in Gen 2: 24 nor here does 'flesh' have that import; for 'becoming one flesh' is not wrong, but becoming one flesh *with a prostitute*. According to the unsophisticated meaning of 'flesh', then, becoming 'one flesh' needs to refer quite simply to physical union through sexual intercourse, and to nothing more.[2] But this works back onto the expression 'become one body', to which the expression 'become one flesh' stands in parallel as a scriptural substantiation and interpretation; i.e., the unsophisticatedly physical meaning of *sarx* from Gen 2: 24 implies an unsophisticatedly physical meaning for *sōma* in Paul's own words.

We can hardly stress too much that the unsophisticatedly physical meaning of *sōma* does not distance the body from the true ego. False alternatives appear in the statement 'Jetzt geht es nicht mehr nur um einen "Teil" des Menschen, es geht

[1] C. K. Barrett, *A Commentary on the First Epistle to the Corinthians*, Harper's New Testament Commentaries (New York, 1968) 149–50.

[2] R. Batey understands Paul to be attacking the pursuit of pleasure for oneself at the expense of regard for the harlot ('The μία σάρξ Union of Christ and the Church', *NTS* 13 [1967] 278–9). But evidence in the text seems lacking.

vielmehr um diesen selbst.'[1] 'Selbst' fails to make a proper contrast to 'Teil'; for a part of the man remains the man himself, though not the whole man. So here, Paul's use of *sōma* does not separate the body from the man, but singles out the body of man for special mention in a discussion of sexual behavior.

Our conclusion naturally runs into opposing considerations. A statement by Josephus is thought to support the interpretation that becoming 'one body' can indicate a personal and moral unity as well as a physical unity – indeed, in Josephus' statement, an entirely non-corporeal unity: 'The parties thus became one body (*hen sōma*).'[2] However, Josephus is describing the way in which the rival factions of Jews within Jerusalem united for a last-ditch stand against the Roman onslaught. Insofar as they shared a common purpose to defend the city, their becoming 'one body' makes a metaphor in some respects reminiscent of I Corinthians 12. But it hardly amounts to the realistic fusion of personalities demanded for a true parallel to the suggested holistic meaning of *sōma* in I Corinthians 6. Moreover, we may doubt that Josephus has in mind very much more than a physical meaning even in his metaphor. He has indicated that the rival factions of Jews maintained spatial, physical separation from one another within the city of Jerusalem. Out of desperation their leaders allowed them to cross the boundaries and line the ramparts together. But Josephus specifically states that they had not buried their differences. 'The parties...thus became one body; and, lining the ramparts' refers to little, and perhaps nothing, more than the physical togetherness of the rival Jewish defenders on the walls. And as noted, any meaning beyond that, being metaphorical at most, would hardly imply that *sōma* means 'person' when used of individual people.

Up to this point we have assumed that the statement which Paul quotes from Gen 2: 24, 'The two shall become one flesh', refers to physical union in the consummation of marriage. Paul of course applies the statement to relationship with a prostitute rather than relationship with one's wife. But we may question whether or not the purview in Genesis is wider than physical

[1] A. Sand, *Der Begriff 'Fleisch' in den paulinischen Hauptbriefen* (Regensburg, 1967) 135, writing on I Cor 6: 16.

[2] Josephus, *JW* 5. 6, 4 §279; A. Wikenhauser, *Die Kirche als der mystische Leib Christi nach dem Apostel Paulus*, 2nd ed. (Münster, Westphalia, 1940) 105.

union and covers the union of the entire persons and lives of husband and wife.

That there is such a larger union cannot be denied; for according to Gen 2: 18–25 God creates Eve as a 'helper fit for him' in lieu of a suitable partner from the animal kingdom, and a man is to leave his father and his mother and cleave to his wife.[1] Morevoer, R. Batey has drawn attention to some rabbinical passages where the union of man and woman appears to be more than a transient physical act.[2] But does becoming one flesh refer to that larger union as a whole, or only to the climactic physical expression of it? The normal meaning of 'flesh' points to the latter. The creation of Eve out of the rib of Adam, the closing up of Adam's side 'with flesh', and Adam's response 'This at last is bone of my bones and flesh of my flesh; she shall be called Woman, because she was taken out of Man' (2: 23) set a physical tone to the passage. So also does the statement 'And the man and his wife were both naked, and were not ashamed' (2: 25). Thus both before and after, references to the human body bound the saying about becoming one flesh. In fact, 'flesh' appears in a purely physical sense three times in the three verses immediately preceding verse 24, from which Paul quotes. That verse therefore refers to physical union alone. Consequently, Paul can naturally apply it to what happens in a casual relationship with a harlot.

We may question whether Paul means that a man and a harlot make up one physical body.[3] But why not, at the time of sexual union? *Prima facie*, that seems to offer the most obvious meaning. To understand that a man and a prostitute become one person by *means* of a physical union (therefore the use of *sōma*) overloads a simple expression with too much conceptual freight. It is more difficult to understand how for Paul an illicit and passing sexual union forms a unified person out of two individuals than to understand Paul in terms of a solely physical union of two bodies in coitus.

[1] Cf. H. Baltensweiler, *Die Ehe im Neuen Testament*, ATANT 52 (Zürich, 1967) 19–22.

[2] 'The μία σάρξ Union', 271–3. The Philonic passages cited by Batey do not support the concept of more than physical union.

[3] Best, *One Body in Christ* (London, 1955) 75.

'One Spirit' (V. 17)

It has been thought, however, that verse 17 indicates a more-than-physical union in the expression 'one body': 'But he who is united to the Lord becomes one spirit with him.' Since 'one spirit' stands in parallelism with the foregoing 'one body (or flesh)', *sōma* (or *sarx*) and *pneuma* are somewhat equivalent. Hence, they refer to man comprehensively rather than partitively, for *pneuma* hardly refers to the physical body in an exclusive way. Why then do we read *hen sōma* and *sarka mian* in verse 16 but *hen pneuma* in verse 17? Because although in both verses the union encompasses the whole person, the union in verse 16 is natural, weak, earthly, and sinful (therefore *sōma* and *sarka*), but that in verse 17 is supernatural, strong, holy, heavenly (therefore *pneuma*). The equivalence of the terms lies in their being each one a comprehensive designation of the whole man, their contrast in the opposition of weakness versus strength, sinfulness versus holiness, and so on.[1]

But this makes a strange and sudden shift in the connotation of *sōma*. Paul has taken pains to emphasize that the body is for the Lord and the Lord for the body, that the body is meant for moral behavior and destined for resurrection, indeed that the body of a believer is a 'member' of Christ. And Paul will yet write that the body is a temple for the Holy Spirit and develop the concept of diversified unity among believers as the Body of Christ. In verses 16–17 does *sōma* refer to the whole man as weak, earthly, and sinful, in opposition to the whole man as strong, heavenly, and holy *pneuma*? Everything Paul writes about the *sōma* in this passage resists such a pejorative connotation. The topic at hand is immorality, and 'flesh', to which 'body' stands in parallel, can bear a pejorative meaning. But as noted above, in view of Paul's many positive statements concerning the body the topic of immorality becomes incidental to the basic definition and connotation of *sōma*; and the

[1] Wikenhauser, *Die Kirche*, 102–8; T. Soiron, *Die Kirche als Leib Christi* (Düsseldorf, 1951) 57–8; B. M. Ahern, 'The Christian's Union with the Body of Christ in Cor., Gal., and Rom.', *CBQ* 23 (1961) 202; A. R. C. Leaney, 'The Doctrine of Man in 1 Corinthians', *SJT* 15 (1962) 395; cf. E. Käsemann, 'Anliegen und Eigenart der paulinischen Abendmahlslehre', *EvT* 7 (1947/48) 282.

neutral use of 'flesh' in Gen 2: 24, quoted here, invalidates importation of a pejorative sense at this point.

Yet another perspective is available. In it we draw a parallel between the two statements 'Your bodies are members of Christ' and 'He who is united to the Lord becomes one spirit with him', cast a glance forward to the discussion of the *sōma pneumatikon* in resurrection (ch. 15), and, synthesizing, draw the conclusion that the believer very realistically becomes a member of the spiritual body with which Christ rose from the dead. Contrary to the view just rejected, this interpretation holds *sōma* and *pneuma* together in a completely positive relationship.[1]

However, such spiritualizing of *sōma* would have played right into the hands of the Corinthian libertines, or proto-gnostics.[2] And we might question the realistic equation between the *sōma pneumatikon* with which Christ arose and the Church as his body. Among other objections, it would seem to create a disparity between the earthiness and mortality of the believer's present body and the glory and immortality of Christ's risen body (cf. the contrasts listed in I Cor 15: 35–6). Yet under this interpretation these oppositely characterized bodies are realistically fused into one. How can this be?

We might think to prove the interpretation by appeal to realistic union with the body and blood of Christ in partaking the Lord's Supper (I Cor 11: 27–34).[3] But the parallel breaks down: the Lord's Supper has to do with the *crucified* body of Christ, not with the new *sōma pneumatikon* of the risen Christ to which, according to the interpretation, the believer is united. Furthermore, it is at least questionable that Paul intends to be taken realistically in writing about participation in the body and blood of Christ at the Lord's Table and that consequently

---

[1] C. M. Proudfoot, 'Imitation or Realistic Participation?', *Int* 17 (1963) 146; P. Benoit, *Exégèse et Théologie* 2 (Paris, 1961) 116–17; cf. E. Schweizer, 'πνεῦμα, πνευματικός', *TDNT* 6 (1968) 419–20.

[2] Cf. E. Percy, *Der Leib Christi*, Lunds Universitets Årsskrift, N.F. (Lund, 1942) 14–15, but without reference to the Corinthian situation. Güttgemanns' counter that Paul never indicates the formation of one body by Christ and the *individual* Christian (*Der leidende Apostel*, 234–5) does not carry conviction because the entire discussion in I Cor 6: 12–20 turns on individual behavior, as shown by the frequent singularity of the personal pronouns and the plurality of *sōma* in v. 15, 'Do you not know that your bodies are members of Christ?'

[3] So Proudfoot, 'Imitation or Realistic Participation?', 146.

the elements of Communion become the poison of mortality for those who partake unworthily. For that would require him to have believed conversely in the *im*mortality of all who partake worthily, in contrast to the sickness and death of those who do not. Yet Paul nowhere suggests that a Christian's survival till the Parousia depends on a worthy eating of the elements in the Lord's Supper. The wording of 11: 27–34 need only mean that an unworthy manner of participation has desecrated a sacred rite by spoiling its meaning, with the result that God has inflicted illness and death – quite apart from making the elements 'poisonous' – upon certain careless participants.[1]

Similarly, we lose the legitimacy of subsidiary appeals to baptism for the dead, understood as realistic participation in the body of Christ in behalf of another through the baptismal rite (I Cor 15: 29), and to the sanctification of unbelieving mates and children, understood as the conveyance of holiness through physical relationships (I Cor 7: 12–16). The meaning of baptism for the dead is highly uncertain; and Paul's speaking in the third person of those who practise it and immediately switching to the first personal pronoun at least opens, if not favors, the possibility that Paul did not himself engage in or approve of it. The passage then becomes either irrelevant to Paul's own view of union with Christ, or, if the change from third person to first implies backhanded disapproval, negative toward the realistic interpretation. And even were we to hold a realistic interpretation of I Cor 7: 12–16, we could hardly think that sanctification of unbelievers by virtue of a Christian mate and/or parent entails the salvific union with Christ of which Paul writes in ch. 6. Whether optimistic or pessimistic, Paul's questions in I Cor 7: 16 decisively exclude such an implication: 'Wife, how do you know whether you will save your husband? Husband, how do you know whether you will save your wife?' Whatever the sanctification is, it does not measure up to the salvation which union with Christ effects. Again the parallel breaks down at the crucial point.

We might make another attempt to establish the parallel:

[1] Cf. G. W. H. Lampe, 'Church Discipline and the Interpretation of the Epistles to the Corinthians', *Christian History and Interpretation: Studies Presented to John Knox*, ed. W. R. Farmer, C. F. D. Moule, and R. R. Niebuhr (Cambridge, 1967) 347.

according to I Cor 6: 12–20 the close and *sinful* relationship of a believer to an unbeliever cancels membership in Christ and the Church; according to I Cor 7: 12–16 the close and *legitimate* relationship of a believer to an unbeliever draws the unbeliever into membership in Christ and the Church.[1] But the parallel rests on an equivocation in the meaning of membership in Christ and the Church. As noted, that membership does not entail salvation in 7: 12–16; but it *does* in 6: 12–20, especially verse 14.

It appears, then, that fundamental differences between I Cor 6: 12–20 on the one hand and 7: 12–16; 11: 27–32; and 15: 29 on the other hand negate arguments drawn from the later passages in favor of a 'realistic' interpretation of 6: 12–20.

Now we may proceed with a closer look at 6: 17 in its immediate context. The *de* with which verse 17 begins, comments E. Best, suggests a certain amount of contrast between 'body' and 'spirit' even though *sōma* refers to the whole person; but the real reason for *de* lies in the use of 'flesh' at the conclusion of verse 16. 'Flesh' highlights the physical side of *sōma*, but 'spirit' contrasts – therefore the adversative *de* – with the emphasis on the physical. Thus the meaning of *pneuma* is 'not really far from the meaning we have already given to σῶμα, but with less stress on the physical side'.[2] The *de* which introduces verse 17 does indeed draw a contrast between emphasis on the physical (v. 16) and emphasis on the spiritual (v. 17). But *sōma* can hardly straddle both emphases. Otherwise unnecessary confusion in the meaning of *sōma* results. *Sarka* highlights the physical side, not of *sōma*, but of *man*. *Sōma* does the same, and only that. *Pneuma* goes in the opposite, non-corporeal direction.[3]

In attacking immorality, Paul does not appeal to a superiority of the *pneuma* over the *sōma*. Three times in the passage he stresses the belonging of the physical body to Christ and his Spirit: 'The body is...for the Lord, and the Lord for the body' (v. 13);[4] 'Do you not know that your bodies are members of

---

[1] Best, *One Body*, 77–8.   [2] *Ibid.* 76.

[3] For a somewhat similar critique of the playing down of the antithesis between *sōma/sarka* and *pneuma*, see J. J. Meuzelaar, *Der Leib des Messias*, Van Gorcum's theologische Bibliothek 35 (Assen, 1961) 144–8.

[4] Robinson relates 'the Lord for the body' to the incarnation: 'Into the body of the old world of sin and death enters the Prince of Life, Himself

Christ?' (v. 15); 'Do you not know that your body is a temple of the Holy Spirit within you?' (v. 19). But only once does Paul mention the union of the spirit with the Lord: 'But he who is united to the Lord becomes one spirit with him' (v. 17). The imbalance of emphasis derives from the Corinthians' acceptance of the spirit's unity with the Lord and rejection of the body's relationship to the Lord. Paul needs to stress what the Corinthians fail to see, or deliberately deny. In Paul's own thought, the twin truths add up to this: the whole man, body and spirit, belongs to the Lord. Therefore, illicit union with a harlot, although it is 'merely' physical, as the Corinthians would say, effects a oneness of physical relationship which contradicts the Lord's claim over the body and creates a disparity between the body (now given over to a harlot) and the spirit (still united to the Lord).

Paul further develops this motif of disparity by proceeding to write about the unique connection between the body and the sin of immorality (v. 18) vis-à-vis the dwelling of the Holy Spirit within the body (vv. 19–20). Paul opposes the disparity between carnal union with a harlot and spiritual union with the Lord because although body and spirit differ, they belong together in the service of Christ. Redemption includes the whole man, of which the body forms as proper and essential a part as does the spirit. This is proved by the coming resurrection and by the present indwelling of the Holy Spirit (vv. 14, 19–20). Hence, contrary to Corinthian belief, the body cannot sin with impunity apart from the spirit.[1]

---

in a body of flesh, to redeem, quicken and transfigure it', with a cross-reference to Gal 4: 3–5 (*The Body*, 34). But nothing in I Corinthians 6 indicates that Paul has the incarnation in mind in v. 13. And 'body' refers to an individual body, not 'the old world of sin and death'.

[1] For the sake of completeness, two other views of v. 17 are here noted. (1) In writing about becoming one spirit with the Lord, Paul steers away from the implication that the believer's relationship to the Lord is of the same kind as coitus with a prostitute. Against this view, although the believer's relationship to the Lord is not sexual, it *is* of the same kind as union with a prostitute insofar as both deal with the body. That is the burden of vv. 13–16, 19–20. (2) Paul wants to say that immorality separates the spirit as well as the body from the Lord. But the crucial point in this interpretation – viz., separation of the believer's spirit from the Lord – does not appear in the text, in contrast to the clear statements concerning separation of the believer's body from the Lord (vv. 15–16).

The Uniqueness of Immorality (V. 18)

We now come to the very difficult eighteenth verse: 'Shun immorality. Every other sin [the Greek text lacks 'other'] which a man commits is outside (*ektos*) the body; but the immoral man sins against (*eis*) his own (*idion*) body.' The last phrase, *eis to...sōma hamartanei*, corresponds to the Hebrew expression חטא בגוף or פשע בגוף.[1] Where used in rabbinical and targumic literature, it means 'to sin by or for oneself alone' (as opposed to leading others into sin) or 'to sin with (or in) the body'. But the Hebrew word גוף hardly means '(whole) person'[2] in the phrase Paul is supposed to have taken over into Greek. That would be necessary to establish, however; otherwise the rabbinical and targumic evidence becomes useless — worse than useless, positively antagonistic to anything more than a purely physical sense.

Since the sexual immorality discussed in I Corinthians involves partnership with a prostitute, the first possible meaning of the rabbinical expression, 'to sin by or for oneself alone' is unlikely. We might therefore opt for the second meaning, 'to sin with (or in) the body',[3] and reason that if *sōma* refers only to physique, it would not hold true that all other sins are committed outside the *sōma*; for sins such as drunkenness, gluttony, and suicide are also physical. A solution to the problem presents itself in a larger meaning of *sōma*, viz., 'person': at the center of his being, a fornicator becomes one person with a prostitute. Of course, other sins — non-physical — strike at the core of personality, too, sins such as pride. They break a believer's relationship with Christ, but in them there is no attachment to another person as in fornication.

Against this explanation, however, other sins *do* involve attachment to another person. 'Let me first go and bury my father.' But more importantly, since many sins other than immorality strike at the center of personality, it really does not matter whether they involve attachment to another person. For they still strike at the center of personality and therefore — if

[1] Str–B 3: 366–7.   [2] See below, pp. 94–6, for the usage of גוף.
[3] So Best (*One Body*, 75–6), who also takes over the RSV, '*against* the body'. But 'against' does not quite correspond to the force of the Hebrew expression.

sōma means 'person' – contradict Paul's implication that only immorality is a sin *eis to idion sōma*.[1] In other words, Paul's exclusivistic statement concerning immorality poses as much a problem for the definition of *sōma* as 'person' as for the popular meaning 'body', for a person never sins apart from his own person.[2]

In another view of verse 18 we take *sōma* as the entire self. Then we look back to verse 13*c* 'The body is not meant for immorality, but for the Lord, and the Lord for the body', and reason that since the two relations to a prostitute and to the Lord mutually exclude each other, it is no exaggeration for Paul to write in verse 18*b* that *only* immorality destroys a person's relation to Christ.[3] But the fact that an immoral relationship excludes relationship to Christ does not rule out the possibility that other sins might also break relationship with Christ. So we have come no closer to identifying the reason behind the exclusivism of Paul's statement. Moreover, the meaning of *sōma* is incidental to the interpretation, which could be held with either of the definitions 'body' and 'person'.

With R. Jewett we may find it necessary to say that for Paul only immorality destroys the corporate relation with Christ 'so completely'.[4] A number of interpreters do the same. Following Calvin, C. K. Barrett thinks that Paul speaks comparatively; other sins do not stain the body so seriously as fornication does.[5] Robertson and Plummer argue that Paul's exclusion of idolaters, thieves, greedy people, drunkards, revilers, and robbers from the kingdom of God along with the immoral, adulterers, and homosexuals (vv. 9–10) demands a comparative sense: 'All other sins are ἐκτὸς τοῦ σ., in the sense that they do not, as *directly* as fornication does, alienate the

[1] For the same reason Güttgemanns' attempt to evade the interpretive difficulty by making *sōma* to mean man as the object of rule from outside fails (*Der leidende Apostel*, 237–8). Although fornication contradicts the rule of Christ over the *sōma* by making it the object of rule by a harlot, other sins, too, contradict the rule of Christ over the Christian.

[2] Again C. T. Craig accuses Paul of illogic in a 'quick generalization which can hardly be substantiated' ('The First Epistle to the Corinthians', *The Interpreter's Bible* 10 [Nashville, 1953] 75). But Paul has just listed sins which exclude people from the kingdom of God (vv. 9–10); he probably still has those sins in mind while dictating, 'Every [other] sin' (v. 18).

[3] Jewett, *Paul's Anthropological Terms*, 261.

[4] *Ibid.*   [5] *First Corinthians*, 150–1.

body from Christ, its Life and Goal.' Robertson and Plummer then draw attention to other absolute statements which turn out on closer inspection to be comparative, notably the sayings 'I will have mercy, and not [meaning "more than"] sacrifice' (Hos 6: 6) and 'Every sin and blasphemy will be forgiven men [meaning "can be forgiven if men repent"], but the blasphemy against the Spirit will not be forgiven' (Matt 12: 31). So also other sins fall 'outside the body' by comparison with immorality.[1] This may be the proper interpretation, but it favors neither the popular nor the proposed larger definition of *sōma*. Indeed, Robertson and Plummer hold it with the one definition and Jewett with the other.

H. Alford holds the comparative view, too, but states the comparison in terms of the origin and purpose of various sins rather than in terms of their seriousness. This is probably the best interpretation:

The assertion [that every sin is outside the body], which has surprised many of the Commentators, is nevertheless *strictly true*. Drunkenness and gluttony, e.g. are sins done *in* and *by* the body, and are sins *by abuse of* the body, – but they are still ἐκτὸς τοῦ σώματος – introduced *from without*, sinful *not* in their *act*, but in their *effect*, which effect it is each man's duty to foresee and avoid. But fornication is the *alienating that body which is the Lord's, and making it a harlot's body* – it is sin *against a man's own body*, in its very nature, – against the *verity and nature* of his body; not an *effect on* the body from participation of things without, but a *contradiction of the truth* of the body, wrought *within itself*.[2]

Grosheide adds that in suicide the pleasure of the body is not sought. In gluttony, the excess of eating and drinking is evil, not the act of eating and drinking *per se*. Besides, drunkenness [and gluttony] stem mainly from conviviality rather than from purely physical desires. In immorality, however, the action itself is sinful, arises within the body, and has as its sole purpose the gratification of the body.[3]

[1] Robertson and Plummer, *First Corinthians*, 127–8 (italics supplied).

[2] H. Alford, *The Greek Testament*, 5th ed. (London, 1865) 2: 518; cf. Meyer, *Corinthians*, 143; A. Schlatter, *Die Korintherbriefe* (Stuttgart, 1950) 75.

[3] F. W. Grosheide, *Commentary on the First Epistle to the Corinthians*, The New International Commentary on the New Testament (Grand Rapids, 1953) 151.

In favor of Alford and Grosheide, the contrast of *eis* with *ektos* favors the meaning '(with)in' for *eis* as opposed to 'outside of' for *ektos*. To be sure, *eis* with *hamartanō* regularly means 'against' throughout Greek literature. But the use of ב in the corresponding Hebrew expressions[1] and the contrast with *ektos* in the immediate context here may well overpower the usual meaning of *eis* with *hamartanō*. If so, there results some substantiation for a stress on the origin of fornication within the physical body.

Other understandings of Paul's statement call for consideration, too. Perhaps sinning against the body means sinning against the Church as the Body of Christ rather than one's physical body.[2] But did Paul expect the Corinthians to read ch. 12 before ch. 6? In 6: 15, 'members of Christ' may hint at what is coming concerning the Church as Christ's Body, but Paul would hardly jump without preparation or warning from an individual use of *sōma* in connection with immoral behavior to an ecclesiastical use. And in the clause 'the immoral man sins within/against his own body', the qualifier 'his own (*idion*)' most naturally points away from the Church by individualizing the noun 'body'.

Or, we may adopt the suggestion that a dialogue appears in verse 18. The Corinthian slogan was *pan hamartēma ho ean poiēsē anthrōpos ektos tou sōmatos estin*, which might be taken to mean that no sin can affect the true personality (*sōma*) of the initiated. Paul's retort is *ho de porneuōn eis to idion sōma hamartanei*, which might be taken to mean that the fornicator *does* sin against his true personality.[3] R. Kempthorne thinks that this understanding receives confirmation from its allowing *pan* to have a natural unqualified sense, with the result that we do not have to interpolate 'other' with the RSV: 'Every *other* sin.'[4] On the other hand, in the estimation of Barrett, Paul states a general proposition and then makes an exception to it, as also in verses 12–13.[5] We might add that the adversative *de*

[1] See above, p. 70.

[2] E. Schweizer, 'σῶμα, σωματικός, σύσσωμος', *TDNT* 7 (1971) 1070.

[3] C. F. D. Moule, *An Idiom-Book of New Testament Greek*, 2nd ed. (Cambridge, 1963) 196–7.

[4] 'Incest and the Body of Christ: A Study of I Corinthians vi. 12–20', *NTS* 14 (1968) 571.

[5] *First Corinthians*, 149–50.

can naturally signify an exceptive contrast and thus justify the interpolation of 'other' in the general statement.

It is neither exegetically necessary nor especially advantageous, then, to adopt the form of dialogue with its implication that *sōma* means 'person'. Of course, the form of dialogue does not in itself require the meaning 'person', but the libertines at Corinth would hardly have divorced all sins from the physical body. Since they would rather have put sin on the side of the physical body and dissociated the true 'I' (consisting in the spirit) from the body with its sin, a slogan from them would more naturally have read, 'Every sin...is outside the *spirit*.' The presence of *sōmatos* where we should have expected *pneumatos* in a libertine slogan would require (if this is indeed a libertine slogan) not that *sōmatos* be used holistically but that it completely reverse its meaning from that which is physical to that which excludes and opposes the physical body. That the libertines used *sōma* for the whole person would need considerable evidence. That they used *sōma* for the true person *in contradistinction to the body* which may sin without impugning the true person requires even greater evidence. That evidence is lacking. So long as any remnant of physicality remains in *sōma*, the libertines could not have used the term for the true self in a slogan designed to separate the true self from the sins of its unessential physique.

Nevertheless, we need to examine a suggested combination of the form of dialogue with the view already mentioned that *sōma* in verse 18 refers to the Church as Christ's Body.[1] According to this interpretation, 6: 12–20 harks back to the case of the incestuous man in ch. 5. In their slogan the libertines were saying that the sin of incest lay outside the ecclesiastical Body because the step-mother was not a Christian. Paul retorts that the man sins against the church because the church is *his* (the man's) body by virtue of his membership in it. With the meaning 'person, self' for *sōma* in Paul's retort, we gain a double meaning: the man sins against the church *and* against himself.[2]

[1] Kempthorne, 'Incest and the Body of Christ', 572. Schweizer specifically rejects dialogue ('σῶμα κτλ.', 1070, n. 439).

[2] Kempthorne strangely attempts to steer away from an emphatic 'his own' to an unemphatic 'his' for *idion*. In reality, his interpretation requires

But we may suspect over-interpretation in the proposal of a double meaning. And the precipitous importation of the Church as the Body of Christ, a theme wholly undiscussed so far in the epistle and presumably unknown to the Corinthians, once again proves problematic. Moreover, the association of 6: 12–20 with ch. 5, by which an individual reference is supplied, raises a doubt. Although *porneia* occurs in both passages, in 6: 12–20 the female partner in immorality is a *pornē*, a prostitute, but in ch. 5 the female partner is the wife of the man's father. An equation between the two therefore seems doubtful, especially if the *pornē* is a temple prostitute as the figure of the temple in verses 19–20 and the local color of the Temple of Aphrodite near Corinth both suggest.

The Body as the Temple of the Holy Spirit (Vv. 19–20)

Paul finishes the section by calling attention to the dwelling of the Holy Spirit within the temple of the body, the divine ownership of the redeemed, and their consequent obligation to glorify God in their body (vv. 19–20). It has been denied that the body as a physical frame alone can be inhabited and controlled by the Holy Spirit 'or else man would be reduced to the worst kind of automaton whose mind and spirit are of no account; rather the Holy Spirit dwells in his whole being or personality'.[1] But so long as the control is conceived to be mechanistic, the 'or else...automaton' cuts equally against the Holy Spirit's control of the whole personality, including mind and spirit. If the Spirit's control of the whole man, including mind and spirit, is not mechanistic and therefore does not make him an automaton, neither does the Spirit's control of the physical body. The mind and spirit keep their significance. But because of the topic at hand – sexual misbehavior – Paul simply has no special need to mention them here. And although it is true that the believer should

the usual strong meaning: the body which is the church and the body which is the whole self, against both of which the incestuous man sins, are *his own* and therefore not irrelevant. Nevertheless, by supplying an individualizing reference even apart from *idion* Kempthorne avoids a serious weakness in Schweizer's generalizing interpretation of the body as the Church, viz., the lack of regard for the force of *idion*. (Even when unemphatic *idios* individualizes.)   [1] Best, *One Body*, 75.

glorify God with his whole person, not just with his physical body, the subject of immorality and the background of sacred prostitutes and hetaerae[1] suit a pointed reference to the physical body as a means and place to glorify God without denial of the larger truth.

The same considerations apply to the doctrines of redemption and sanctification as expressed in verses 19–20. Once again, the alternation of the personal pronoun 'you' with *sōma* fails to enlarge the meaning of *sōma*. Instead, *sōma* restricts the reference of the pronoun to the physical side of believers. This interpretation becomes superficial only if *sōma* as a physical organism is demeaned. However, Paul's very point of emphasis here and throughout the section is that the body as a physical organism is not to be demeaned.

If the interpretation of *sōma* as the Church were to gain our favor in preceding verses, we might bring it into verses 19–20. In support we might cite the singular number of *sōma* in its two appearances and of the noun 'temple', over against the individualizing plural in verse 15 ('your bodies'; cf. Eph 5: 28 and the v.l. *ta sōmata* in I Cor 6: 19). This, we might think, outweighs the plural *hymōn*, which occurs twice with *sōma* in verses 19–20. Thus, *sōma hymōn* would mean 'the Body (of Christ) of which you are members', and Paul would be exhorting the Corinthians to keep the Body which is the church holy by removal of the incestuous man (cf. 3: 17).[2]

An ecclesiastical use of *sōma* in these verses would of course eliminate them from the debate over the anthropological meaning of *sōma*. But they are not so easily eliminated. The difficulty of equating the incest in ch. 5 with the prostitution here still militates against the interpretation. So also does the delay in Paul's exposition of the Body of Christ until ch. 12. We should not read too much into the singular form of *sōma*. Although the plural appears in verse 15, thereafter Paul consistently uses the singular. It is only natural for him to continue with the singular and to imply a distributive sense with the plural possessive pronoun *hymōn*. N. Turner notes that

[1] See Baltensweiler, *Die Ehe*, 197–8.

[2] Kempthorne, 'Incest and the Body of Christ', 572–3; see also P. S. Minear, *Images of the Church in the New Testament* (Philadelphia, 1960) 180–2.

sōma appears as a distributive singular in two other passages: (1) 'always carrying in the body the death of Jesus, so that the life of Jesus may also be manifested in our body ["bodies" in ℵ 1739 *pc r* vg sy^p Or]' (II Cor 4: 10); (2) 'the redemption of our body' (Rom 8: 23).[1]

We may try to evade the force of these cross-references by making Paul refer to himself alone in II Cor 4: 10 and to the Body of Christ in Rom 8: 23.[2] But in II Corinthians the context both near and distant abounds in plural forms of the first personal pronoun which appear to include Paul and his missionary partners and sometimes perhaps the Corinthians themselves. At least colleagues such as Timothy (1: 1) and Titus (2: 13) who had shared his recent sufferings must come into view along with the apostle himself in 4: 10. Paul writes in the first person singular when he wishes to refer to himself alone in the early chapters of II Corinthians (see 1: 12–2: 13). Similarly, plural forms of the first personal pronoun surround the phrase in which the singular of *sōma* occurs in Rom 8: 23. And Paul is writing about the hardships endured by the physical creation, including our own physical hardships. That motif favors nothing more than the normal meaning of *sōma*.

The distributive singulars stand fast in the two cross-references, then, and thereby support an identical understanding of the singulars in I Cor 6: 19–20. We may compare a similar situation in Rom 12: 1–2, where *sōma* appears in the plural and its coordinates in the singular. Paul exhorts his readers to present their 'bodies' (plural) to God as a living 'sacrifice' (singular) and to be transformed by the renewal of their 'mind' (singular). The singulars take on a distributive meaning from the plural. In all these passages the singular may imply a certain commonness of action or experience, but in context they carry a distributive (and therefore plural) sense.

We have discovered no convincing reason to make us think that Paul speaks of anything other or more than the physical body in writing of the *sōma* as the temple of the Holy Spirit and as the place where God is to be glorified. The very meaning of

[1] J. H. Moulton, W. F. Howard, and N. Turner, *A Grammar of New Testament Greek*, III, *Syntax* (Edinburgh, 1963) 23–4.

[2] Kempthorne, 'Incest and the Body of Christ', 572–3; Robinson, *The Body, passim*.

'temple' as a physical structure favors the simple and usual definition of *sōma*, especially if Paul antithetically alludes to the physical structure of the Temple of Aphrodite near Corinth. Final confirmation comes from a similar Pauline statement: 'If the Spirit of him who raised Jesus from the dead dwells in you, he who raised Christ Jesus from the dead will give life to your mortal bodies also through his Spirit which dwells in you' (Rom 8: 11). The motif of the indwelling Spirit corresponds exactly to I Cor 6: 19–20. And the plural 'bodies' confirms the distributive sense of the singulars in I Cor 6: 19–20.

Oscillation versus *constancy of meaning*

Bultmann's interpretation of I Cor 6: 13–20 varies so frequently in its understandings of *sōma* that it has been reserved till last for consideration all at once. 'The nuances of meaning in the word *soma* melt into one another in a strange fashion.'[1] In the denial that the body is meant for immorality, *sōma* refers to the body 'insofar as it is the seat of sex-life'. Presumably, then, the connotation is physical, and to that we may assent. But, states Bultmann, the sexual implication can scarcely adhere to the affirmation that the body is for the Lord and the Lord for the body. There is no *sexual* implication, we agree, but there may still be a *physical* implication, which is all that is needed – and it *is* needed – for the discussion of moral versus immoral behavior. The physical implication gains support from the immediate reference to resurrection *pace* Bultmann, who sees *sōma* as 'self, person' hovering 'in the background' because of alternation with the personal pronoun.

Further oscillation of meaning occurs in verse 15, where according to Bultmann 'your bodies' has the larger meaning 'you' in the question, 'Do you not know that your bodies are members of Christ?' But in the ensuing question, 'Shall I therefore take the members of Christ and make them members of a prostitute?', we are back to the physical meaning, which continues in verse 16 in the becoming 'one body' with a prostitute. In this latter expression Bultmann detects a figurative tendency, 'unity, one-ness'. But the oneness of coitus with a

[1] Bultmann, *Theology of the New Testament* 1: 194–5, followed by Baltensweiler, *Die Ehe*, 194–5.

prostitute is hardly figurative and the idea of oneness comes from *hen* and from the statement as a whole rather than from a special meaning for *sōma*.

In verse 18, though the meaning is 'hard to determine', we are essentially back to 'self' because *sōma* is here 'most intimately connected with man'. But, we may respond, for Paul the *physical* body is most intimately connected with man. Hence, we need not see a further or different reference. And regarding verse 19, after concession that 'one is at first inclined to think of his physical body as the temple (cf. Rom 8: 11) in keeping with the basic tenor of the exhortation – that the Christian keep his body clean from immorality', Bultmann falls back on the argument from the alternation of *sōma* and personal pronouns in order to demonstrate the meaning 'whole person, not just his body'. The result is that 'the meaning fluctuates strangely'. 'On the other hand, *soma* in the exhortation, "So glorify God in your *soma*" (v. 20), probably means "body" – i.e. within the whole context it means: do not yield your body to unchastity.' That is well said. Greater attention to this motif would have forestalled the overloading of Paul's simple use of *sōma* with superfluous and erratic meanings.

Summary and Conclusion

In summary, Paul admits that the present physical body will perish, but does not allow the deduction that its actions are morally indifferent. Rather, this body belongs to the Lord, as is shown by its resurrection (which Paul will yet show entails transformation) and by its present function as the habitation of the Holy Spirit. Therefore, physical fusion with a prostitute in an act of intercourse contradicts the redemption and sanctification of the body.

We conclude that in neither the Pauline epistles, nor the literature of the NT outside those epistles, nor the LXX, nor extra-Biblical ancient Greek literature does the definition 'whole person' find convincing support. This is not to deny that (outside the Platonic tradition) emphasis falls on the unity of man's being. But it is a unity of parts, inner and outer, rather than a monadic unity. Ancient writers do not usually treat *sōma* in isolation. Rather, apart from its use for a corpse, *sōma* refers to the physical body in its proper and intended union with the soul/spirit. The body and its counterpart are portrayed as united but distinct – and separable, though unnaturally and unwantedly separated. The *sōma* may *represent* the whole person simply because the *sōma* lives in union with the soul/spirit. But *sōma* does not *mean* 'whole person', because its use is designed to call attention to the physical object which is the body of the person rather than to the whole personality. Where used of whole people, *sōma* directs attention to their bodies, not to the wholeness of their being.

PART II

SŌMA IN THE FRAMEWORK OF ANTHROPOLOGICAL DUALITY

CHAPTER 8

Anthropological Duality and Classical Greek Thought

If Paul never uses *sōma* as a technical term for the whole person but always of man's physique, the possibility of a certain anthropological dualism arises. In fact, the strictly physical meaning of *sōma* demands qualification of the unitary view of man. (We may presume that Paul's use of terms for the incorporeal side of man prohibits thorough-going materialism.) For reasons yet to be explored, however, it will appear that 'dualism' too strongly dichotomizes Pauline anthropology. And the traditional term 'dichotomy', being purely ontological in its connotation, lacks dynamism. 'Duality' – just because it sounds like a hybrid of 'dual' and 'unity' and poses the possibility of a functional as well as ontological understanding – better expresses Paul's way of thinking. Even then careful explanation must accompany the term.

For the avoidance of misunderstanding we need to issue a number of disclaimers even prior to discussion of the evidence in favor of anthropological duality. There is no making of Paul into a Greek. The distance of Paul from Philo, who attempted to combine Jewish theology and Hellenistic philosophy, clearly shows the comparatively un-Hellenistic character of Pauline anthropology.[1] Rather, the Hebrew concept of man was not monadic even though it was unitary. The anthropological duality of the OT, yet to be considered here, developed clearer exposition in Judaism of the Hellenistic age but usually resisted a dualism in which body and soul oppose each other. Paul's recognition of the duality of man reflects the Jewish theology of his time and neither contradicts the OT nor denies the unity (but not monism) of man as a whole being.

Again, anthropological duality does not imply a metaphysical dualism according to which the body or flesh is evil, but affirms that man is made up of two substances which belong

---

[1] See W. D. Stacey, *The Pauline View of Man* (London, 1956) 215–22. For Philo's use of *sōma, sarx, psychē, pneuma,* and *nous,* see E. Hatch, *Essays in Biblical Greek* (Oxford, 1889) 110–29.

together though they possess the capability of separation.[1] *Sarx* does not necessarily refer to evil; but when it does, the term no longer refers to a physical substance as such. On the other hand, *sōma* never refers to evil but always to an organization of physical substance. Thus, *sarx* can be used in a variety of meanings, but *sōma* possesses a constancy of physical meaning.[2]

Nor does the difference and separability of the corporeal and the incorporeal in man imply any inferiority on the part of the corporeal. For Paul, actions performed through the body count quite as much as contemplation and feeling. The true man is the whole man – corporeal and incorporeal together, the incorporeal acting through the corporeal, each equally deficient without the other. Hence, the true man is not the inner man alone, for although the body is outward, it is not unessential. The body is to be sanctified and will be resurrected. No inferiority here!

Furthermore, anthropological duality in Paul does not typically take the form of *sōma* and *psychē*. In spite of the frequency of נפש in the Hebrew OT as well as of *psychē* in the LXX and extra-Biblical Greek literature, Paul likes to use *pneuma* more than *psychē* – and then seldom of the human spirit (though that receives mention) but more often of the Holy Spirit because of the experience of divine initiative in redemption.[3] As a matter of fact, Paul's anthropological duality does not display itself in a formally consistent use of any two terms. *Sōma* always refers to the physique, but so does *sarx* at times. A number of words refer to the incorporeal side of man and functions thereof: *pneuma, psychē, kardia, nous, dianoia, phrenes, syneidēsis, ho esō anthrōpos*. For the whole man, Paul uses *anthrōpos*. In other words, there is an ontological duality, a functional pluralism, and an overarching unity. No emphasis lies on the duality, however. It is just there. Paul is not interested in

---

[1] See D. E. H. Whiteley, *The Theology of St Paul* (Philadelphia, 1964) 32–3, on different types of dualism. He attributes the recent dominance of the holistic view over the dualistic view to reaction against nineteenth century idealism, to materialistic progress in the modern world, and to psychosomaticism in current medical science and behavioristic psychology – in addition to Biblical exegesis.

[2] This is not to deny metaphorical usage, which, however, rests on an understanding of *sōma* as the physical body.

[3] See W. D. Stacey, 'St Paul and the "Soul" ', *ExpT* 66 (1955) 274–7.

anthropology as an independent motif. Rather, he treats man as the object of divine dealings and as the subject of activity in the order which God created. Despite the informality of his anthropology, it appears that Paul regularly thought of man as a unity of the tangible and the intangible. Into this way of thinking fits *sōma* as a term consistently used for the physical body.

Having aired these caveats, we may proceed to evidences of duality in Pauline anthropology. We shall work from the background materials into Paul himself the better to assess the milieu in which he wrote and thereby the probable meaning of his statements which may be claimed for a duality in his view of man.

The anthropological dualism in Greek tradition is so well known that it requires little space here. In the Homeric period body and soul are distinguished and death consists in their separation, but the difference between them is unimportant. Indeed, *sōma* normally refers to a corpse. The persistence of the soul after death is not a benign existence; true immortality requires body and soul in unity. Especially under the influence of Orphism, Pythagoreanism, and the mysteries, the distinction between body and soul becomes more important shortly before Plato and in Plato. Death continues to be the separation of body and soul, but now they are pitted against each other in earthly life.

Although in Aristotle the soul becomes one with the body as the latter's form, by this time the dualistic mode of thought prevails so strongly that even Aristotle partially capitulates by making the mind that which stands over against the body in that it can exist in isolation and thus survive the body.[1] Within Stoicism develops the idea of soul as a pervasive, rarefied substance. Epicurus accepts nothing but the body, with the result that the soul becomes a part of it. By NT times, revival of Platonic ideas has firmly established within Greek tradition the distinction and opposition between body and soul, although some continue to think of the mind as distinct from the soul and of the soul as a pervasive rarefied substance. *Sōma* and

[1] But mind belongs only to a few men; there is no general individual immortality in Aristotle (Stacey, *The Pauline View of Man*, 74–5). See Sir David Ross, *Aristotle*, 5th ed. (London, 1949) 131–5.

4   GSB

psychē are not the only terms used to express this disjunction. For instance, the outer man and the inner man contrast. *Sōma* also stands opposite *nous*, *phrenes*, and *gnōmē*. Thus, although *psychē* is not alone and undergoes a variety of treatments, *sōma* possesses a general constancy of meaning in its distinction from and, frequently, opposition to another part or other parts of man which are intangible, or at least less tangible.[1]

[1] As indicated above, the general knowledge of and agreement upon the Greek material relieves us of the necessity to go into greater detail with specific citations of the primary sources. Besides, most of the questions in this area have to do with historical origins and with the meaning of *psychē* rather than with *sōma*. One can pursue almost innumerable references given in Liddell, Scott, and Jones, *A Greek–English Lexicon* and *TDNT* under the relevant terms; the classic work by E. Rohde, *Psyche: The Cult of Souls and Belief in Immortality among the Greeks*, 2 vols. (New York, 1966 reprint); W. Jaeger, 'The Greek Ideas of Immortality', *Immortality and Resurrection*, ed. K. Stendahl (New York, 1965) 97–114; D. R. G. Owen, *Body and Soul* (Philadelphia, 1956); and other works too many to mention here.

CHAPTER 9

Anthropological Duality in the Judaism
of NT Times

In moving to Jewish literature of the intertestamental and NT
period, we confront an anthropological duality so clear and
widespread that it can justly be described as the normative
view within late Judaism. Judith says, 'And there will not lack
of his men one flesh [in the sense of body] or spirit of life'
(Jdt 10: 13). Here the individualizing use of *sarx* and *pneuma*
identifies the two basic components of man. In II Mac 6: 30
pain in the body (*kata to sōma*) and gladness in the soul (*kata
psychēn*) contrast. In the statement, 'I give up body and soul'
(II Mac 7: 37), the complementary nouns sum up the whole
man. So also does the statement in II Mac 14: 38 about the
risking of body and soul. Judas Maccabeus is described as 'the
man who was ever in body and soul the defender of his fellow
citizens' (II Mac 15: 30). A number of passages in IV Macca-
bees distinguish soul and body (1: 20, 26–7, 32; 14: 6; and
especially 10: 4, where it is said that men may torment the
body, but not the soul; see also ch. 13 as a whole).[1]

Jesus the son of Sirach talks of the hot *psychē* of a man who
fornicates *en sōmati sarkos autou*, a possible reference to mastur-
bation (Sir 23: 17). The Testament of Dan warns against
anger, which overpowers both soul and body (3: 1–6). God
makes the body to suit the spirit which it contains just as the
potter suits a vessel to its intended contents, according to
T Naph 2: 2–4. And in the *Biblical Antiquities* of Philo 3: 10
God is reported to say, 'I judge between soul and body.'

But above all, we see the duality of man's constitution in
statements regarding the separation of soul/spirit and body at
death, the conscious existence of the soul/spirit after death, the
reuniting of soul/spirit and body at resurrection, and, occasionally, the bodiless pre-existence of souls. Tobit prays for the

[1] E. Brandenburger notes that, contrary to Greek thought, in IV Macca-
bees the soul is immortal only by divine gift on account of obedience to the
Law (14: 6; 18: 23; 15: 1–13; cf. 9: 2; 11: 12; *Fleisch und Geist*, WMANT 29
[Neukirchen-Vluyn, 1968] 71–2).

4-2

release of his 'spirit' in death for enjoyment of the 'everlasting place' (Tob. 3: 6; cf. Phil 1: 23). Jesus the son of Sirach advises the bereaved to be consoled when the spirit of the deceased departs (*en exodō pneumatos autou* – 38: 23).

As we would expect, a number of passages in the strongly Hellenistic Wisdom of Solomon display anthropological duality. 'Wisdom will not enter a deceitful soul, nor dwell in a body enslaved to sin' (1: 4). The immortality of righteous souls appears in 3: 1–4. The molding of the body prior to birth in 7: 1–2 stands opposite the statement, 'a good soul fell to my lot; or rather, being good, I entered an undefiled body', in 8: 19–20.[1] Though undefiled at first, the body is perishable – *phthartos*, corruptible not in the sense of sinful by nature but in the sense of liable to sin and decay – and as such 'weighs down the soul'. The duality is plain, but even here we have not reached the full dualism of Hellenistic thought, in which evil is more closely allied with the body. At death the body returns to the earth and the soul to God who lent it (15: 8; cf. v. 11).

In Bar 2: 17 the dead are those 'who are in Hades, whose spirit has been taken from their bodies'.[2] II Apoc Bar 23: 4 speaks of the pre-existence and post-mortem existence of souls (cf. 3: 8). II Apoc Bar 30: 2–5 deals again with the post-mortem existence of souls, and also with the uniting of the souls and bodies of the righteous at the resurrection[3] and the grief-laden continuation of bodiless existence for the souls of the wicked. Quite differently but just as dichotomously, Job 23: 31 describes the final state of the righteous in terms of death for the body and blessed immortality for the spirit: 'And their bones shall rest in the earth, and their spirits shall have much joy.'

[1] Cf. II Enoch 23: 5 for pre-existence, and rabbinic literature cited in the note of Forbes and Charles, in *APOT* 2: 444; W. D. Stacey, *The Pauline View of Man* (London, 1956) 110.

[2] O. C. Whitehouse, the editor of Baruch in *APOT* 1: 586, thinks that *pneuma* here means 'breath'. But the consistency with which death is pictured during this period as the separation of spirit, or soul, from body works against such an understanding unless the spirit is thought to reside in the breath.

[3] This seems to be the implication of the statement 'Then all those who have fallen asleep in hope of Him shall rise again', followed by an indication that at the same time their souls will be released from the 'treasures' where they have been preserved. Contra Brandenburger, who thinks that a spiritualized concept of heavenly bliss has subsumed corporeal resurrection (*Fleisch und Geist*, 78–9).

According to I Enoch 9: 3, 10, the souls of righteous martyrs make suit to God; and 22: 5–7 speaks of the spirit of the martyr Abel, the spirit which had gone out of him at his murder by Cain. In 22: 3 we read that certain 'hollow places have been created for this very purpose, that the spirits of the souls of the dead should assemble therein', and verses 9–14 assign the divisions of Sheol to different classes of spirits of the dead for the suffering of pain or the enjoyment of bliss, according to deserts. 'And in those days shall the earth also give back that which has been entrusted to it [viz., bodies], and Sheol shall also give back that which it has received, and hell shall give back that which it owes [viz., spirits, or souls]' (51: 1).[1] In 67: 8–9 we read, '...for the healing of the body, but for the punishment of the spirit; now their spirit is full of lust, that they be punished in their body...And in proportion as the burning of their bodies becomes severe, a corresponding change shall take place in their spirit for ever and ever.' 'Their spirits shall be cast into the furnace of fire' (98: 3). The spirits of the righteous will enjoy bliss, but the souls of the wicked will suffer punishment (103: 3–8). 'Fear not, ye souls of the righteous...and grieve not if your soul into Sheol has descended in grief, and that in your life your body fared not according to your goodness' (102: 4). Upon ascending into heaven, Enoch himself says, 'And my whole body became relaxed, and my spirit was transfigured' (71: 11).[2]

[1] See R. H. Charles, *The Book of Enoch* (Oxford, 1912) 98–100.

[2] In I Enoch and elsewhere in the apocrypha and pseudepigrapha Brandenburger tries to show that a spiritualized doctrine of afterlife is juxtaposed with the rather different doctrine of physical resurrection, and sometimes dominates (*Fleisch und Geist*, 59–85). Since the sole purpose here is to demonstrate anthropological duality, it would be otiose to evaluate in detail Brandenburger's thesis, which includes an eschatological dualism deriving from the wisdom tradition. We may suspect that Brandenburger and others too often set the notion of spiritual translation into heavenly company with the angels opposite the notion of physical resurrection. At least in some passages the two notions seem to sit easily with each other. Not even the seeming contradiction between earthly and heavenly bliss is decisive since the canonical Apocalypse shows that it was possible to think of a uniting of the heavenly and earthly spheres (Revelation 21–2). The Lukan and Johannine narratives of the appearance of the risen Jesus show that materiality and pneumatic, glorified corporeality need not have been thought incompatible: Jesus appears out of nowhere, in spite of closed

According to II Esdr 7: 75–101, at death the soul of the righteous returns to God to adore him and the soul of the wicked wanders in torture, grief, and sadness. Verse 100 specifically mentions the separation of soul from body. Similarly, 'Six days hence, his soul shall go off his body and when it shall have gone out...' (Adam and Eve 43: 1). And, 'Adam thy husband hath gone out of his body. Rise up and behold his spirit borne aloft to his Maker' (Apoc Mos 32: 4). There follows a contrast between Adam's dead body on earth and his soul in heaven. In 42: 8, Eve says, ' "God of All, receive my spirit", and straightway she delivered up her spirit to God.' Her body is then buried.

In the Testament of Abraham, Abraham's death consists in the taking of his soul from his body. His soul goes to be with God. There it is wrapped in 'divinely woven linen'. And angels deal with the bodiless souls of the deceased in general.

According to Josephus, for the Essenes soul and body together make up the whole man (*JW* 2. 8, 6 §136). The Essenes resign their souls confident of receiving them again (*JW* 2. 8, 10 §153) and believe that their bodies are perishable because of the impermanence of matter, but that their souls are immortal forever. Moreover, souls emanate from very fine ether, become entangled in the prison-house of the body and dragged down thereby, and are released at death from the bonds of flesh. Righteous souls are borne aloft to enjoy bliss in a paradise beyond the ocean; wicked souls plunge into a dungeon full of punishments (*JW* 2. 8, 11 §§154–8; *Ant.* 28. 1, 5 §18). Josephus goes on to make a favorable comparison with Greek views. Similarly, Josephus reports that the Pharisees believe every soul is immortal and imperishable, that the souls of the wicked suffer eternal punishment and the souls of the righteous enjoy reward, and that only the souls of good men go into another body (*JW* 2. 8, 14 §163; *Ant.* 18. 1, 3 §14). Only the Sadducees believe that souls perish along with bodies (*JW* 2. 8, 14 §165; *Ant.* 18. 1, 4 §16). In *JW* 3. 8, 7 §§ 344–50 Josephus reports Eleazar as saying that death liberates the soul from its bodily prison to depart for its own pure abode, and that sleep provides

doors, and vanishes; yet he presents himself as flesh and bones, scarred from crucifixion, and capable of partaking food, perhaps even hungry for it (Luke 24: 31, 36, 39–43; John 20: 11–29).

a temporary liberation of the same sort. A statement similar to Eleazar's appears in a Jewish epigraph dating from the beginning of the Christian era,[1] and H. Gressmann has collected both archeological and literary evidence of Jewish as well as Gentile use of the dove to portray the departed human spirit.[2] In all of this we may suspect that Josephus has an apologetic purpose in view of his non-Jewish readers. But enough material containing similar anthropology has already been noted in other Jewish literature of the time to show that Josephus had little or no need to distort his information for an apologetic point. The least we can say is that Judaistic anthropology was not so far from certain Hellenistic views of man as to resist correlation.

As for the view of Josephus himself, in *JW* 5. 9, 3 §368 we read of men who 'in [their] souls and bodies' were far superior to others and in 6. 1, 6 §55 of a soldier with an emaciated body in which dwelled a heroic soul. Earlier, Josephus has told of his urging fellow Jews against suicidal resistance to the Romans: 'Why separate the very fond friends body and soul?' (*JW* 3. 8, 5 §362). Farther on in the same passage he sets the mortal body opposite the immortal soul, defines death as their separation, and sees the soul of the righteous as going to heaven to await the resurrected body. Similarly, in *AgAp* 2. 24 §203 Josephus writes that souls are planted in bodies at conception and separated therefrom at death.

Since the anthropological dualism in Philo is universally recognized, it needs no delineation. For a representative statement, we may cite *De opificio mundi* ch. 46 §135 (ed. Mangey, I, 32).[3]

In rabbinical literature the word גוף refers as early as the second century B.C. to a physical container filled with the soul/spirit.[4] Hillel the Elder asks, 'Is not the poor soul a guest within

---

[1] J.-B. Frey, *Corpus inscriptionum iudaicarum* (Rome, 1952) 2:n. 1510, p. 422.

[2] 'Die Sage von der Taufe Jesu und die vorderorientalische Taubengöttin', *Archiv für Religionswissenschaft* 20 (1920/21) 327–30.

[3] See further Brandenburger, *Fleisch und Geist*, 114–21.

[4] Whether the soul was conceived to be completely immaterial and spoken of as though it were material or whether the soul was thought to consist of highly rarefied substance does not significantly affect our discussion. Even under the latter view, a great contrast still exists between body and soul/spirit.

the body? Today it is here and tomorrow it is gone' (*Leviticus Rabbah* xxxiv, 3). R. Johanan ben Zakkai weeps while dying because, as he says, his soul will survive his body to face the judgement of God (*Berakhoth*, 28*b*).[1]

R. Judah tells the fable of a lame man and a blind man who helped each other rob an orchard of figs and received punishment together. 'So will the Holy One, blessed be He, bring the soul, [re]place it in the body, and judge them together' (*Sanhedrin*, 91*a*). R. Judah goes on to discuss the timing of the placement of the soul in man (*Sanhedrin*, 91*b*).

According to *Genesis Rabbah* xiv, 9, the soul fills the body during the day, warms it, and leaves to refresh itself in heaven during sleep. This notion goes back to the third Tannaitic generation.

Death consists in the withdrawal of souls from bodies according to *Qoheleth Rabbah* iii, 20–1 and *Mekilta* to Exod 15: 1. It does also in *Deuteronomy Rabbah* xi, 10, where according to the legend of Moses' death God commands Michael and Sammael, 'Go forth and bring Moses' soul', but finally does so himself – 'from the midst of the body'. Correspondingly, at the beginning of life the soul is formed in forty days and then placed in the embryo according to *Menahoth*, 99*b*.

R. Simai teaches that man's soul is from heaven and his body from the earth,[2] as does also R. Simeon ben Lakish (*Tanḥuma*, ed. Buber, *Bereshit* 15).[3] Montefiore and Loewe quote an old rabbinic prayer from the Jewish Prayer Book (Singer): 'Thou didst breathe it [the soul] into me, thou preservest it within me; and thou wilt take it from me, but wilt restore it hereafter. So long as the soul is within me, I will give thanks unto thee, O Lord...who restorest souls unto dead bodies.'[4]

---

[1] The view of H. A. Wolfson that Jesus also wept because he believed his soul was immortal and faced judgement is more problematic ('Immortality and Resurrection in the Philosophy of the Church Fathers', *Immortality and Resurrection*, ed. K. Stendahl [New York, 1965] 55).

[2] Cited by G. F. Moore, *Judaism* (Cambridge, Mass., 1962) 2: 451–2; W. Bacher, *Die Agada der Tannaiten und Amoräer* (Strassburg, 1902) 2: 543ff.

[3] Cited by Moore, *Judaism* 2: 451–2; Bacher, *Die Agada der palästinensischen Amoräer* (Strassburg, 1892) 1: 412–13. See further references in R. Meyer, *Hellenistisches in der rabbinischen Anthropologie*, BWANT 4/2 (Stuttgart, 1937) 15–16, 27.

[4] C. G. Montefiore and H. Loewe, *A Rabbinic Anthology* (London, 1938) 312.

Further, rabbinical literature contains indications of belief in the consciousness of departed souls/spirits and at least some activity on their part, as when R. Ḥiyya tells R. Jonathan not to insult the dead by allowing the fringe of his garment to trail the ground. R. Jonathan asks whether the dead know so much, and R. Ḥiyya argues that they do (*Berakhoth*, 18*b*). We read also concerning R. Ḥiyya's knowledge, after his own death, of his sons' troubles (*Berakhoth*, 18*b*) and concerning the activities on behalf of Aḥer of R. Meir and R. Johanan immediately upon their deaths (*Hagigah*, 15*b*). It was thought that one could hear the voice of a dead man (*Hagigah*, 16*b*). Later folklore regarding the activities of departed souls/spirits is also available.[1]

Finally, there is rabbinical belief in the pre-existence of souls, with the metaphorical use of גוף for the region filled with the souls of the unborn (*Niddah* 13*b*; *Genesis Rabbah* VIII, 7).[2] The metaphor rests on an understanding of the body as the physical container of the soul.

In view of the evidence, it is difficult to comprehend failure to see duality in rabbinic anthropology.[3] We can hardly claim that the division between physical and spiritual did not occur to the rabbis and that their only dualism was aspectual. For they speak of the different origins of soul/spirit and body, their separation at death, conscious existence of the soul during the interim, and the reuniting of soul/spirit and body at resurrection. In rabbinical writings the body is not corrupt *per se*, and both body and soul share in the evil and the glory of man. Anthropological duality, however, hardly depends on the notion that the body is the source of evil.

---

[1] R. Meyer, *Hellenistisches*, 2ff., cf. 145; P. Hoffmann, *Die Toten in Christus*, Neutestamentliche Abhandlungen 2/2 (Münster, 1966) 156–72. It is obvious that there is disagreement here with Meyer's view that tales concerning the activities of the dead represent a lingering holistic anthropology. They rather represent a belief, based on dichotomous anthropology, in the continued and conscious existence of departed spirits, a belief going back to the OT itself (as we shall see).

[2] See further R. Meyer, *Hellenistisches*, 49–61, 63–4, 78ff.

[3] Such as that in Stacey, *The Pauline View of Man*, 114–16.

Excursus on the Meaning of גוף, גופא, גשם, *and* גשמא *in Rabbinical Literature*

In passing we have already noted the appeal to certain definitions of גוף, גופא, גשם, and גשמא in the standard lexicons to rabbinical literature for support of the holistic definition of *sōma* as 'person'. J. Levy and M. Jastrow list several references for the set of meanings 'body, person, self'.[1] The first reference has to do with the release of Hebrew servants in the seventh year, according to Exod 21: 3–4: בגופו נכנס וכ', 'With his body he entered...' (*Kiddushin*, 20a). This is taken to mean, 'Of himself he entered...' However, the statement refers either to the release of a Hebrew servant with his body just as intact as when he entered servitude, in contrast to Gentile servants released because of their having been maimed (cf. Exod 21: 26–7), or to the release of the servant with his own body alone, i.e., without wife or children (so the LXX). Both interpretations appear in *Kiddushin*, 20a, and under either the stress lies, not on the slave as a person, but on his body as a physical object. Moreover, we have here a parallel to the use of *sōma* for slaves as things.

The next reference cited by Levy and Jastrow is one previously considered here, *Sanhedrin*, 91a, where R. Judah speaks of the replacing of the soul in the body for mutual judgement – clearly a dichotomous rather than holistic use of גוף. In yet another reference we read of חובת הגוף, 'obligations of the body', as distinct from חובת קרקע, 'obligations of the soil' (*Kiddushin*, 37a). But translation of the first expression by the phrase 'personal duty' may mislead us into thinking of גוף holistically. Rather, a contrast obtains between the laws which attach to the body wherever it is, even outside Palestine, and the laws which apply only on Palestinian soil. Physical location is in view. Of course, the rest of the person is in the place where the body is, but that is not the point of גוף in context.

In *Rosh ha-Shanah*, 17a and elsewhere Rab speaks of 'Wrong-

---

[1] J. Levy, *Wörterbuch über die Talmudim und Midraschim*, 2nd ed. (Berlin, 1924) s.v.; and his *Neuhebräisches und Chaldäisches Wörterbuch über die Talmudim und Midraschim* (Leipzig, 1876) s.v.; M. Jastrow, *A Dictionary of the Targumim, the Talmud Babli and Yerushalmi, and the Midrashic Literature* (New York, 1950) s.v.

doers...who sin with their body (בגופן)...go down to Gehin-nom...After twelve months their body is consumed and their soul is burned.' If that is not clearly dichotomous in itself, the following statement should dispel any doubt. Rab describes the wrongdoers of Israel who sin with their body as 'the cranium which does not put on the phylactery' and the wrongdoers of the Gentiles who sin with their body as those who engage in sexual immorality. The meaning of גוף continues to be physical.

Accordng to *Aboth*, iv.8, 'R. Jose said: Whoever honors the Torah is himself honored (גופו מכבד) by men, and whoever dishonors the Torah is himself dishonored (גופו מחלל) by men.' A more literal translation reads, 'Whoever honors the Torah, his body is honored by men, and whoever dishonors the Torah, his body is dishonored by men.' Whether honor of the Torah refers to reverential handling of the scrolls themselves (so most older commentators), to zealous obedience to the precepts of the Torah (Herford),[1] or to both (J. Israelstam in the Soncino edition), the honor of the body of him who honors the Torah refers to respectful bearing towards Torah scholars *in their physical presence*. Disrespectful bearing belongs to those who fail to honor the Torah. Here we have a parallel to the use of *sōma* in Greek literature for physical presence as opposed to reputa-tion, written records, and the like. Similarly, the phrase איתו הגוף הקדוש 'that holy body', with reference to the saintly Rabbi Yose ben Halafta (Jerusalem Talmud, *Taanith* 1.64d top) probably calls attention to the aura of holiness one feels in the physical presence of such a man. Moreover, the immediate context of the expression deals with ablutions after sexual inter-course and nocturnal emission of semen. 'That holy body' refers, then, to the physical side of a man who is ritually clean, or cleansed.

For *Aboth*, 1.17 the Soncino translation has, 'I have found nothing better for a person (לגוף) than silence.' Herford translates לגוף, 'for one'. But a more restricted under-standing, 'for a *body*', is preferable because the immediately following statement reads, 'Simeon, his [Rabban Gamaliel's] son, used to say:...study is not the most important thing, but deed; whoever indulges in too many words brings about sin.' The גוף, then, is a physical organ for active deeds rather than

---

[1] R. T. Herford, *Pirke Aboth* (New York, 1962 reprint) 103.

sedentary recitation. (In ancient Jewish culture one studied by reciting aloud, whereas speaking was not an integral part of physical labor.)

We can dismiss quickly those passages where גופא is said to mean 'self' in relationship to various laws and rabbinical interpretations thereof: היא גופא גזרה. 'This [law] is itself [only] a preventive measure', or more literally, 'This body is a preventive measure' (*Betzah*, 3*a*); הא גופא קשיא, 'This contains a contradiction in itself', or more literally, 'This body is a contradiction' (*Niddah*, 46*a* and *Erubin*, 13*a*). Persons do not at all come into the picture. In these statements גופא appears metaphorically for emphasis on the referents as specific entities. (Cf. our speaking of a '*material* contradiction'.) Thingness rather than personhood is in view.

Concerning גשם/גשמא defined as 'body, self', the meaning in Dan 4: 30; 5: 21 is obviously and exclusively physical: 'his body was wet with the dew of heaven'. But in *Lamentations Rabbah* 1, 5, § 31 R. Johanan b. Zakkai is reported as saying, 'I thought that so long as the stores [of food in Jerusalem] were intact the people would not expose themselves (לא יהבין גשמיהון) to the dangers of battle.' Levy, Jastrow, and A. Cohen[1] translate גשם as a general reflexive for the whole person. However, the statement deals with the risking of the physical body in warfare. There is no need to see any enlargement of the corporal sense. On the contrary, considerations of context both here and in the foregoing rabbinical passages cited for holistic meanings uniformly favor a simply physical connotation for the words in question.

The kind of anthropological duality which appears in the apocrypha, pseudepigrapha, and rabbinical literature appears also in the sectarian writings among the DSS. That is what we should expect since a number of the apocrypha and pseudepigrapha have also been discovered near Qumran.

We read in 1QM 7: 4–5, 'They shall all be freely enlisted for war, perfect in spirit and flesh (תמימי רוח ובשר).' Together spirit and flesh make up the whole man. Hardly less clear is 1QS 3: 8–9: 'And by humble submission of his soul (נפשו) to all the commandments of God his flesh (בשרו) will be cleansed

---

[1] In *Midrash Rabbah: Lamentations*, ed. H. Freedman and M. Simon (London, 1939) 101.

by sprinkling with water for purification.' Inner submission results in true ritual cleansing of the flesh, that outer, physical part of man which in the DSS is portrayed as weak and prone to be overcome by sin. We may compare 1QS 4: 20–1, according to which God will remove every spirit of evil from man's flesh. We might think that this passage refers to the doctrine of the two spirits in man (1QS 3–4), with the result that we are here dealing with cosmic and ethical dualism rather than anthropological duality. That is true up to a point. However, this very cosmic and ethical dualism at least implies a distinction between the inner man and the outer man, for we read that ultimately the elect will have only the spirit of truth housed within their flesh. Moreover, God parcels out the two spirits in such a manner that they are men's *own* spirits. The psalmist therefore writes '*my* spirit' (1QS 9: 12 [*bis*]; 8: 29) parallel to 'my soul'. The terms are therefore anthropological[1] despite the cosmic dualism in 3 and 4. Cf. '*every* spirit' in 1QH 15: 13, and 22: 'You formed the spirit', with reference to the making of man. Alternatively, in these texts man has his own human spirit in addition to the spirits of truth and falsehood. Under either understanding, an anthropological duality is apparent when the spirit and the flesh stand in a relationship which is contrastive as well as complementary.

The psalmist even speaks of the separation of his spirit, as in death: 'And with the dead ones[2] my spirit is detached (or for-

---

[1] Contra A. Sand (*Der Begriff 'Fleisch' in den paulinischen Hauptbriefen* [Regensburg, 1967] 266), who says that 'flesh' refers to the whole man dominated either by the evil spirit or by the holy spirit (cf. F. Nötscher, *Zur theologischen Terminologie der Qumran-Texte*, BBB 10 [Bonn, 1956] 85–6). But if the spirit is the psalmist's own and is housed within his flesh, a duality is evident. To this extent K. G. Kuhn's statements should be modified, or interpreted ('New Light on Temptation, Sin, and Flesh in the New Testament', *The Scrolls and the New Testament*, ed. K. Stendahl [New York, 1957] 101). For further discussion see R. E. Murphy, 'Bśr in the Qumran Literature and Sarks in the Epistle to the Romans', *Sacra Pagina* 2 (1959) 63ff., who thinks that the expression 'within me (בתכמי)' in 1QH 17: 25, where we might have expected 'within my flesh', suggests the meaning 'person' for בשר. But this is to suppose erroneously that the personal pronoun must broaden the meaning of בשר. Rather, בשר here restricts the meaning of the personal pronoun.

[2] עם מתים might also be taken as coming from מַת, 'man'. Even so, the immediate reference to the Pit requires that the men be dead.

saken),[1] because (my life) has reached the Pit, (and within me) faints my soul day and night with no rest' (1QH 8: 28–30). Since the surrounding context deals with physical illness, it is apparent that the terms are anthropological and that the illness of the outer man has affected the inner man – his 'spirit', 'soul', or 'heart' – to the extent that the psalmist even imagines his spirit as departed to dwell among the dead.

This same duality appears less hyperbolically in the next two lines: 'to destroy (my) flesh...and my soul in me (עלי) languishes...my strength has gone out from my body and my heart has flowed out like water' (1QH 8: 31–2). Flesh/body and soul/strength/heart stand side by side in a complementary but dichotomous fashion. The exit of the soul/strength/heart from the flesh/body approaches the idea of the spirit's exit to dwell among the dead in the Pit in the preceding lines.

The mood changes even more dichotomously in 1QH 9: 7–8, 12. No longer is the soul languishing. The psalmist rather writes, 'My soul meditates on your marvelous works...my soul delights in the abundance of your mercies.' And the psalmist rejoices in God's upholding and establishing his 'spirit'. This stands in contrast to his still-continuing physical pains, which he delineates in some detail. Though the body suffers, the soul/spirit exults.

In 1QH 9: 15–16 we read, 'One person (אנוש) may be more righteous than another person. And one man (גבר) may be more wise than (another man). And one body (בשר) may be more glorious than another formation (of clay). And one spirit (רוח) may be more powerful than another spirit.' In the last sentence quoted, the psalmist does not refer to the two spirits of

---

[1] יחפש is probably the *pual* of חפש, 'to be freed, detached', in the bad sense of 'forsaken' as in Ps 88: 6: 'like one forsaken among the dead (במתים חפשי כמו)'. But it may be taken as the *pual* of חפש, 'to be searched for' and thus 'hidden'. Or by comparison with Arabic and Ugaritic parallels it may mean 'to be low', or by comparison with Aramaic, 'to deliver'. See the discussions in M. Mansoor, *The Thanksgiving Hymns*, Studies on the Texts of the Desert of Judah 3 (Grand Rapids, 1961) 156; S. Holm-Nielsen, *Hodayot. Psalms from Qumran*, Acta Theologica Danica 2 (Aarhus, 1960) 144, 157; T. H. Gaster, *The Dead Sea Scriptures* (Garden City, 1956) 219, n. 23. Cf. 1QH 10: 33. Whatever the proper translation, the spirit of the psalmist is with the dead in the Pit and therefore gone from his body. This presence with the dead and the parallel in Ps 88: 6 favor a derivation from חפש with its specific meaning of detachment.

truth and falsehood and their relative strengths; for the passage speaks only of comparisons between men and men, and in the larger context between man and God. Thus רוח is anthropological. What is significant for our purpose is the way in which, following the two holistic references to man under the terms אנוש and גבר, the psalmist synecdochically mentions the two components which make up the whole man, viz., בשר and רוח.

Similarly, the phrase 'spirit of flesh (רוח בשר)' in 1QH 13: 13; 17: 25 means 'a spirit embodied, or housed, in flesh', and thus a dually composed human being. This is confirmed by the subsequent figure of speech 'building of dust' and the statement that a spirit of straying rules *in* him (בו) in 13: 15–16. For 'building (מבנה)' as a metaphor for the physical body, cf. 1QH 7: 4, where the term occurs in association with 'arm', 'foot', 'eyes', 'ears', 'heart', 'bones', and 'bowels'. We might translate, '*breath* of flesh',[1] but the usage of רוח elsewhere in 1QH and the entire corpus of the DSS favors 'spirit', as recognized by most translators of and commentators on these passages. By context 'flesh' additionally connotes the frailty of the human being. That gives no reason, however, to ignore the duality of the human constitution with a generalizing interpretation, 'a creature with fleshly, i.e., human character'.[2]

In 1QH 15, we confront a series of contrasts between flesh and spirit/soul. 'And I have loved you with voluntariness and with all the heart and with all the soul...and I know by your knowledge that not by the hand of flesh...and I know that by your hand is the formation of every spirit' (15: 10, 12–13). The context is anthropological, with reference to human incapability and to divine predetermination of men to good or evil. Here 'flesh' bears the more general sense of 'mankind' – a frequent meaning in the DSS[3] – but mankind from the visible

---

[1] As does Mansoor, *The Thanksgiving Hymns*, 178–9.

[2] H. Ringgren, *The Faith of Qumran* (Philadelphia, 1963) 99. Cf. Mansoor, *The Thanksgiving Hymns*, 178–9. Sand interprets 'spirit' and 'flesh' aspectually in order to avoid anthropological dualism; each term denotes the totality of man, but each from a different side (*Der Begriff 'Fleisch'*, 265). But since two different sides of man are not only distinguishable but also separable, we ought not to engage in a monadically unitary interpretation.

[3] See especially 1QS 11: 6–7, where 'the assembly of flesh' is parallel to 'men' and 'the sons of men'.

side of his frail physique. Thus, there lies in the background an anthropological duality of 'flesh' and 'spirit'. In other words, the psalmist is attaching his love for God to his 'soul' (alternately, 'heart') and conversely is denying any positive relationship between his piety and 'flesh' but rather attributing to God the good inclination of his 'spirit' (a synonym for 'soul' and 'heart', previously used). Similarly, the psalmist elsewhere contrasts the unworthiness of human flesh with the good spirit created within men by God (1QH 4: 29–33).[1]

Then in 1QH 15: 15–17 the psalmist writes, 'You established him [the righteous]...in order to open up all the straitness of his soul (נפשו) unto everlasting salvation and perpetual peace and absence of need, and you will raise up his glory (or liver) from flesh (ותרם מבשר כבודו).' The opening up all the straitness of the soul unto everlasting salvation corresponds to the raising up of the glory from flesh. Thus, 'his soul' and 'his glory' are equivalent. This equivalence follows the pattern of a number of OT passages in which 'glory' parallels and stands for the 'soul' and 'heart' as the inner part of man (Ps 16: 9; 7: 6; 30: 13; 57: 9; 108: 2; Gen 49: 6).[2] In effect, then, the statement 'you will raise up his *glory* from flesh' means 'you will raise up his *soul* from flesh'. I.e., 'everlasting salvation and perpetual peace and absence of need' come about through the opening up of 'all the straitness of his soul'. And that opening up *is* the raising up of 'his glory [= his soul] from flesh'. Whether 'flesh' is individual flesh or the flesh of mankind in general, the statement fairly cries out for interpretation in terms of the immortality of the soul apart from flesh.

That would both agree with the other Essene features of the Qumran community and literature and absolve Josephus from

[1] Cf. D. Flusser, 'The Dualism of Flesh and Spirit in the Dead Sea Scrolls', *Tarbiz* 27 (1958) 158–65.

[2] It is wrong, therefore, to interpret 'glory' here as the position and role God has destined for the righteous, a state of holiness, with reference to CD 3: 20 and 1QS 4: 23 (contra Murphy, 'Bśr', 67). Cf. J. van der Ploeg, 'The Belief in Immortality in the Writings of Qumrân', *BO* 18 (1961) 122, who adds 1QH 17: 15. The 'glory of Adam' in CD 3: 20; 1QS 4: 23; and 1QH 17: 15 is the reward of the righteous, but the 'glory' of the righteous in 1QH 15: 15–17 is an anthropological term parallel to 'soul' in contrast to 'flesh', and thus is an entity, not just a way of being. Van der Ploeg recognizes the possibility that 'glory' is equivalent to 'soul', but he dismisses the possibility without discussion.

the charge of excessive Hellenization of the Essenes in his statements about their belief in the immortality of the soul apart from the body.[1] Indeed, Josephus' account of Essene belief confirms the most natural reading of the present text. Thus the agreement between 1QH and Josephus, even to the point of identical emphasis on the upward direction of the soul at death, goes far to substantiate the basic accuracy of Josephus' remarks as well as to support the identity of the sectarians at Qumran with the Essenes. Josephus had just as much reason to Hellenize Pharisaic beliefs as he had reason to Hellenize Essene beliefs – perhaps more reason, in view of his own Pharisaism. Yet he does not delete bodily resurrection from Pharisaic belief as a feature objectionable to his Hellenistic readers. It is likely, then, that he accurately reports the Pharisaic doctrine of bodily resurrection and the Essene doctrine of the immortality of the soul.

For the consistent meaning of רום מן as removal (here, separation of the soul/glory, or liver, from flesh), see Lev 2:9; 4:8, 19; 6:8; Num 18:26, 28, 29, 30, 32; I Sam 2:8; Ps 119:7; Isa 57:14; cf. 1QH 11:12. BDB give the definition, 'lift up and take away, remove'. Finally, the passage indicates that flesh confines the soul; apart from it the soul will be free ('open') and experience no material needs (אין מחסור). For אין מחסור as absence of material need, we may note Judg 18:10; 19:19; Ps 34:10, which contain all the appearances of the expression in the OT. Also, מחסור always carries the meaning of material

---

[1] *JW* 2. 8, 11 §§154–8; *Ant.* 18. 1, 5 §18. This goes against Hippolytus' statement that the Essenes held to resurrection of the body as well as immortality of the soul (*Refutatio Omnium Haeresium* 9.27). M. Black is inclined to prefer Hippolytus' account of the Essenes because of its greater simplicity in comparison with the Josephan description (*The Scrolls and Christian Origins* [New York, 1961] 188–91). However, Hippolytus may be smoothing out and simplifying Josephus' text. The 'Christian' touches in Hippolytus' description – and the doctrine of resurrection might be one of them – may represent conscious or unconscious assimilation to Christian phraseology and belief for the purpose of better understanding on the part of readers. Or, preferably, Hippolytus may bring over resurrection of the body from the Pharisees because of his view that they and the Essenes have largely identical beliefs and practices. For a somewhat different critique of Black's view, see G. W. E. Nickelsburg, Jnr, *Resurrection, Immortality, and Eternal Life in Intertestamental Judaism*, Harvard Theological Studies 26 (Cambridge, Mass., 1972) 167–9.

need when used apart from אֵין.[1] Thus, the exegetical details
point forward to the freeing of the soul from the flesh, from its
confinement and material requirements, and militate against
our understanding the passage in terms of a *present* salvation
which will continue for a long time (but not endlessly) on
earth. Cf. also the corresponding 'day of massacre' for the
wicked (line 17), surely future to the psalmist. We might take
'straitness' figuratively of adversity were it not for the
parallelism of removal from flesh. As it is, the parallelism of
'raise up his glory from flesh' favors a literal meaning for 'open
all the straitness of his soul'. Cf. 1QH 9: 27–8. In lines 21–2
the psalmist sets 'flesh' as 'dust' opposite man's 'spirit', formed
and established in its works by God. Thus, an anthropological
duality of flesh and soul/spirit/glory dominates the whole of
1QH 15.

Immortality of the soul appears also in 1QH 11: 12–14:
'...to raise from dust (להרים מעפר) the worm of men (מתים) to
the counsel [of your truth] and from the perverted spirit to the
understanding [which comes from you] and to stand in station
before you with the eternal host and the spirits [of holiness],
to be renewed with every being, and with the knowing ones in
unison shout with joy'. Apart from column 15, we might think
that in column 11 the psalmist refers merely to the raising of
the elect from the hoi polloi of mankind to a favored position
before God, in association with heavenly beings but in location
still on earth. However, the rather clear indications in column 15
of an eschatologically future raising of the soul away from the
flesh and away from its limitations through physical needs
suggest at least something of the same here. Thus, although the
raising of the 'worm of men' from dust to divine counsel has
already begun through their spiritual enlightenment, their
standing in station before God along with the heavenly hosts of
spirits refers ultimately and mainly to blessed immortality of
the soul far above the plane of flesh, not just to that proleptic
association with angels while the convenanters are still
earthbound.

Certain factors suggest that the expression 'raise from dust'
here means more than elevation from commonness ('dust'

---

[1] Deut 15: 8; Judg 19: 20; Prov 6: 11; 11: 24; 14: 23; 21: 5, 17; 22: 16;
24: 34; 28: 27.

as men in general – I Kgs 16: 2) or from distress ('dust' as wretchedness – I Sam 2: 8; Ps 113: 7). In the hymns 'dust' frequently stands for the physical constitution of man as flesh. 'What then is man? He is earth. He is nipped off [from clay], and to dust is his return...I am dust and ashes' (1QH 10: 3–5; see also line 12 and 1QS 11: 21–2; Gen 18: 27; Ps 103: 14). The psalmist at Qumran is playing upon the creation of man's body from the dust and the dissolution of his body back to dust. Moreover, man's physique does not merely come from and return to dust. It *is* dust, as in line 3 of the very column (11) we are considering: 'You have dealt wondrously with dust, even with a formation of clay', with reference to divine revelation and deliverance. 'And behold, I [was taken] from dust...a heap of dust [I am]...a returning to dust [is] for the formation of clay...and what shall dust...reply?' (1QH 12: 24–7; see also the subsequent lines). 'And you disclosed to the ear of dust...to dust like myself...and what is flesh?...to recount to flesh...and you disclosed to a heart of dust...in an ear of dust...and I am a formation of dust' (1QH 18, excerpts). Here we may note the synonymy of 'dust' and 'flesh'. In his frail and perishable physique, man is dust/flesh. Moreover, elevation from dust parallels station in God's presence with the eternal host and the spirits of holiness. Therefore, the elevation of the elect from dust to stand eternally before God with the heavenly spirits denotes elevation of the soul from the dusty 'flesh', or body, just as indicated in column 15.

[Note: In the expression 'worm of men' (1QH 11: 12–14), it is possible to treat מתים as coming from מות (thus, 'the dead ones') instead of from מת (thus, 'men'). For discussion of the question see Holm-Nielsen, *Hodayot*, 184, 187; Mansoor, *The Thanksgiving Hymns*, 147, with further references. For parallels to the entire expression, see 1QH 6: 34; Isa 41: 14; 66: 24; Ps 22: 7; Job 25: 6. We might detect a doctrine of bodily resurrection in 1QH 11. However, separation from the dust (= flesh) and association with the angelic hosts and spirits militates against that understanding. Furthermore, there are the notorious lack of unequivocal evidence in the sectarian scrolls for belief in bodily resurrection and the statements of Josephus that the Essenes rejected that belief in favor of immortality of the soul alone. In 1QH 6: 34, 'You worm of men' parallels 'You who lie (or dwell) in the dust' and therefore has been thought to refer to the resurrection of corpses. However, since the men in dust prepare for battle, the expressions probably refer to wretchedness rather than to a condition of actual death. Cf. 1QH 3: 13, where 'those who lie (or dwell) in the dust' certainly are not corpses, but land-lubbers as opposed to sailors. *Living* men are 'worms' also in 1QS 11: 10. The wording of Dan 12: 2, ורבים מישני אדמת־עפר יקיצו, is not close to that of 1QH 6: 34, ושוכבי עפר הרימו תרן, and therefore provides scant support for interpretation in terms of resurrection.

K. Schubert argues to the contrary that for the sectarians at Qumran, as for Biblical writers and Semites generally, there can be no life without corporeality. Therefore, in the DSS all passages concerning afterlife presuppose bodily resurrection. Only a polemic against corporeality can upset this presupposition. In particular, Schubert reasons that in intertestamental literature the attribution of bodily functions (such as thirst) and physical torments (such as binding and burning) to spirits, or souls, demonstrates that the spirits, or souls, are not immaterial but have resurrected bodies (*The Dead Sea Community* [New York, 1959] 108–11; also his 'Die Entwicklung der Auferstehungslehre von der nachexilischen bis zur frührabbinischen Zeit', *BZ* 6 [1962] 177–214; and 'Das Problem der Auferstehungshoffnung in den Qumrântexten und in der frührabbinischen Literatur', *Wissenschaftliche Zeitschrift der Königlichen Universität in München* 56 [1960] 154–67).

Schubert correctly insists that resurrection is not to be denied simply because it is not mentioned explicitly in a passage. But the converse that resurrection must be assumed wherever it is not explicitly denied is equally wrong. We shall see that incorporeal afterlife of a reduced but not nihilistic sort appears in the OT. Cf. Jub 23: 31: 'And their bones shall rest in the earth, and their spirits shall have much joy.' Moreover, Schubert underestimates Hellenistic influence and seems to forget that the doctrine of physical resurrection bloomed late and therefore, as the Sadducees' rejection of that doctrine shows, cannot be presumed to have taken over Jewish theology quite so thoroughly as he supposes. Perhaps the OT idea of shades, different from the solid bodies which return to dust at death, continued alone in some circles, i.e., without addition of belief in bodily resurrection and possibly with some encouragement from the Hellenistic idea of the soul's immortality.

Finally, the argument that attribution of physical functions and corporal torments to spirits, or souls, must imply bodily resurrection clearly needs refutation. In the Testament of Abraham *passim* heavenly spirits are portrayed as *asōmata*, neither eating nor drinking, yet as having feet which Abraham washes and Sarah embraces. In I Enoch 22 the departed 'spirits' of the wicked are 'scourged' '*till* the great day of judgement'. No resurrection is presupposed, for the wicked who have not yet died still persecute the righteous (see esp. v. 7). Similarly, in Rev 6: 9–11 the souls of the martyrs are given white robes to wear in spite of the futurity of the first resurrection. In Luke 16: 19–30 resurrection is held in view but has not yet occurred (*ean tis ek nekrōn anastē*, v. 31). Nevertheless Jesus speaks of the rich man, Lazarus, and their respective fates in physical terms – 'tongue' and 'finger', 'flame' and 'Abraham's bosom'. We should probably conclude that such language was intended to be taken analogically. Such an intention seems rather clearly implied in I Enoch 100: 9: 'In blazing flames burning *worse than fire* shall ye burn.' Alternatively, the soul/spirit was thought to possess its own 'physique' separately from the body.]

In 1QH 11 and 15, then, the removal from dust/flesh to the presence of God and his angels militates against an interpretation in terms of present salvation. Thus, we are disposed to doubt that in 1QH 3: 19–23 the fellowship of the cleansed 'spirit' of the psalmist and other righteous men with the 'host of the holy ones' and the 'congregation of the sons of heaven' in the 'everlasting height' refers only, if at all, to present salvation and communion with heavenly beings.[1] It is the '*soul*' of him whom God 'shaped from dust' that God has redeemed from the Pit and from the Sheol of Abaddon and has destined 'for the everlasting council' in the 'everlasting height'. 'Soul' and 'dust, (for the body) contrast. Again by contrast with the 'dust'/body, it is the '*spirit*' which enters into communion with the 'holy ones' and 'sons of heaven'. The following lines in 1QH 3 reemphasize the contrast in terms of the fleshly side of man as 'a formation of clay' 'kneaded with water'. And the lengthy sections which open and close this column sound exactly like the Messianic woes and final judgement upon the wicked as described in other literature of the period. Hence, the future is in view, not the present; and for the righteous the prospect is heavenly rather than earthly.

Likewise in 1QH 4 the judgement of the wicked is future, as especially in line 20, according to which '*all* men of deceit'

[1] Contra R. B. Laurin, 'The Question of Immortality in the Qumran "*Hodayot*"', *JSS* 3 (1958) 344–55; Ringgren, *The Faith of Qumran*, 149–50, with references to further literature. Laurin too often has to resort to hyperbole in the texts, and his appeal to earthiness in comparable passages in the OT overlooks the possibility of reinterpretation by the sectarians at Qumran. He does not discuss the contrast between 'soul/ spirit' and 'flesh/dust'.

will be 'cut off in judgement' and 'seers of error will not be found *any more*' – hardly true at the psalmist's time of writing. By the same token, the psalmist must be speaking of the eternal state in the immediately following statements concerning the eternal position before God of those who please him. To be sure, deliverances already experienced preview final vindication, and the fellowship of the community at Qumran anticipates heavenly communion. But eschatology has not been realized to any large degree. And as elsewhere, in lines 29–32 the psalmist contrasts the unworthiness of his flesh with the spirit which God has created for him.

The psalmist again describes the final vindication and ever-lasting bliss of the righteous with the 'angels of the presence' in 1QH 6, especially lines 10–17, 29–31: 'And all the sons of wrong-doing shall *not be any more.*' It is somewhat unclear whether here and in 1QS 4: 7–8 the dénouement of the present age is followed by a paradisaical era of limited duration on earth and then the eternal state, whether the heavenly, eternal state is described in terms of an earthly paradise, whether heaven and earth unite for the eternal state, or whether the deceased righteous will live immortally in heaven while the surviving righteous continue to live blissfully on earth for a while. This much *is* clear: throughout the passages just discussed the souls, or spirits, of the righteous – in contradistinction to their flesh, made of dust, or clay – enjoy immortality in the immediate presence of God and other heavenly beings (cf. also 1QH 9: 27–8; 10: 27; 11: 20ff.; 1QH frag. 7: 5; 1QS 4: 6–8, cf. 11–13; 1QSb 4: 26; 1QM 1: 8–9). Anthropological duality is inescapable under such a belief.

Anthropological duality appears in yet further statements. 'I belong to wicked mankind, to the company of ungodly flesh. My iniquities, rebellions, and sins, together with the perversity of my heart...' (1QS 11: 9–10, here according to Vermes' translation). The psalmist views himself outwardly as 'flesh' along with other men and inwardly as 'heart'. As in most other Jewish literature of the time, sin attaches to both the outer man and the inner man.[1] The result is a constitutional

---

[1] For sin in the heart, spirit, or soul, see 1QS 1: 6; 2: 11–18, 25–3: 3; 5: 4–5; 7: 22–4; 11: 1; cf. 10: 21; 1QH 6: 21–2; and *Discoveries in the Judaean Desert* v, 81 (Fgmt. 183, col. 11, l. 6). The associations of sin and flesh are too numerous to list.

duality in man *without* a correlative ethical dualism. At the same time, we have seen that in the sectarian scrolls the piety of the righteous derives from the man's good spirit cleansed or formed within him by God, while the flesh is consistently associated with a proclivity to sin.[1] The flesh may receive ritual purification now,[2] but in the final state it is dropped altogether.[3]

We conclude therefore that the DSS display the same anthropological duality which characterizes other Jewish literature of the period. As to subspecies, the Hymns rather emphasize that duality through the doctrine of immortality of the soul/ spirit apart from the flesh. Of course, any number of passages evince the intertwining of soul or spirit with bodily functions during earthly lifetime. This is so especially in complaints concerning illness and other distresses. Nevertheless, there exists an ontological difference between the soul/spirit and the flesh/ body, even to the extent of their separation at death with retention of conscious existence by the soul/spirit in the absence of physical limitations and needs.

In surveying the literature of late Judaism we might have merely stated conclusions and listed references. But it is not fully appreciated for purposes of interpreting the Pauline usage of *sōma* how extensive and uniform is the anthropological duality in the Jewish beliefs which formed a major part of the milieu of Paul's own thought. In this connection we should not forget Paul's rabbinical training as a Pharisee. R. H. Charles does not overstate the case by writing that 'in all the remaining

---

[1] See especially 1QH 1.   [2] 1QS 3: 8–9; 1QM 7: 4–5.

[3] See the preceding discussion of immortality of righteous souls. Of course, statements about immortality are limited to the Hymns. But it is only natural that the Hymns should contain the clearest expressions of hope for afterlife. The subject matter of the other sectarian DSS would not lead us to require in them expressions of individual hope for immortality. Not even a writing so eschatological as the War Scroll would lead to such a requirement, for there the concern lies with an earthly battle against the forces of darkness. Sectarian DSS other than the Hymns do, nevertheless, contain statements evincing an anthropological duality which dovetails very well with that same duality as it occurs in the Hymns in association with immortality of the soul. Finally, agreement between the Hymns and Josephus' description of Essene belief in immortality of the soul apart from the body strongly suggests that the doctrine was not peculiar to the author(s) of the Hymns, but characterized the Essene community in general.

literature of this period there is only a dichotomy – either the spirit and body, or the soul and body'.[1] All of this adds up to presumptive evidence in favor of a simply physical meaning for *sōma*.

To be sure, most if not all of the Jewish writers and rabbis do not go the way of making the body the source and seat of sin and the soul a paragon of purity when not defiled by the body. For the rabbis, body and soul cooperate in sinning (*Sanhedrin*, 91*a*). And the one cannot lead a normal life without the other. Granted these qualifications, it remains true to say that an anthropological duality runs through the Jewish literature of the period. It is more than aspectual; it is partitive. Souls pre-exist. Together, body and soul/spirit make up the man. The soul/spirit inhabits the body during life and leaves it at death.[2] Despite incompleteness, the soul/spirit of the righteous consciously enjoys bliss; that of the wicked consciously suffers torment. At the resurrection (if that is held) body and soul reunite.

It is commonly thought that such an anthropology derives from Greek influence upon Jewish thinking. To some extent that is true – especially in Philo, to take the most outstanding example.[3] However, we should bear in mind the remarkable phenomena that generally Jewish writers and rabbis do not attribute sin to the body in opposition to the soul and that a good number of them regard a soul's divestiture of its body

[1] *Eschatology* (New York, 1963 reprint) 288.

[2] See A. T. Nikolainen, *Der Auferstehungsglauben in der Bibel und ihrer Umwelt*, Annales Academiae Scientiarum Fennicae, B XLIX, 3 (Helsinki, 1944) 1: 1–95, for another survey of material concerning the widespread belief in death as separation of the soul from the body. Nikolainen's conclusions differ, however.

[3] Stacey reasons that the occasional use of *sōma* for בשר (as well as for גויה) in the LXX and the great upsurge of *sōma* in the apocrypha and pseudepigrapha 'can only mean that the conception of the physical as a unified order of existence, perhaps in contrast to some other, was being learnt by the Jews from the Greeks' (*The Pauline View of Man*, 103). But בשר frequently means 'body' in the Hebrew OT (see below, p. 118, for references) and as such sometimes receives the translation *sarx* in the LXX. The phenomenon to which Stacey appeals is due to literal translation in the LXX rather than to the lack of a concept concerning the body on the part of the Hebrews. When, instead of translating Hebrew, later Jewish authors write on their own in Greek, they naturally feel more free to use *sōma* for what in Hebrew would be בשר and in translation Greek would be *sarx*.

as undesirable and affirm resurrection of the body. Borrowing from the Greeks does not entirely suit these phenomena. Of course, we may say that the OT heritage fortified most Jewish thinkers against complete capitulation to Hellenistic dualism. But concerning the doctrine most offensive to Greek thinking – viz., bodily resurrection – the OT has not very much to say and therefore provides little fortification.

K. Hanhart thinks that the anthropological duality in Jewish theology of this period derives, not from Hellenistic influence, but from speculation on OT passages with the help of Greek terminology.[1] In his favor, full scale dualism might have appeared more frequently and consistently under borrowing from Greek anthropology. Actually, we have a mixed bag. What Hanhart thinks probably holds true for some of the literature. But we can detect Hellenistic influence in other literature. And a mixture of both occurs elsewhere.

The question of origin aside, what is most remarkable is the constancy with which man is portrayed as made up of body and soul/spirit. Some affirm the resurrection. Others do not. It is disagreed whether the body is a hindrance or a help. But consistently body and soul/spirit form the constituent parts of man – throughout the period in question and regardless of the geographical provenance of the literature. From the inter-testamental literature to the later rabbinical statements, from Palestinian as well as extra-Palestinian sources, we hear the same opinion: man is body plus soul/spirit, united but divisible.

[1] *The Intermediate State in the New Testament* (Franeker, 1966) 96ff.

CHAPTER 10

Anthropological Duality in the NT
Outside Pauline Literature

We come now to an investigation of the anthropology displayed in the writings of the NT apart from Pauline literature. As we might expect by now, a duality is evident.

'The spirit indeed is willing, but the flesh is weak' (Mark 14: 38; parallel Matt 26: 41). In the Garden of Gethsemane, the spirit of the disciples, desiring to pray, has succumbed to the fatigue of the body. It is possible, on the contrary, that the contrast lies between the *Holy Spirit* and flesh. This would not be along Pauline lines; for there the Holy Spirit is the eschatological gift granted not until the exaltation of Jesus, and here 'flesh' relates to physical tiredness rather than proclivity toward evil, as in the Pauline dualism. Rather, in the manner of the OT the contrast would put the Holy Spirit as the source of divine strength opposite flesh as characterized by human weakness. Cf. the 'willing spirit', perhaps parallel to 'your holy Spirit', for which the psalmist prays in Ps 51: 14 (and 12–13).

However, in the OT 'spirit' and 'flesh' appear together without reference to the divine spirit.[1] Moreover, we may at least doubt that 'a willing spirit' in Ps 51: 14 refers to 'thy holy Spirit' of verse 13; for the psalmist *already possesses* (but fears to lose) the 'holy Spirit', which corresponds to 'thy presence', whereas 'a willing (obedient) spirit' better corresponds to the 'clean heart' and 'new and right spirit' which the psalmist wants to *receive* in verse 12. By parallelism with 'clean heart', 'a new and steadfast spirit' is human rather than divine (v. 12). So then is 'a willing spirit' (v. 14). The correspondence of these anthropological expressions in contradistinction to the divine Spirit (v. 13) receives confirmation from the positive form of the petitions in verses 12 and 14 in contrast to the negative form of the petitions in verse 13. Thus the three verses present an a–b–a pattern in form and meaning: positive–negative–positive; anthropological–theological–anthropologi-

---

[1] Num 16: 22; 27: 16: 'the God of the spirits of all flesh'.

cal. This in turn confirms the anthropological meaning of the willing spirit in Jesus' statement and the resultant duality of flesh and spirit.[1]

In Heb 9: 1 – 10: 25 the contrast between heavenly reality and earthly copy takes on anthropological significance in the pitting of 'regulations of flesh (*dikaiōmata sarkos*)' – food and drink and various ablutions (9: 10) – and 'purification of the flesh' (9: 13) against purification of the 'conscience' (9: 14) and the writing of God's laws on 'hearts' and 'minds' (10: 16). The anthropological duality receives succinct expression in 10: 22: 'our hearts sprinkled clean from an evil conscience and our bodies washed with pure water'. Similarly, in 4: 12 the sword-like word of God pierces 'to the division of soul and spirit, of joints and marrow'. The author does not mean that the word separates soul *from* spirit any more than he thinks that a sword separates joints *from* marrow. Rather, the word penetrates the inner man ('soul and spirit') just as a sword penetrates the outer man, or body ('joints and marrow'). As 'sword' is a metaphor for 'word of God', so 'joints and marrow' are a metaphor for 'soul and spirit'. But the metaphors rest on a distinction between the corporeal and the incorporeal.

In Matt 5: 27–8 Jesus correlates physical adultery and adultery 'in the heart'. Against 'heart' stand 'eye', 'hand', 'members', and 'body' in verses 29–30. With reference to dietary laws, Jesus contrasts the heart and the stomach (Mark 7: 19; parallel Matt 15: 17), and the heart and the mouth with reference to the ultimate and immediate sources, respectively, of sins (Mark 7: 20–3; parallel Matt 15: 18–19). The heart represents the inner man (cf. *esōthen*), the stomach and mouth, man's body. The same sort of contrast appears in the quotation of Isa 29: 13: 'This people honors me with their *lips*, but their *heart* is far from me' (Mark 7: 6; parallel Matt 15: 8); and in Matt 12: 34; parallel Luke 6: 45: 'For out of the abundance of the *heart* the *mouth* speaks.' ('Heart' had long since lost its physical connotation in such statements.[2]) The contrast between the inner man and the outer man appears again in

---

[1] Cf. K. H. Rengstorf, 'πρόθυμος, προθυμία', *TDNT* 6 (1968) 695–7, on the anthropological use of *pneuma* as practically synonymous with *kardia*.

[2] See below, p. 126.

Jesus' denunciation of the Pharisees' concern for ritual purity at the expense of spiritual cleanness, in terms of the inside and outside of cups, plates, and tombs (Matt 23: 25-8; Luke 11: 39-40).[1]

Jas 4: 8 echoes the same duality of body ('hands') and inner man ('hearts...mind'): 'Cleanse your hands, you sinners, and purify your hearts, you men of double mind (*dipsychoi*).' I Pet 3: 21 is similar: 'not as a removal of dirt from the flesh but as an appeal to God for a clear conscience'. Here, as a counterpart to *sarkos* in the sense of 'body', 'conscience' is an aspect of the incorporeal part of man's constitution. Just possibly, the exhortation 'abstain from the passions of the flesh (*sarkikōn*) that wage war against your soul' (I Pet 2: 11) pits body against soul. Commentators often take 'flesh' in its special Pauline sense, proclivity toward evil. That requires 'soul' to be taken in the sense of 'self'. On the other hand, Paul would have put flesh against *Spirit*. The fact that 'soul' instead of Spirit stands opposite 'flesh' raises the possibility that the use of 'flesh' is not Pauline. *Sarkikos* occurs only here in 1 Peter; but noteworthily, *sarx* elsewhere in I Peter does not carry the special Pauline connotation (with the possible exception of 4: 1*b*; the word occurs also in 1: 24; 3: 18, 21; 4: 1*a*, 2, 6). Even Paul can use *sarkikos* in a physical sense (Rom 15: 27; I Cor 9: 11; II Cor 10: 4). Thus, I Pet 2: 11 may contain a warning against immorality in which physical passions war against the incorporeal soul (cf. II Pet 2: 10, 18).

The two halves of the human constitution come into view in the exhortation that Christian wives adorn the 'hidden person (*anthrōpos*) of the heart' with a 'gentle and quiet spirit' rather than the body with 'outward adorning' in the 'braiding of hair, decoration of gold, and wearing of robes' (I Pet 3: 3-4). In a somewhat similar fashion, the prayer for prosperity and (physical) health in correspondence with the prosperity of the soul (III John 2) exhibits the same duality.

It looks as though the writers of the NT habitually viewed man as a unity of parts, body and soul (or synonyms and synecdochic expressions thereof). Conceivably, under the

---

[1] Since we are dealing only with the milieu of Paul's use of *sōma*, we need not determine the authenticity or inauthenticity of the reported dominical sayings.

holistic hypothesis we might say that the foregoing citations only evince two vantage points from which an indivisibility is viewed. The frequency of the double viewpoint, however, and the high degree of contrast sometimes evident both suggest a partitive rather than monadic unity. Even more tellingly, a whole series of passages concerning the body and soul in matters of life and death establish the partitive interpretation.

'The body apart from the spirit is dead' according to Jas 2: 26. Paul pronounces Eutychus alive since 'his soul is in him' (Acts 20: 10).[1] God tells the rich fool, 'This night your soul is required of you *(apo sou)*' (Luke 12: 20). *Tēn psychēn sou* cannot mean merely life, for in the preceding verse the rich man addresses his soul; and the point of the judgemental word is that apart from the body the soul cannot enjoy the material wealth the man has heaped up.

The background for Martha's statement concerning Lazarus, 'he has been dead four days' (John 11: 39), appears to be the belief attested elsewhere that the soul returns to the corpse on the third day, but finding the onset of corruption abandons the body to irreversible decay from the fourth day onward.[2] By way of contrast, 'You will not abandon my soul to Hades, nor let your Holy One see corruption' (Acts 2: 27 [in quotation of Ps 15: 10 LXX] and 31) displays confidence in God's preservation of soul and body together, over against death, in which the body wastes away in the grave while the soul languishes in Hades. We may compare the expressions 'being in the body' (Heb 13: 3), 'the rest of the time in the flesh' (I Pet 4: 2), 'though we live in the flesh' (II Cor 10: 3), 'the life I now live in the flesh' (Gal 2: 20; cf. Phil 1: 22-4 below), 'in the days of his flesh' (Heb 5: 7), and on the other hand Jesus' promise to the repentant thief – despite his physical fate – 'Truly, I say to you, today you will be with me in Paradise' and the dictum with reference to Abraham, Isaac, and Jacob (their bodies long since buried) that God is the God of the

---

[1] We might translate *psychē* 'life' as does the RSV, but the other passages here discussed, including others in Luke Acts, favor the meaning 'soul' as that entity (rather than mere quality) which animates the body.

[2] See references in Str-B 2: 544-5; G. Dalman, *Jesus-Jeshua* (New York, 1971 reprint) 220; and commentaries on John.

living (Mark 12: 26–7; parallel Matt 20: 31–2 and Luke 20: 37–8).[1]

Luke describes Jesus' own death in the following manner: 'Then Jesus, crying with a loud voice, said, "Father, into thy hands I commit my spirit!" And having said this he breathed his last *(exepneusen)*' (Luke 23: 46). Mark 15: 37 has *exepneusen*, though without the 'Last Word', which is based on Ps 30: 6 LXX. And according to Matt 27: 50 Jesus 'let his spirit go *(aphēken to pneuma)*'. Dying, Stephen prays, 'Lord Jesus, receive my spirit' (Acts 7: 59). In these passages death consists in the departure of the human spirit from the body.

Perhaps Luke 16: 19–31 belongs here. Upon dying, the rich man goes to Hades, poor Lazarus to Abraham's bosom. The use of 'Hades' in verse 23 favors a reference to the intermediate state.[2] The putting of the resurrection in the future *(ean tis ek nekrōn anastē*, v. 30) confirms that understanding. Hence, the intermediate state of the soul apart from the body is described in terms analogous to physical life.

Jesus warns, 'Do not fear those who kill the body but cannot kill the soul; rather fear him who can destroy both soul and body in Gehenna' (Matt 10: 28).[3] The distinction between body and soul is clear. So also is their separability in that man

---

[1] This last observation comes from G. de Rosa, 'Immortalità dell'anima e rivelazione cristiana', *Divinitas* 4 (1960) 93–4.

[2] See J. Jeremias, 'ᾅδης', *TDNT* 1 (1964) 147–8.

[3] The duality is not so clear in the parallel, Luke 12: 4–5: 'do not fear those who kill the body, and after that have no more that they can do... fear him who, after he has killed, has power to cast into Gehenna'. J. Schmid thinks that Luke suppresses the distinction between body and soul in favor of the general thought that men can kill the body, but only God can cast a person into hell ('Der Begriff der Seele im Neuen Testament', *Einsicht und Glaube*, Festschrift for G. Söhngen, ed. J. Ratzinger and H. Fries, 2nd ed. [Freiburg, 1962] 144–5 and *Das Evangelium nach Matthäus* [Regensburg, 1956] 182–3; also G. Dautzenberg, *Sein Leben bewahren: Ψυχή in den Herrenworten der Evangelien* [München, 1966] 138–53; R. Schnackenburg, *Christian Existence in the New Testament* [Notre Dame, 1968] 1: 7–8). I. H. Marshall recognizes the dichotomy ('Uncomfortable Words. VI. "Fear him who can destroy both soul and body in hell" [Mt 10: 28 R.S.V.]', *ExpT* 81 [1970] 277). Obviously Luke does not give clear expression to a dichotomy, for he does not even mention the soul. Nevertheless, since God must have something to cast into Gehenna after he has killed the body, the Lukan form of the saying implies the casting into Gehenna of either a bodiless soul or (in accordance with the Matthaean version) the body and soul together.

can kill the body but not the soul. We might reason in the opposite direction that the destruction of *both* soul *and* body in hell shows the unity of man even in death.[1] In that case the antithesis does not lie between body and soul, but between merely earthly death and far more serious eternal damnation.[2] It is true, of course, that the destruction of soul and body together constitutes eternal damnation. But man's ability to destroy the body *apart from* the soul still shows that the two are distinct and separable.[3] In speaking of divine destruction of both soul and body Jesus does not refer to an intermediate state, for then he could not have included the body. He refers rather to the final state in which reunited soul and body undergo divine judgement.

The distinction between spirit and body comes out clearly in Luke 24: 37, 39: 'But they were startled and frightened, and supposed that they saw a spirit... "See my hands and my feet, that it is I myself; handle me, and see; for a spirit has not flesh and bones as you see that I have."' The author of Heb 12: 23 refers to 'the spirits of just men made perfect' in heaven. In Rev 6: 9 we read that 'the souls of those who had been slain for the word of God and for the witness they had borne' wait under the heavenly altar for vindication. They are visible; they cry out loudly; they wear white robes (vv. 9–11). Thus they are not nonentities. On the other hand, the futurity of their resurrection (20: 4, 6) shows that they are bodiless despite their visibility and ability to speak and wear clothing. Either they are described in terms analogous to earthly life, or their souls are considered to be composed of fine substance.

Since the departed are bodiless spirits, or souls, death consists in the separation of body and soul/spirit and in the dissolution of the body. That is the implication of the expression in

[1] So J. N. Sevenster, 'Die Anthropologie des Neuen Testaments', *Anthropologie Religieuse*, ed. C. J. Bleeker, Studies in the History of Religions (Supplements to *Numen*) 2 (Leiden, 1955) 176–7.

[2] So R. Schnackenburg, 'Man Before God: Toward a Biblical View of Man', *Man Before God: Toward a Theology of Man* (New York, 1966) 5–6.

[3] To escape the dichotomy Nikolainen adopts a generalizing interpretation that God has power over man's *life* (*Der Auferstehungsglauben in der Bibel und ihrer Umwelt* (Helsinki, 1944) 2: 24–5). This sidesteps the pairing of soul with body by Jesus and his indication that one may be destroyed without the other.

II Pet 1 : 14, 'the putting off of my tent'. According to I Peter 3 : 18 Christ was killed as to flesh but vivified as to spirit. Only later do references to his resurrection and ascension occur (vv. 21–2).[1] Similarly, the dead who have been 'judged as to flesh according to men' and 'live as to spirit according to God' (I Pet 4 : 6) appear to be Christians whose bodies have died but whose spirits continue to live in communion with God.[2]

Then we confront passages in which *psychē* has the meanings of 'self' and 'life'. Yet *psychē* remains an entity, not just a quality, for it refers to the incorporeal part of man which animates the body and thereby constitutes the inner man. So Jesus speaks about saving and losing one's soul/life/self, and about gaining the whole world but losing one's soul/life/self (Mark 8 : 35–7; Matt 16 : 25–6; Luke 9 : 24–5; John 12 : 25 – all parallel). Similar are Heb 10 : 39, 'But we are not of those who shrink back and are destroyed, but of those who have faith and keep their souls'; Jas 1 : 21, 'save your souls'; I Pet 1 : 9, 'the salvation of your souls'; Matt 11 : 29, 'rest for your souls'; I Pet 1 : 22, 'having purified your souls'; and I Pet 4 : 19, 'Therefore let those who suffer according to God's will do right and entrust their souls to a faithful Creator.'

The spread of these dichotomous statements throughout the NT (outside Pauline literature) further demonstrates the prevalence of anthropological duality in early Christian thinking. Only I and II John and Jude fail to be represented among the passages here considered, and there is quite a heavy concentration in the synoptic gospels as well as Hebrews and I Peter.

[1] See further R. H. Gundry, 'The Form, Meaning and Background of the Hymn Quoted in I Timothy 3 : 16', *Apostolic History and the Gospel: Biblical and Historical Essays Presented to F. F. Bruce on His Sixtieth Birthday,* ed. W. Gasque and R. P. Martin (Grand Rapids, Mich., 1970) 211–14.

[2] E. G. Selwyn, *The First Epistle of St Peter* (London, 1958) 214–15, 337–9.

Anthropological Duality in the OT

We have established that a consistent use of *sōma* by Paul in a purely physical sense would agree with the anthropological duality which prevailed in Christianity, Judaism, and the Hellenistic world of thought outside Christianity and Judaism. But in the interests of a holistic definition of *sōma* in Pauline passages some might say that Paul went directly to the OT, where the anthropology is monadic rather than dichotomous. We turn then to the OT view of man.

It is sometimes stated that the Hebrews were so holistic in their view of man that they lacked even the concept of the physical body as a discrete entity. For example, Stacey writes that the proper Hebrew word for body, גויה, occurs only fourteen times in the OT because the distinction between physical and psychical simply was not made.[1] Similarly, J. A. T. Robinson states that 'the Hebrews had no term for the "body"'. In the Septuagint the Greek word σῶμα translates no less than eleven Hebrew words (with cognates, thirteen), for none of which is it a true equivalent.'[2] The statement is qualified with the comment, 'It would be more accurate to say that Hebrew has no word for "the body" which is in any sense *technical or doctrinally significant*.'[3] גופה (1 Chr 10: 12), נבלה (Deut 21: 23; Josh 8: 29; I Kgs 13: 22, 24, 28, 29), and פגר (Gen 15: 11; Isa 37: 36) refer only to a corpse, and גויה, which is 'much nearer to "body" proper', has 'no theological significance'. That word also means 'corpse' in a number of instances (I Sam 31: 10, 12; Ps 110: 6; Nah 3: 3). It does refer, however, to living human bodies in Gen 47: 18; Neh 9: 37; Dan 10: 6 (torso); and Ezek 1: 11, 23 (torso). Finally, Robinson discounts גשם as a word for the living human body because of its Chaldean origin and its limitation to the Book of Daniel (3: 27–8; 4: 30; 5: 21; 7: 11).

---

[1] W. D. Stacey, *The Pauline View of Man* (London, 1956) 94.

[2] J. A. T. Robinson, *The Body: A Study in Pauline Theology*, SBT 1/5 (London, 1952) 11.　　　[3] *Ibid.*, italics supplied.

But the lack of a word in a language would not necessarily imply the lack of a concept. Moreover, in the OT we fall far short of possessing a complete vocabulary of ancient Hebrew. Even were these considerations not apropos, we should note that גויה in the sense of the living human body, infrequent though it is, shows that the Hebrews *did* have a concept of the body as a discrete entity. And we should not overlook the possibility that גו and גוה mean 'body' instead of 'back' in several OT passages.[1] However, what is most damaging to the notion that the Hebrews lacked the concept of the body is the frequent use of בשר in this sense (Exod 30: 32; Lev 6: 3; 14: 9; 15: 13, 16; 16: 4, 24, 26, 28; 17: 16; 19: 28; 21: 5; 22: 6; Num 8: 7; 19: 7–8; I Kgs 21: 27; II Kgs 6: 30; Job 4: 15; 14: 22; 19: 26; Ps 16: 9; 63: 2; 84: 3; 119: 120; Prov 14: 30; Eccl 2: 3; 4: 5; 5: 5; 11: 10; 12: 12; Isa 10: 18; 17: 4).[2] In many of these passages, the RSV translates with 'body'. The fact that the identical phrase על בשרו (with reference to the donning of sackcloth) in I Kgs 21: 27 and II Kgs 6: 30 appears in the LXX as *epi to sōma autou* and *epi tēs sarkos autou* respectively demonstrates בשר and *sarx* can refer to the body. That בשר has other meanings, too – flesh as a substance, mankind, kinsfolk, the penis – does not give us the right to say that the word is 'essentially not "body" but "flesh".'[3] For a mere glance at the passages just cited will show that in them בשר refers to flesh, not as a substance or some other generality, but as organized into an individual body. The flesh as a body is anointed, washed, clothed, cut, pained. It thirsts, trembles, faints, grows weary through excessive study. בשר can be modified by כל ('all, entire, whole') *even when used of individuals* (Lev 15: 16; Num 8: 7). It simply includes the sense 'body' alongside other meanings. The Hebrews did know and frequently use, then, the same concept as that which is conveyed in the popular meaning of *sōma*. For that concept they happened to use בשר more often than גויה.

Beyond the meaning and usage of Hebrew words for the body, we confront a current understanding of OT anthropology by

---

[1] See above, p. 19.   [2] See BDB, בָּשָׂר s.v.
[3] Robinson, *The Body*, 12. Cf. the flat denial by Tresmontant that 'flesh' ever conveys what we mean by 'body' (*A Study of Hebrew Thought* [New York, 1960] 95).

now so common that its maxims need no quotation marks. It is that in the OT body and soul do not contrast. Man is an animated body rather than an incarnated soul. The breath which God breathed into molded clay at the creation represents the principle of life; and the soul that resulted is the human person as a whole. Thus man does not *have* a body; he *is* a body – a psychophysical unity. The body is the soul in its outward form. Hence the various members and organs of the body think and act as representations of the soul, or person. The soul, then, is simultaneously visible and invisible and constitutes the whole man. Since flesh stands on the same continuum with soul, the flesh likewise constitutes the whole man. Indeed, the term 'flesh' sometimes stands where we would have expected the term 'soul' (Eccl 5: 5; Prov 4: 22; 14: 30; Lev 13: 18). Consequently, at death the soul does not survive the body or flesh. It simply goes out, drains away with the blood, for death afflicts the soul and flesh alike since both refer to the person as a whole (Isa 10: 18, and Num 23: 10 for death to the soul). Therefore the dead are not designated 'souls', but 'shadows, shades'. As such, they are unsubstantial but not immaterial – ethereally material, we might say. Under this view death becomes, not extinction, but drastic reduction of the vigor of life. It is the weakest form of life.[1]

To the extent that this reading of OT anthropology emphasizes that body and soul belong together we may heartily agree. But at the point where a distinction of kind between body and soul is denied, we should disagree. Of course, even J. Pedersen admits that 'the Israelites are quite able to distinguish between soul and body, as when Isaiah says: He shall consume both soul and flesh (10, 18)'. However, that distinction for Pedersen

---

[1] H. W. Robinson, 'Hebrew Psychology in Relation to Pauline Anthropology', *Mansfield College Essays* (London, 1909) 265–86, *The Christian Doctrine of Man*, 2nd ed. (Edinburgh, 1913) ch. 1, 'Hebrew Psychology', *The People and the Book*, ed. A. S. Peake (Oxford, 1925) 353–82, and *Inspiration and Revelation in the Old Testament* (Oxford, 1946) 69–70; J. Pedersen, *Israel: Its Life and Culture I–II* (London, 1926) 99–181; A. R. Johnson, *The One and the Many in the Israelite Conception of God* (Cardiff, 1961) 3–4, and *The Vitality of the Individual in the Thought of Ancient Israel*, 2nd ed. (Cardiff, 1964) 87–109; M. E. Dahl, *The Resurrection of the Body*, SBT 1/36 (London, 1962) 59–60, 62, 71–2; Tresmontant, *Hebrew Thought*, 43–9, 90, 93–5; D. Lys, *Nèphèsh*, Etudes d'histoire et de philosophie religieuses 50 (Paris, 1959) *passim*; Käsemann, *Leib und Leib Christi* (Tübingen, 1933) 1–23.

is not a distinction in kind but in degree of vigor; the soul is the stronger manifestation of the person, the flesh the weaker: 'But no distinction is made between them as two fundamental forms of existence. The flesh is the weaker...the soul the stronger. The soul is more than the body, but the body is a perfectly valid manifestation of the soul...Soul and body are so intimately united that a distinction cannot be made between them. They are more than "united": the body is the soul in its outward form.'[1]

Despite all his emphasis on the identity of body with soul, Pedersen allows that the soul is 'more than' the body. I.e., although 'flesh' may be comprehended under 'soul', 'soul' cannot be comprehended under 'flesh'. Not only are there divine souls without flesh, but man as soul is 'more than' flesh, so much so that after the dissolution of the body, the 'shade' is still a soul, but one bereft of strength.[2] (Pedersen here contradicts his other statement that the soul does not survive but drains away.) But what is this 'more than'? Does it not indicate a distinction in kind as well as in degree of strength, and thus represent a certain duality, especially since it survives the dissolution of the body? It is, indeed, a wedge within the holistic anthropology. We shall see from the OT that Pedersen's 'more than' cannot be eliminated. And it suggests the possibility that man is a unity of parts rather than a monadic unity.

Since the soul is more than the body, we may suspect that the soul interpenetrates the body and its members, rather than identify the body with the soul. That in turn raises the possibility that death is not *initially* a reduction in the vigor of life, but separation of the soul and flesh, or body. Cf. also the return of the soul to the body. Reduction of vigor then follows only as a consequence of that separation. Moreover, under such an understanding death touches the soul as much as the body. For death is not cessation, but a separation in which each part suffers. The body lacks vigor through absence of the soul; the soul lacks means of action through absence of the body. Maybe that is the reason the deceased ordinarily are no longer designated 'souls', a word which connotes vitality, but 'shades'.

[1] Pedersen, *Israel I–II*, 170–1. [2] *Ibid.* 180.

Under a holistic anthropology there is an unresolved problem in that at death the soul drains away – but to where? Into nothingness? Hardly, for death is not extinction, and man *is* soul. Does not even the holistic anthropology need to recognize, against its wish, the continued existence of man as soul in the inhibited form of a shade? Pedersen does. For the OT knows that the flesh returns to dust and that the bones lie in the grave.[1] The *whole* man as he now exists in flesh hardly survives, then, even in weak form. Though the shade is pictured as a weak body, we cannot identify the shade with the body which comes from earthly lifetime. *That* flesh has gone back to dust and those bones may still be dug up. Therefore shades are portrayed in physical terms simply by way of analogy.

Without identification of the soul which leaves the body at death with the shade which survives the corpse, the soul is left at loose ends even though the person continues to exist, and the shade lacks continuity with the person who has lived on earth. It seems more natural to make an identification between the soul and the shade and to explain the shift in terminology by means of the respective connotations of the terms, vitality and unsubstantiality. This would fit into an anthropology which emphasizes the intended unity of man as body and soul, but recognizes the distinction between the two, laments their unnatural separation through death, and, finally, looks forward to their reunion.

Further consequences follow from such an anthropology. The designations 'animated body' and 'incarnated soul' no longer oppose each other, for because of their interpenetration the soul *is* the animation of the body and the body *is* the incarnation of the soul. The soul *has* a body and the body *has* a soul and man as a whole *is* both, a psychophysical unity – but a unity, not a monad.

Because of the interpenetration (not identity) of soul and body, psychological functions are attributed to the body and its parts, and physical functions to the soul. Synecdoche of both the terms 'soul' and 'flesh' for the whole man (or mankind) becomes very natural, 'soul' to indicate man as a living

[1] See K. Bornhäuser, 'Die Gebeine der Toten: Ein Beitrag zum Verständnis der Anschauungen von der Totenauferstehung zur Zeit des Neuen Testaments', *Beiträge zur Förderung christlicher Theologie* 26 (1921) 123–78.

being[1] and 'flesh' to indicate him as a visible, tangible creature. Parts of the body stand for the whole man in the same way, with emphases differing according to the term used. Already A. R. Johnson, himself an advocate of a modified holistic ('synthetic') anthropology, has shown that 'diffused consciousness' overstates what should be regarded as simple synecdoche due to the phenomenon of poetic parallelism.[2] Identification of the body with the soul is not necessary to explain this well-known phenomenon, in which the soul is nauseated by tasteless food (Num 21: 5) and the navel healed by the fear of the Lord (Prov 3: 8) – to take but two of many possible examples. All that is needed to account for such statements is psychosomatic unity, not atomic indivisibility.

Here should be put references which Pedersen cites as demonstrations of the identity of flesh with soul since in these passages we should have expected נפש instead of בשר: 'A tranquil mind gives life to the flesh, but passion makes the bones rot' (Prov 14: 30).[3] We may doubt that here 'soul' would have been expected in place of 'flesh'. The proverb simply indicates effects upon the body of psychic characteristics. Similar is Prov 4: 22. 'For they [wise words] are life to him who finds them, and healing to his flesh.' Eccl 5: 5 is somewhat different: 'Let not your mouth cause your flesh to sin.' 'Soul' would have surprised us hardly less. We expect a simple 'you'. Evidently 'flesh' appears in synecdoche for 'you' because of its connotation of weakness and consequent proneness to sin, as frequently in later Jewish literature. Pedersen's reference to Lev 13: 18 is mystifying, because the passage has a purely physical import: 'And when there is in the skin of one's body (בשר) a boil that has healed...'

For a dichotomy within the unity of man's constitution the

---

[1] Gen 2: 7. Under any view the 'dead soul' of Lev 21: 11 and Num 6: 6 is odd, as also 'soul' in the sense of 'corpse' in Lev 19: 28; 21: 1; Num 5: 2; 9: 6–7, 10. Does the usage reflect a notion that the soul lingered near the corpse for a while, until dissolution? Cf. the soul's feeling the worms as they gnaw on the body (Job 14: 22) and see above, p. 113, n. 2. In any case, 'dead' may modify the normal connotation of 'soul', and the need for the modification in two instances shows that 'soul' ordinarily connotes vitality.

[2] *The Vitality of the Individual*, 1–2, 37–87. Cf. J. Barr's criticism of holism (*The Semantics of Biblical Language* [London, 1961] 89–106).

[3] Pedersen, *Israel I–II*, 176.

OT offers evidence beyond that which turns up in an examination of evidence for the holistic view. In a number of passages terms for the corporeal and the incorporeal stand side by side or in parallelism, sometimes by way of contrast, sometimes by way of complement, to denote the whole man as composed of two basic parts which are happily united in life and unfortunately separated in death.

'I will take my flesh in my teeth, and put my soul in my hand' (Job 13: 14).[1] 'But his flesh is in pain over himself, and his soul laments over himself' (Job 14: 22). In Ezek 44: 7, 9 we read of 'foreigners, uncircumcised in heart and flesh'. And in Ezek 36: 26 the 'new heart', or 'heart of flesh', must be metaphorical, for it stands in a contrastive parallel to a 'heart of stone', which cannot be taken literally. Moreover, 'heart of flesh' is paralleled synonymously by 'a new spirit'. The putting of the 'new spirit' (or, metaphorically, 'new heart') into the physical 'flesh' through which obedience to divine law will be carried out (v. 27) rests on a duality of spirit/heart and body/flesh. Similar are Eccl 2: 3, 'I searched with my heart how to cheer my flesh', and 11: 10, 'Remove vexation from your heart and put away pain from your flesh'.

'The Lord will destroy both soul and body (literally, from soul even to body, מנפש ועד בשר) and it will be as when a sick man wastes away' (Isa 10: 18). To avoid duality, we might take נפש to mean the throat as the channel of breathing and בשר to mean the genitals as the organs of reproduction.[2] However, the infrequency of those meanings and the frequency of dichotomous anthropological expressions combine to favor the usual translation and understanding. The dual expression 'body and soul' then denotes the two parts which make up the whole man who falls under divine judgement. Cf. 'the spirits of all flesh' (Num 16: 22; 27: 1).

'Therefore my heart is glad and my glory (or liver) rejoices; my flesh also dwells secure' (Ps 16: 9). In the first colon 'heart' and 'glory (or liver)' denote the inner man. In the second colon 'flesh' represents the outer man. Together, they represent the whole man. Similarly, 'My heart and flesh sing for joy'

---

[1] The RSV misses the duality with the translation 'life' for נפש.

[2] O. Sander, 'Leib–Seele-Dualismus im Alten Testament?', *ZAW* 77 (1965) 329–32.

(Ps 84: 3*b*). 'My flesh (שׁארי) and my heart may fail' (Ps 73: 26*a*). 'My soul thirsts for you; my flesh faints for you' (Ps 63: 2). 'A man who is kind benefits his soul, but a cruel man hurts his flesh (שׁארו)' (Prov 11: 17).

In the last quotation, both 'soul' and 'flesh' by synecdoche act like reflexive pronouns for the whole man. But the point to notice is that for the parallel synecdoches, the composer of the proverb chooses two terms which denote the inner man and the outer man respectively and, in combination, the whole man. The passages from the Psalms certainly indicate the unity of flesh and soul/heart in their acting in unison and upon each other; but it is a unity of parts. If these terms denoted a mere difference of degree in vigor on a continuum, rather than a difference in kind, such pairing would probably have not appeared so frequently.

'The Egyptians are men, and not God; and their horses are flesh, and not spirit' (Isa 31: 3). Here we are not dealing with a contrast within man, and 'flesh' connotes weakness whereas 'spirit' connotes strength. Nevertheless, the contrast between the terms is instructive. It is stated so strongly that we receive the impression of a qualitative rather than merely quantitative distinction between flesh and spirit as the reason for the difference between their respective weakness and strength. This receives confirmation from the parallel contrast between men and God, surely a qualitative one for Isaiah (see ch. 6).

'I am bringing evil upon all flesh, says the Lord; but I will give you your soul as a prize of war' (Jer 45: 5). 'Flesh' here means mankind, but from the side of his physical mortality, to which נפשׁ as the animus within flesh stands in contrast: flesh/death–soul/life.

'And the dust returns to the earth as it was, and the spirit returns to God who gave it' (Eccl 12: 7; cf. 3: 21). The dust is the body of flesh. The differing origins and fates of body and spirit make the duality unmistakable. Although the statement by context expresses a sceptical view concerning afterlife rather than blessed immortality for the spirit, the thought rests on a commonly understood distinction in kind between flesh and spirit.

'If he should take back his spirit to himself, and gather to himself his breath, all flesh would perish together, and man would return to dust' (Job 34: 14–15). 'His [God's] spirit/ breath' is not the Holy Spirit, but the divinely given spirit/ breath of man in contrast to the flesh of man which comes from and returns to dust (see Eccl 12: 7; Gen 2: 7; Isa 42: 5; Zech 12: 1; cf. Num 16: 22; 27: 16).[1]

'Then the Lord said, ''My spirit shall not abide in man forever'', for he is flesh, but his days shall be a hundred and twenty years' (Gen 6: 3). Under this probable reading of the text, the spirit which man has within him from God contrasts with the flesh which constitutes his body.

In the last several passages, death consists in the withdrawal of the spirit from the flesh. So also in Ezek 37: 1–14 the bones, sinews, and skin of the human body contrast with the רוח. Here the use of רוח plays upon several meanings, 'breath', 'wind', and 'spirit'. But as applied to men, רוח does not refer simply to physical breath, for it is associated also with God's spirit (v. 14), if not identified with it. The bodies live again only when spirit from God enters them.

In Ps 103: 1–2, 14, 'my soul' is equivalent to 'all that is in the midst of me (כל קרבי)', and these two expressions contrast with 'our frame (יצרנו)...dust', which refers to man's physique as formed by God prior to the breathing in of life (Gen 2: 7). In Job 4: 19 men are 'those who dwell in houses of clay, whose foundation is in the dust'. Cf. 10: 11: 'You *clothed* me with skin and flesh.' The figure of houses with foundations seems to imply that bodies are inhabited by souls, or spirits. The figure of clothing seems to imply that the soul, or spirit, wears the body.

The interior part of man receives mention also in Ps 51: 12, 'Create for me a clean heart, O God, and renew a right spirit in the inward part of me (בקרבי)', and Zech 12: 1, ''Thus says the Lord, who...formed the spirit of man in the midst of him (בקרבו).' Of course, we might regard קרב (and 'heart' and other designations of the inner man) as merely the invisible interior of the indivisible entity which appears out-

---

[1] It is arbitrary for W. Eichrodt to distinguish sharply between the individual spirit of man and the divine spirit within him (*Theology of the Old Testament*, The Old Testament Library [Philadelphia, 1967] 2:47–8, 131–4). In Job 27: 3 'my breath...in me' stands in synonymous parallelism with 'the spirit of God...in my nostrils'.

wardly as body. But the separability clearly stated in passages cited above and below rules out that understanding and requires a partitive interpretation instead. Moreover, the indication in Job 10: 4 that God is not flesh (cf. Isa 31: 3) shows an awareness in the OT of incorporeal reality as well as corporeal reality. Thus the physical etymologies of words such as נפש and רוח should not prejudice our interpretation of the actual usage of the words where they clearly complement, and even contrast with, the physical.

Of course this does not imply that נפש, e.g., cannot carry other meanings. We might hypothesize that the meaning 'life' quite naturally came to refer to the person who bears life, 'the living being', and from there came to the additional meaning, 'self'. But yet another meaning developed, viz., 'soul' as that part of man which animates his body and leaves it at death. Since the נפש in this sense may leave, exist apart from the body, and even come back to the body, it is properly called a 'part' of man's constitution. We may trace a similar evolution of meaning in the term רוח from 'wind', or 'breath', to 'spirit' as distinct from the body, or flesh.

The contrast between the inner man and the outer man appears also in the difference between the mouth and the reins (Jer 12: 2) and between the mouth/lips and the heart (Isa 29: 13). Similarly, the outward appearance and the heart (I Sam 16: 7) and circumcision of the heart and circumcision of the flesh contrast (Jer 4: 4; 9: 25; Deut 10: 16; 30: 6; cf. Rom 2: 28; Jer 31: 33). It is worth mentioning here that although the term 'heart' started with a physical connotation, in passages such as these it has developed a metaphorical meaning which leaves behind the physical. I.e., 'heart' does not refer to the inside of the body, let alone the single organ of the heart. For what could circumcision of the foreskin of the heart possibly mean unless the term 'heart' has lost its physical connotation? Literal circumcision of a physical heart or of the inner aspect of the body is out of the question. Nor can we take literally the melting of the heart with fear.[1]

W. Eichrodt does not exaggerate, then, in writing, 'The dis-

[1] A. R. Johnson, *The Vitality of the Individual*, 82. See also P. Dhorme, *L'emploi métaphorique des noms de parties du corps en hébreu et accidien* (Paris, 1923) 109–28, for the progression from the literal to the metaphorical.

tinction between an inner, spiritual aspect and a physical aspect of human nature...is...a constituent element of the whole Old Testament view of Man.'[1] In view of this duality, we may suspect to be wrong the frequently made statement that at death the soul as life simply dissipates. As a matter of fact, not only the general duality of OT anthropology, but also clear indications in the text prove the falsity of that view and in turn confirm the anthropological duality we have found elsewhere. The soul as the inner part of the person goes to Sheol. Once there, the soul is called a 'shade'. The soul may also return from Sheol.

'He keeps back his soul from the Pit...His flesh is so wasted away that it cannot be seen; and his bones which were not seen stick out. His soul draws near the Pit...He has redeemed my soul from going down into the Pit...to bring back his soul from the Pit, that he may see the light of life' (Job 33: 18, 21, 22, 28, 30). We note (a) that through sickness and death the soul may approach and descend into the Pit (= Sheol) and yet come back, and (b) that by contrast the body wastes away as the soul goes toward the Pit.

'Because you have not abandoned my soul to Sheol nor given your godly one to see the Pit' (Ps 16: 10). The synonymous parallelism suggests that the soul is not the force of life in an impersonal way but the individual person as a living being, the 'godly one' himself. Moreover, 'abandoned...to' parallels 'given...to see'. The psalmist therefore implies that his soul might have *experienced* Sheol. If we take the translation 'see corruption' at the close of the verse, we have a parallel between the abandonment of the soul to the underworld and the return of the flesh to dust.

Sheol holds the soul in its grip: 'What strong man can live and not see death, [and] deliver his soul from the hand of Sheol?' (Ps 89: 49). But God can and does deliver a righteous man's soul from Sheol: 'O Lord, you have brought up from Sheol my soul; my life you have restored from among those who have gone down to the Pit' (Ps 30: 4). Again, the soul may experience Sheol, and its restoration therefrom brings renewed life. Similar are Ps 49: 16, 'But God will ransom my soul from the hand of Sheol', Prov 23: 13–14, 'You will save his soul

[1] *Theology of the Old Testament* 2: 131.

from Sheol', and Ps 86: 13, 'You have delivered my soul from the depths of Sheol.' In the last passage we detect poetic hyperbole in that the distress of the psalmist represents, not merely the outskirts of Sheol encroaching upon present life, but the deadly depths of the Pit. And immediately prior to the exultation in Ps 49: 16 appears an indication that in death the physique wastes away while Sheol becomes the abode of the soul. That is the inference from the following reference to redemption of the soul from Sheol.

In his psalm of thanksgiving, Hezekiah recalls his illness: 'I said, In the noontide of my days I must depart; I am consigned to the gates of Sheol' (Isa 38: 10). In what form? Verse 17 supplies the answer, 'You have held back *my soul* from the pit of destruction.' נפש should not here be translated 'life', for according to verse 10 Hezekiah fears that *he himself* will go to Sheol. Moreover, his removal to Sheol entails separation from his body: 'My dwelling is plucked up and removed from me like a shepherd's tent' (v. 12). In summary, Hezekiah fears that in soulish form he will depart to confinement in Sheol when the tent-habitation, his body, folds up. This separability of soul from body shows that we are not dealing with inner and outer viewpoints of an indivisible entity.

The soul does not evaporate, then, but goes to Sheol for confinement. In this way we are to understand statements that the soul at death departs, or is breathed or poured out (Gen 35: 18; Job 11: 20; 31: 39; Isa 53: 12; Jer 15: 9; Lam 2: 12; cf. 1: 11, 19 and Ps 23: 3). Thus also the soul as a personal entity comes from somewhere – viz., Sheol – when it returns into the inward part of a man (על קרבו – I Kgs 17: 21–2 *bis*).[1]

Statements about the gathering of the deceased to his ancestors also indicate that the soul continues to exist in a place. These statements do not refer primarily to interment of the corpse in a family sepulchre, but to association with the shades of one's ancestors in the underworld. This is evident from instances in which a person goes to his ancestors in spite of burial

---

[1] We therefore should not accept Nikolainen's argument that the killing of a נפש implies the soul's nonexistence after the body's death (Num 23: 10; 31: 19; 35: 15; Josh 20: 3, 9; Judg 16: 30; Ezek 22: 25, 27; *Der Auferstehungsglauben in der Bibel und ihrer Umwelt* [Helsinki, 1944] 107). In such passages נפש bears the meaning 'living being' rather than 'soul'. Cf. Lys. *Nèphèsh*, 124–5.

far from a family sepulchre. Abraham receives the promise that he will go to his fathers in peace (Gen 15: 15), yet he is 'gathered to his people' and buried in the cave of Machpelah, a long way from Mesopotamia (Gen 25: 8–9). Jacob 'was gathered to his people' in Egypt and buried in the family sepulchre not until seventy days of mourning plus a journey to the Land of Canaan (Gen 49: 28 – 50: 14).

Indeed, the gathering to ancestors consistently occurs at the moment of death and thereby precedes burial. Isaac 'died and was gathered to his people'; only then did Esau and Jacob bury him (Gen 35: 29). It is foretold of both Aaron and Moses that they will be gathered to their people; yet both die and are buried alone (Num 20: 24, 26; 27: 13; 31: 2; Deut 31: 16; 32: 50). David 'slept[1] with his fathers', but was buried in Jerusalem, not Bethlehem (I Kgs 2: 10). Omri 'slept with his fathers', but was buried in Samaria, the city he had newly built (I Kgs 16: 28). Manasseh 'slept with his fathers', but was buried in the garden of his house (II Kgs 21: 18). And Jacob's lament, ' I shall go down to Sheol to my son, mourning' (Gen 37: 35), cannot refer to common destiny in a single sepulchre, for Jacob thought that beasts had devoured the body of Joseph and at best had left scattered remnants of his body uneaten and unburied (v. 33). Therefore the phrase 'to my son' implies more than common burial, say, a degree of conscious reunion.[2]

We might suppose that the concept of a gathering to one's fathers *originally* denoted burial in a family sepulchre, but became a euphemism for death so stereotyped that it could be used indifferently of those who died and were buried in other places.[3] However, the distinction between the gathering to one's

[1] N. J. Tromp notes the distinction between the verbs for being gathered to and sleeping with one's fathers (*Primitive Conceptions of Death and the Nether World in the Old Testament*, BibOr 21 [Rome, 1969] 168–71). Since both expressions carry a dichotomous implication for anthropology, the difference in the verbs does not concern us.

[2] J. Héring, 'Entre la mort et la résurrection', *RHPR* 40 (1960) 339.

[3] So Eichrodt, *Theology of the Old Testament* 2: 213–14. Nevertheless he admits that the concern to be united with one's family in death 'clearly derives from a belief that the dead still survive in some way or other in the grave'. What survives, though, is not the soul or spirit, according to Eichrodt, but the shadow of the whole man. But how can the *whole* man have been thought to survive when it is well known in the OT that the body

ancestors at the moment of death and the burial of the corpse (sometimes considerably later) militates against the supposition that the euphemism initially referred to death and burial as a single concept with reference to a family sepulchre. Moreover, it is exeedingly strange that in the OT the euphemism almost invariably refers to an exception to the supposed original meaning.

Isaiah says concerning the king of Babylon, 'Sheol beneath is stirred up to meet you when you come, it rouses the shades to greet you, all who were leaders of the earth; it raises from their thrones all who were kings of the nations' (Isa 14: 9). These shades in conclave are clearly different from the corpses, or bones, which individually lie 'each in his own tomb' (v. 18). In particular, the descent of the king of Babylon to the company of the shades can have nothing to do with burial, for Isaiah addresses him, 'You are cast out, away from your sepulchre...You will not be joined with them in burial' (vv. 19–20).

This passage also indicates that Sheol is a place of some activity even though that activity is minimal. The shades rise to greet and address the king of Babylon. In other words, they have certain powers of movement and speech. For their power of speech, we may also note Isa 29: 4, 'your voice shall come from the ground like the voice of a ghost', and parallel lines, and Ezek 32: 21, 'The mighty chiefs shall speak...out of the midst of Sheol: "They have come down, they lie still, the uncircumcised, slain by the sword"'; and for movement, Job 26: 5: 'The shades below tremble.'

Furthermore, the deceased, or the mediums whom they inform, are called the 'knowing ones' (Lev 19: 31; 20: 6; Isa 19: 3). 'Should they consult the dead on behalf of the living?' (Isa 8: 19; cf. the practice of incubation in 65: 4).[1] It is evident that the shades are thought to possess knowledge superior to that of living people. The shade of Samuel, called up by the witch of Endor, forecasts the future; but that may

returns to dust? Why cannot the shade be the soul bereft of the body, which had been its means of action?

[1] Perhaps there is some significance in deceased Rachel's mourning for the captives of Israel (Jer 31: 15), though this might be merely figurative. Cf. Isa 63: 16.

be due to his prophetic gift also during life. He does come up from Sheol, however, and say directly to Saul that the very next day Saul and his sons will be with him in Sheol (I Sam 27: 3–19). In view of Samuel's conscious state, 'with me' probably implies conscious association in Sheol.[1] The prohibitions of necromancy (Exod 22: 18; Lev 20: 27; Deut 18: 10–12) and of offerings to the dead (Deut 26: 14; cf. Ps 102: 28) further show that the people of the OT think of the dead as alive apart from the flesh, which has returned to dust.[2]

R. H. Charles writes: 'The leading characteristic of these survivals may be said to be the comparatively large measure of life, movement, knowledge, and likewise power attributed to the departed in Sheol.'[3] This is surely an overstatement. Charles is interested to establish a Sheol full of active spirits as an early concept drawn from heathen ancestor worship and the like over against a Sheol of nothingness as a later concept produced by the this-worldly ethics of Yahwism. Nevertheless, Charles could never have made his extravagant statement without good evidence of at least some consciousness and activity in Sheol.

On the other side, it is pointed out that the excitement in Sheol over the descent of the king of Babylon appears to be unusual.[4] That may be true, but the indications just discussed

---

[1] Cf. P. Torge, *Seelenglaube und Unsterblichkeit im Alten Testament* (Leipzig, 1909) 45ff.

[2] The story of Saul, the witch of Endor, and Samuel and the designation 'knowing ones' undermine E. F. Sutcliffe's suggestion that the prohibition of necromancy indicates Israelite unbelief in superior knowledge on the part of the dead (*The Old Testament and the Future Life*, The Bellarmine Series 8 [London, 1946] 24). רפאים, 'shades', possibly comes from רפא, 'to heal, mend, darn, repair', and relates to the *rephaim* in the literature from Ras Shamra, in which they are divine beings active in providence, especially in the increasing of fertility. Such a derivation would favor our understanding the *rephaim* of the OT as more than practical nonentities. Nevertheless, other derivations are possible, such as רפה, 'to sink, decline, abate, relax, abandon, enfeeble', with the result that the רפאים are those weakened by loss of bodily expression. See R. Martin-Achard, *From Death to Life* (Edinburgh, 1960) 34–5; B. Margulis, 'A Ugaritic Psalm (RŠ 24. 252)', *JBL* 89 (1970) 299–302; and G. R. Driver's review of H. H. Rowley's commentary on Job in *JTS* N.S. 22 (1971) 77.

[3] *Eschatology* (New York, 1973) 41.

[4] A. Murtonen, *The Living Soul*, StudOr 23/1 (Helsinki, 1958) 33; Eichrodt, *Theology of the Old Testament* 2: 211.

concerning the state of the dead in Sheol show that the excitement is unusual by contrast with *relative* inactivity rather than by contrast wth complete unconsciousness.

Still other passages are sometimes thought to prove that Sheol is a place of nullity:

For in death there is no remembrance of you; in Sheol who can praise you? (Ps 6: 6).

What profit is there in my blood, when I descend to the Pit? Will the dust praise you? Will it proclaim your faithfulness? (Ps 30: 10).

Do you work marvels for the dead? Do the shades stand up to praise you? Is your steadfast love recounted in the grave, your faithfulness in Abaddon? Are your marvels known in the darkness, and your vindicative acts in the land of forgetfulness? (Ps 88: 11–13).

My soul would soon have dwelt in the land of silence (Ps 94: 17).

The dead do not praise the Lord, nor do any who go down into silence (Ps 115: 17).

For Sheol cannot thank you, death cannot praise you; for those who descend into the Pit cannot hope for your faithfulness. The living, the living, he thanks you, as I do this day; the father makes known to his children your faithfulness (Isa 38: 18).

But we should assess the meaning of these passages with care not to overstate what they say in context. They do not imply total silence in Sheol. Rather, death takes away the reason for which the living praise God, viz., his deliverance of them from death. The dead are silent and fail to remember (i.e., recount) God's salvific deeds, not because as shades they lack capabilities of speech and memory, but because they can hardly call upon God or praise him for salvation from death after death has taken place. 'The land of forgetfulness', then, is the place where in the very nature of the situation men cannot recount divine deliverances from mortal danger.

Added to this is the inability of shades to join the congregation assembled at the sanctuary for worship of God. Following Ps 115: 17 'The dead do not praise the Lord, nor do any that go down into silence' is the contrast, 'But we will bless the Lord' (v. 18). The dead are cut off from the cultic ritual at the sanctuary where they might praise God for salvation. And we should remember that praise consisted in public recitation of divine deliverances.[1] Nor can the deceased father recount God's faithfulness to his surviving children (Isa 38: 18). Thus these passages fail to prove that Sheol is altogether a kind of zero.

Two passages for nullity remain:

His sons come to honor, and he does not know it; they are brought low, and he perceives it not (Job 14: 21, cf. 10).

The dead know nothing... There is no work or thought or knowledge or wisdom in Sheol, to which you are going (Eccl 9: 5, 10).

We cannot deny the nihilism of these statements; but we need to examine their frameworks. They occur in passages of wisdom literature where pessimism reaches its depth. It would be methodologically wrong to let the extremes of Job's despair and the Preacher's scepticism govern our understanding of the rest of the OT. Significantly, it is only in these special settings that nihilism concerning the state of the dead appears. The normal view of Sheol is reductive, but not nihilistic.[2]

Sometimes a point is made that the shades cannot be the souls of the deceased because their physical traits show them to be traces of the whole man, body included. They are visible, even recognizable. Samuel looks old and wears a robe (I Sam 28: 14). They may be uncircumcised and scarred by the sword (Ezek 32: 21-32). But this last passage may refer to the *corpses* of the shades. At any rate, it did not take very much intelligence and observation for ancient man to see that the present body goes back to the earth upon death. The OT fully recognizes this: 'Dust to dust'.[3] In view of this recognition, we can hardly say that the description of shades in physical terms is meant to indicate that the present physical body contributes to the make-up of the shade. And so long as the present flesh does not contribute to the shade, a duality of the present body and the deprived soul, or shade, is evident.

We have seen evidence enough that shades are souls bereft of bodies but described in bodily terms and reduced in activity by their lack of a body. This comes remarkably close to the Homeric view of the dead as souls existing in the under-

---

[1] See C. Westermann, *The Praise of God in the Psalms* (Richmond, 1965).

[2] Cf. Sutcliffe, *The Old Testament and the Future Life*, 55–69.

[3] See Gen 3: 19; Job 10: 9; 34: 15; Ps 104: 29; Eccl 3: 20; 12: 7.

world but not enjoying a full life.[1] Indeed, the agreement with Homeric views may well support our understanding of the OT data.

[1] See esp. Homer's *Odyssey* XI. For specific similarities between early Greek and Hebrew anthropology, see the excellent discussion, with numerous references, by R. B. Onians, *The Origins of European Thought about the Body, the Mind, the Soul, the World, Time, and Fate*, 2nd ed. (Cambridge, 1954) esp. 93ff., 254ff., 480ff.

CHAPTER 12

Anthropological Duality in Pauline Literature

Our question now becomes this: Did Paul forsake the anthropological duality of the other early Christian writers, current Judaistic beliefs, the OT, and Hellenistic thought by going his own way into a monadic view of the human constitution? A negative answer lies in a string of dichotomous passages running through his epistles.

'Though our outer man is wasting away, yet our inner man is being renewed every day' (II Cor 4: 16). The contrast between inner man and outer man was native to Hellenistic thought.[1] But unlike Hellenistic thinkers, Paul does not denigrate the outer man as evil or irrational. And the eschatological frame of reference (see the following vv.) contrasts with Hellenistic thinking. Despite these differences, however, Paul makes the same basic distinction between the physical and the non-physical. We might deny this by attaching other meanings to the inner man and the outer man and by making both refer to the indivisible personality seen from within and seen from without. Indivisibility is hard to accept, however, because the outer man even now is passing away while the inner man gains in vigor. Ultimately the inner exists without the outer, or rather, receives a new outer man (5: 1–5).

The attempt to redefine the inner man and the outer man usually runs in the direction of treating the inner man as the 'new man' in Christ (Eph 4: 24; Col 3: 10; cf. the corporate new man in Eph 2: 15). This requires equation of the outer man with the 'old man' (Rom 6: 6; Eph 4: 22; Col 3: 9). Thus the inner man and the outer man, ontologically understood in the Greek tradition, take on the rather different functional meanings of the old man and the new man: both the inner man and the outer man refer to the total 'self in its new aeon status and, as a process, to the self in its moral transformation and in its increasing apprehension and comprehension of the mystery

[1] See references in J. Jeremias, 'ἄνθρωπος, ἀνθρώπινος', *TDNT* 1 (1964) 365; J. Behm, 'ἔσω', *TDNT* 2 (1964) 699.

of Christ. This pattern does not lend itself in the least to an anthropological dualism.'[1]

But does such an interpretation agree with the contents of the relevant passages? All the appearances of the '*old* man' are hamartiological in nature, as shown by their contexts: 'that we might no longer be enslaved to sin' (Rom 6: 6); 'your former manner of life...corrupt through deceitful lusts' (Eph 4: 22); 'immorality, impurity, passion, evil desire, and covetousness, which is idolatry...anger, wrath, malice, slander, and foul talk...' (Col 3: 5–9, excerpts). The old man has already been crucified (Rom 6: 6) and is to be put off (Eph 4: 22; Col 3: 9).

But the '*outer* man' simply wastes away. Moreover, the associations of the outer man are not hamartiological, but have to do with physical hardships, especially those endured in the spread of the gospel: 'For this slight momentary affliction is preparing us for an eternal weight of glory' (II Cor 4: 17); 'We are afflicted in every way...crushed...perplexed... persecuted...struck down...always carrying in the body the death of Jesus, so that the life of Jesus may also be manifested in our bodies. For while we live we are always being given up to death for Jesus' sake' (II Cor 4: 8–11, excerpts; cf. 1: 3–11). The outer man is not the old man of sin, then, but the physical body subject to hardship, decay, and death.[2]

Similarly, the '*new* man' is to be put on and has to do with sanctification: 'created after the likeness of God in true righteousness and holiness' (Eph 4: 24); 'renewed in knowledge after the image of its creator' (Col 3: 10). But the '*inner* man' in II Cor 4: 16 is renewed, not in sanctification, but in buoyancy of spirit: 'not crushed...not driven to despair...Since we have the same spirit of faith as he had who wrote, "I believed,

[1] E. E. Ellis, *Paul and His Recent Interpreters* (Grand Rapids, Mich., 1961) 39.

[2] Because of its identical context, the expression 'earthen vessels' in II Cor 4: 7 probably is a figure of speech for the physical bodies of those who spread the gospel. For the figure, see the references in A. Plummer, *A Critical and Exegetical Commentary on the Second Epistle of St Paul to the Corinthians*, ICC (Edinburgh, 1915) 126–7. Instead of referring to the whole persons of Christian missionaries, Paul emphasizes their bodies as instruments of action and objects of hardship and persecution in evangelistic endeavor.

and so I spoke", we too believe, and so we speak, knowing that
he who raised the Lord Jesus will raise us also with Jesus and
bring us with you into his presence...So we do not lose heart'
(II Cor 4: 8–16a, excerpts; cf. 1: 3–11). And there is no indication that the inner man is to be put on, as the new man. They
are to be distinguished. The new man is the new style of righteous
conduct. The inner man is the human spirit, the center of
psychical feelings. We cannot evade anthropological duality
in II Cor 4: 16.

In the same fashion the 'inner man' of Eph 3: 16 correlates
with 'your hearts' in the following verse. In Rom 7: 22–3
Paul associates the 'inner man' quite Hellenistically with the
'mind' opposite the 'members', 'flesh', and 'body'. To be
sure, the term 'flesh' in the earlier clause, 'when we were in
the flesh' (7: 5), cannot mean the physical body; for then
Paul would ridiculously and self-contradictingly be implying
that Christians are now bodiless. There, 'flesh' bears its
hamartiological meaning. With the section that begins at
7: 13, however, Paul reverts to the normal sense of 'flesh'.
This is shown by the parallelisms with 'members' and 'body'
in opposition to 'mind' and 'inner man'.[1] However, by increasing association of weak physical flesh with the domination
of sin, Paul finally comes back to the connotation of flesh as
itself the principle of, or proneness to, evil (8: 4–13).

Thus, 'I am fleshly, sold under sin' (7: 14) does not imply
that flesh is an incorporeal evil force. Neither does it mean
that corporeal flesh is inherently evil. Rather, corporeal flesh is
weak because of its physical needs and desires, and therefore
easy prey for sin. 'For I know that nothing good dwells within
me, that is in my flesh. I can will what is right, but I cannot do
it' (7: 18). This verse indicates that the flesh as the physical
body does not possess the resolve to do good. It is therefore
victimized by sin, which is stronger than the 'mind', or
'inner man' (vv. 22–3), which wants to do good. At least sin
has an advantageous bridgehead (*aphormē*) in the needs and
desires of the body from which to work against the resolve of
the mind, or inner man. We are dealing here with the same

---

[1] Just as in the OT בשר occurs for the body, Paul here uses *sarx* for the
body, not as in older Greek usage for the soft, fleshy part of the body as
distinct from the bones.

contrast that is expressed in Mark 14: 38; parallel Matt 26: 41, 'The spirit indeed is willing, but the flesh is weak', concerning the defeat of the spirit's resolve to pray because of the body's desire to sleep.

But the body is not to be blamed, as though the conflict took place simply between the inner man and the body. The real conflict occurs between the inner man and *sin*, with the body caught in the middle and dominated by sin rather than the mind. There is anthropological duality, then, but not a correlative ethical dualism in which the body is evil *per se*.

In 7: 23 Paul continues his delineation of the battle between the law of sin in his 'members' (or, body; see 6: 12–13, 19; cf. I Cor 12: 17–27) and the law of his 'mind'. Verse 24 contains a cry for rescue 'from (*ek*) this body of death', i.e., this body destined to die through the dominion of sin, which leads to death. Except that Paul does not make sin inherent to physicality, the ejaculation, left here, would go the full length of Greek and Gnostic dualism.[1] However, Paul does not leave it unqualified. He picks up the theme again in 8: 10*a* with his statement that this body is so certain to pass away as to be called even now 'dead'. But he proceeds in 8: 10*b*–11 to write about the resurrection of the body by the power of the Holy Spirit. That is hardly Greek or Gnostic.

Again in 7: 25, Paul writes of serving the law of God with the 'mind' versus serving the law of sin with the 'flesh'. The term 'flesh' still does not mean the principle of evil in man, but refers to the physical body as the vehicle of specific actions. The statement in 8: 3 that the law 'is weak through the flesh' harks back to the body's susceptibility to attack from sin because of physical needs and desires. Because of the foregoing context, 'the flesh of sin' in the same verse refers to the physical body – the agent of activity and conduct – as dominated by sin, not to the physique as inherently sinful or to flesh as the inward proclivity toward evil. Again in the same verse, 'sin in the flesh' simply means sin that takes control in the body and determines its deeds.

Paul has associated evil with 'flesh' (in the sense of the body) so closely and frequently, however, that now he begins practically to identify 'flesh' with evil. From verse 4 onward, then,

---

[1] Cf. R. Jewett, *Paul's Anthropological Terms* (Leiden, 1971) 294–5.

he writes of walking and not walking 'according to the flesh', of being and not being 'in the flesh', and thus comes full circle to the usage in 7: 5: 'While we were in the flesh...' But for our purpose, what is significant is the consistent dichotomy between 'inner man'/'mind' and 'members'/'body'/'flesh' in 7: 13 – 8: 3.

Furthermore, that dichotomy in all probability has to do with the unregenerate man. Thus the 'inner man'/'mind' is native to the human constitution as a counterpart to the body and cannot be treated as the new man in Christ. At least the dramatic change from the dismal tone of the latter part of ch. 7 to the triumphant note sounded throughout ch. 8 makes it natural to see unregenerate man without the Spirit of Christ in ch. 7. Moreover, ch. 7 presupposes a subjection to the law which is not true of Christians (contrast 6: 12 – 7: 6 with 7: 7–25 in this respect).

W. G. Kümmel correctly emphasizes that in Romans 7 the 'I', sinful man as a whole being, does not escape responsibility for his will and actions and that man knows he does wrong against a holy law.[1] But though it is correct that 'mind' and 'flesh' belong equally to the 'I', we do not quite hit the mark to say that the mind is dominated by flesh. *Here* 'flesh' is not equivalent to sin. More accurately (as we have seen) flesh is the equivalent of 'body' and 'members' as the physical means of activity. Therefore we should not say that the mind is dominated by the flesh, but that the flesh is dominated by sin. The mind would like to dominate the 'flesh'/'body'/'members', but fails to win its battle with sin for control thereof. It is a mistake to interpret 'mind' and 'flesh' as functions rather than parts of man and accordingly to treat 'flesh' as the equivalent of sin. On the contrary, since sin rather than goodness dwells *in* the flesh (7: 17–18), sin and flesh are distinct even though associated as resident and residence respectively. Moreover, Paul uses 'flesh', 'body', and 'members' interchangeably. Consequently, in this passage flesh does not represent sin, but the physical body, or members, which sin occupies and uses as an instrument for the performance of evil.

---

[1] *Römer 7 und die Bekehrung des Paulus*, Untersuchungen zum Neuen Testament 17 (Leipzig, 1929) 27; and his *Man in the New Testament*, 2nd ed. (London, 1963) 57–61.

We need also to question the claim that the mind, or inner man, does not stand closer to God in its wanting to follow God's law. Paul writes that the mind/inner man wants to do, indeed, delights in the good law.[1] *In that respect* it stands closer to God – but without practical benefit in actual conduct because it fails to seize control of the body from that usurper, sin. Because of the unity of the inner man and the outer man in a living human being, the whole 'I' becomes a sinner. In his salvific purpose, however, God will not abandon the body to sin in favor of the mind/inner man. He will save the whole man in both his parts or not at all. For what kind of a salvation would it be to save only half a man – a mind without a physical means of expression?

As in Romans 7, so also in Rom 12: 1–2 Paul distinguishes between the body and the mind: 'present your bodies...be transformed by the renewal of your mind'. In other places Paul refers to the inner man by the term 'spirit', in its human sense as distinct from the Holy Spirit. 'For what person knows a man's thoughts except the spirit of the man which is in him? So also no one comprehends the thoughts of God except the Spirit of God' (I Cor 2: 11). 'I serve [God] with my spirit' (Rom 1: 9). 'It is the Spirit himself bearing witness with our spirit' (Rom 8: 16). 'For they refreshed my spirit as well as yours' (I Cor 16: 18). 'The grace of our Lord Jesus Christ be with your spirit' (Gal 6: 18; Phil 4: 23; Phlm 25). Cf. the collective 'one spirit' which is parallel to 'one soul' in Phil 1: 27.

That the human spirit is distinct from the body becomes evident from several passages. 'And the unmarried woman or girl is anxious about the affairs of the Lord, how to be holy in [both]² body and spirit; but the married woman is anxious

---

[1] Paul can also regard the mind as sinfully disposed. See Rom 1: 28; Eph 4: 17; Col 2: 18; I Tim 6: 5; II Tim 3: 8; Tit 1: 15. The contexts of these vv. uniformly suggest, however, that corruptness of mind characterizes an advanced stage of degeneration, as though in the beginning the mind had known and desired better. In any case, although the mind may stand on the side of the flesh, it does so morally rather than ontologically. Hence, there is no loss of the duality of mind and body in the human constitution.

[2] J. Weiss suggests that the *kai* before *sōmati*, missing in P¹⁵, ⁴⁶ A D 33 *al t* vg^{s, cl} sy^p, was inserted to indicate that marital sexual relationship precluded

about worldly affairs, how to please her husband' (I Cor 7: 34). The body and the spirit do not diverge but unite in consecration to God, for Paul does not correlate the body with worldly affairs and the spirit with the affairs of the Lord or pit the body as evil against the spirit as good. Nevertheless, his choice of 'spirit' and 'body' does seem to be analytic as a specification of the two basic human parts to be sanctified in common service to the Lord.[1]

A similar distinction, plus contrast, appears in I Cor 5: 3–5:

> For though absent in body I am present in spirit, and as if present, I have already pronounced judgement in the name of the Lord Jesus on the man who has done such a thing. When you and my spirit are assembled, with the power of our Lord Jesus, you are to deliver this man to Satan for the destruction of the flesh, that his spirit may be saved in the day of the Lord Jesus.

Anthropological duality appears first in the contrast between absence in body and presence in spirit. Paul refers to his own spirit – '*my* spirit' – not to the Holy Spirit. And it is a real presence, not merely a presence within Paul's mind, for Paul writes, 'When you and my spirit are assembled'.[2] Paul clearly conceives of his spirit's presence in a place far removed from that where his body stands. Such separability can hardly agree with a concept of man as an indivisible whole viewed from inside and out. It is true that Paul's dealing with the Corinthians 'with the power of our Lord Jesus' suggests an endowment of Paul with the Holy Spirit. But evasion of anthropological duality through fusion of Paul's spirit and the

holiness in body (*Der erste Korintherbrief*, Meyer 5, 9th ed. [Göttingen, 1910] 203–4). Perhaps so, but the same meaning could be derived from the text with the omission, too. See H. Baltensweiler, *Die Ehe im Neuen Testament*, ATANT 52 (Zürich, 1967) 167–74, that Paul does not here derogate marriage because of its physicalness.

[1] For this reason we may doubt Bultmann's assertion that Paul deprecates the physical aspect of marriage in a Gnostic fashion (*Theology of the New Testament* [New York, 1951] 1: 202). Paul's treatment is merely utilitarian; i.e., celibacy is good for greater usefulness in Christian service, and marriage is good in that it reduces temptation to illicit love.

[2] Best, *One Body in Christ* (London, 1955) 208, contra D. E. H. Whiteley, who thinks 'spirit' may refer to thought or intention (*The Theology of St Paul* [Philadelphia, 1965] 38).

Holy Spirit[1] is illegitimate: Paul distinguishes the two (I Cor 2: 11; Rom 8: 16; cf. 1: 9; II Cor 7: 1–13). It is also unsuccessful: so long as the spirit remains Paul's *to any degree*, contrast with the body evinces a duality of parts in the human make-up.

Col 2: 5 repeats the contrast between absence in body and presence in spirit: 'For though I am absent in flesh, yet I am with you in spirit, rejoicing to see your good order and the firmness of your faith in Christ.'

Anthropological duality appears a second time in I Cor 5: 3–5 in the contrast between destruction of the flesh and salvation of the spirit. We might, of course, treat 'flesh' as a reference to the whole man as a sinner. 'Spirit' would then refer to the whole man as a saint. So man as a sinner suffers destruction. The same man as a saint receives final salvation.[2] The main argument in support of this view is that to understand flesh

---

[1] *Kümmel, Römer* 7, 17, 31; cf. E. Schweizer, 'πνεῦμα, πνευματικός', *TDNT* 6 (1968) 435–6. In the same vein H.-D. Wendland appeals to the double-I in Gal 2: 20 ('Das Wirken des Heiligen Geistes in den Gläubigen nach Paulus', *Pro Veritate*, Festgabe for L. Jaeger and W. Stählin, ed. E. Schlink and H. Volk [Münster–Kassel, 1963] 154). Having interpreted Paul as referring in earlier passages to the human spirit as the apportioned divine spirit, Jewett suggests that in line with I Cor 2: 11 Paul here distinguishes the human and divine spirits in order to undermine Gnostic inferences from amalgamation of the two (*Paul's Anthropological Terms*, 175–200). But the argument for the human spirit as the apportioned divine spirit from the use of *pneuma* in the singular with the plural *hymōn* (I Thes 5: 23; Gal 6: 18; Phil 4: 23) overlooks the singularity of *psychē* and *sōma*, too, in I Thes 5: 23 and the use of a term very similar to *pneuma* – viz., *kardia* – as a distributive singular with a possessive pronoun in the plural (Rom 1: 21; II Cor 3: 15; 6: 11; Eph 5: 19; 6: 5). Elsewhere *kardia* appears frequently in the plural and there is no apparent difference of meaning between the distributive singular and the plural. The inadequacy of viewing the human spirit as the apportioned divine spirit becomes apparent when Jewett is forced to say that in Rom 8: 16 God's Spirit gives confirmation to himself (*ibid.* 198–9).

[2] So A. Sand, *Der Begriff 'Fleisch' in den paulinischen Hauptbriefen* (Regensburg, 1967) 143–5; J. Cambier, 'La Chair et l'Esprit en I Cor. v. 5', *NTS* 15 (1969) 221–32. Cambier's argument that a dichotomous interpretation would be un-Pauline assumes the very point in question. 'Flesh' might be taken as the principle of sin rather than man as a sinner. But that would seem to require that the counterpart 'spirit' be taken as the principle of righteousness – and it is hard to think that Paul is writing about the destruction and salvation of principles rather than the being of a man himself.

and spirit ontologically (with the result that 'flesh' becomes equivalent to 'body') makes Paul contradict his other statements concerning the resurrection of the body (above all, I Cor 15). But Paul need refer only to the *present* body of the sinful Christian, the flesh which is now indulged through gross immorality. The destruction of the present physical body, or flesh, contradicts the doctrine of a transformed body at the resurrection no more here than in Rom 7: 24; 8: 10–11; II Cor 4: 16 – 5: 10. Paul simply leaves it for later discussion that the salvation of the spirit 'in the day of the Lord Jesus' will entail the resurrection of the body as well. Attention focuses quite naturally on that body which is currently the agent of sin.

Paul may have chosen the term 'flesh' rather than 'body' – even though the meaning be the same – because of the evil coloring 'flesh' carries elsewhere on occasion. On the other hand, the topic of sexual immorality strongly favors an understanding of 'flesh' as physical. So also does the parallel in 11: 29–30 concerning the bodily ailments and deaths of those who have desecrated the Lord's table. Moreover, 'destruction' (*olethros*) seems too strong a word for the overcoming of the *phronēma sarkos* through penitence, and delivery to Satan too strong for excommunication from fellowship. Rather, it appears to be a curse of execration[1] with special reference to Satanic affliction of the body. Cf. Satan's work on the body of Job, Paul's thorn in the flesh (apparently some physical malady) as 'a messenger of Satan' (II Cor 12: 7), and the disciplinary deaths of Ananias and Sapphira (Acts 5: 1–11). The phrase 'with the power of our Lord Jesus' probably echoes part of the formula in such a curse. The object is that the sinner should be brought to repentance through his illness or, if necessary, through the throes of physical death itself.[2] And so the probable meaning of the contrast between destruction of the flesh and salvation of the spirit supports anthropological duality, to the point of disjunction of flesh and spirit at death.

[1] For curses of execration in general, see Gal 1: 8–9; I Cor 16: 22; Rom 9: 3; I Tim 1: 20.

[2] See the admirable discussion by G. W. H. Lampe, 'Church Discipline and the Interpretation of the Epistles to the Corinthians' in *Christian History and Interpretation: Studies Presented to John Knox* (Cambridge, 1967) 394–55.

Three parallel texts from II Corinthians are instructive: (a) 'I had no relief in my spirit' (2: 13); (b) 'our flesh had no relief' (7: 5); (c) 'his [Titus'] spirit has been set at rest by you all' (7: 13). If the statements are taken apart from their contexts, the parallelism between 'spirit' and 'flesh' in practically identical expressions seems to indicate a holistic anthropology in which the two terms stand equally for the entire man. Attention to contexts, however, leaves a different impression. In 2: 13 Paul writes of his *inward* distress through anxiousness to hear Titus' report concerning the Corinthians – therefore *pneuma*. In 7: 5 Paul refers to *physical* distress through hardship and persecution in Macedonia – therefore *sarx*. (That this 'fighting without' led to 'fear within' does not broaden the meaning of 'flesh' to include the inner man, but merely indicates the source of the inward fear in physical suffering and external danger.) In 7: 13 Paul alludes to the *inward* relief of Titus through the favorable response of the majority at Corinth – therefore *pneuma*. Thus in the three passages Paul carefully chooses his terms after the pattern of an anthropological duality of flesh as body and spirit as the incorporeal part of man.

The first two lines of the early Christian hymn quoted in I Tim 3: 16 also put 'flesh' and 'spirit' somewhat in contrast:

> 'Who was manifested in flesh,
> vindicated in spirit'

Several considerations militate against our taking *en pneumati* as a reference to the Holy Spirit: (1) the absence of a modifier to indicate the divine Spirit (in contrast to Rom 1: 4, in other respects somewhat similar); (2) the parallelism with *en sarki*, a phrase referring to the appearance of Jesus in his physical body and favoring a corresponding reference to his human spirit; (3) the close similarity to I Pet 3: 18, where Jesus' own flesh and spirit are in view.[1]

The same pattern appears elsewhere with varying terms, and so repeatedly that we may conclude this to be Paul's

[1] For greater detail and references to the exegetical literature, see R. H. Gundry, 'The Form, Meaning and Background of the Hymn Quoted in I Timothy 3: 16' in W. Gasque and R. P. Martin (eds.), *Apostolic History and the Gospel: Biblical and Historical Essays Presented to F. F. Bruce on his Sixtieth Birthday* (Grand Rapids, Mich., 1970) 209–14.

habitual way of thinking about man's constitution. The 'lusts of their [men's] hearts' leads to the 'dishonoring of their bodies' (Rom 1: 24). 'The mind of his flesh' probably means the mind as dominated by sensuousness (Col 2: 18).[1] 'Let us cleanse ourselves from every defilement of flesh and spirit' (II Cor 7: 1). 'Flesh' here means body, for flesh as the principle of sin could hardly be cleansed. And 'spirit' refers to the human spirit to the exclusion of the Holy Spirit, for the Holy Spirit would hardly need cleansing from defilement. Hence 'flesh' and 'spirit' comprehend man as a unity of two parts. It is further notable that Paul indicates capability of defilement on the part of the human spirit as well as the physical body.[2] There are no simple equations between spirit and goodness, bodily flesh and evil.

The complementary relationship between 'mouth' and 'heart' in Rom 10: 9–10 – 'if you confess with your mouth... and believe in your heart...For man believes with his heart... and confesses with his mouth' – again exhibits Paul's dichotomous mode of thought. 'Mouth' represents the corporeal part of man; 'heart' the incorporeal part of man. 'Heart' and 'mouth' function similarly in II Cor 6: 11: 'Our mouth is open to you, Corinthians; our heart is wide.'[3] The same impli-

---

[1] C. F. D. Moule, *The Epistles of Paul the Apostle to the Colossians and to Philemon*, Cambridge Greek Testament Commentary (Cambridge, 1958) 106.

[2] If the genitives *sarkos* and *pneumatos* are objective, Paul simply refers to the defilement of the whole man in the unity of his two basic parts. If the genitives are subjective, he means that the sinful actions of the body and the sinful thinking and willing of the spirit defile a man. But perhaps we are not supposed to make such a fine distinction. Jewett argues that Paul refers to the divine spirit apportioned to men since that spirit is capable of defilement according to the T Naph 10. 9 and CD 5. 11–12; 7. 4, 12 (*Paul's Anthropological Terms*, 184–5). This is possible, but a difficulty in using those texts to explicate Paul's meaning is that they qualify the term 'spirit' as 'holy' and of or from God, whereas Paul does not. And even though Jewett's interpretation be accepted, in the extra-Biblical texts the 'holy spirit' which God has put in men is clearly anthropological (whatever its relation to the Spirit of God; cf. T Naph 2: 2). Naturally, the value of II Cor 7: 1 as evidence for anthropological duality in Paul becomes somewhat less if he here quotes a source, and nil if the verse is a later interpolation (see, e.g., H. D. Betz, '2 Cor 6: 14 – 7: 1: an Anti-Pauline Fragment', *JBL* 92 [1973] 88–108, and earlier literature there cited).

[3] The use of *kardia* by Paul is not semi-physical, for he links the term closely with *noēma* and *nous*. See Rom 1: 21, 28; 2: 5; 12: 2; 16: 18; II Cor

cation for anthropology derives from the contrasts between 'face' and 'heart', 'eye and ear' and 'heart', 'circumcision in the flesh' and 'circumcision of the heart', and 'eye' and 'heart, soul, mind' in the following passages:

We were bereft of you, brethren, for a short time – in face, not heart (I Thes 2: 17).

[They] pride themselves in face and not in heart (II Cor 5: 12).

What no eye has seen, nor ear heard, nor the heart of man conceived (I Cor 2: 9, a conflation of Isa 64: 4 and Jer 3: 16).

For he is not a real Jew who is one outwardly, nor is true circumcision external in the flesh. But he is a Jew who is one inwardly, and real circumcision is a matter of the heart – in spirit,[1] not in letter (Rom 2: 28–9; cf. Eph 2: 11: 'circumcision which is made in the flesh by hands').

Slaves, be obedient...in singleness of heart...not in the way of eyeservice...but...from the soul, with a well-disposed mind (Eph 6: 5–7).

Slaves, obey...not with eyeservice...but in singleness of heart... from the soul (Col 3: 22 3).

Such contrasts would not be possible or appear so often did not Paul (and the originators of whatever traditional material he used) naturally think in dichotomous rather than monadic categories.

Anthropological duality of flesh and spirit lies behind Paul's contrast between 'spiritual things' (the gospel) and 'fleshly things' (physical sustenance): 'If we have sown spiritual things among you, is it too much if we reap your fleshly things?' (I Cor 9: 11); 'for if the Gentiles have come to share in their [the Jewish Christians'] spiritual things, they ought also to be of service to them in fleshly things' (Rom 15: 27).

The separability of the inner man from the body comes out unequivocally in II Cor 12: 2–3: 'I know a man in Christ who fourteen years ago was caught up to the third heaven – whether in the body or out of the body I do not know, God

3: 14; 4: 4, 6; 11: 3; W. D. Stacey, *The Pauline View of Man* (London, 1956) 196.

[1] It is uncertain whether *en pneumati* refers to the human spirit as the locale of true circumcision or to the Holy Spirit as the agent of true circumcision. Even with the latter understanding, the contrast between 'flesh' and 'heart' still supports anthropological duality.

knows. And I know that this man was caught up into Paradise – whether in the body or out of the body I do not know, God knows.' Paul does not certainly indicate a bodiless state, but he does hold it out as a possibility equal to the other. It is not necessary that Paul should assert bodilessness for proof of anthropological duality in his thinking, but only that he conceive the possibility thereof – and this he does.

It is unsatisfactory to say, "This, we must admit, is a case of anthropological dualism', but claim that the view is 'peripheral' to Paul's thought elsewhere, not 'central and normative', and appeal to the pressure from opponents under which Paul was writing.[1] To be sure, ecstatic *visions* are exceptional in Pauline theology. But the dichotomous material already cited is so massive as to show that neither in Pauline literature nor elsewhere should the possibility of separation of the inner man from the body occasion any surprise on our part. If Paul be monadic in his anthropology, he need not even mention the possibility of *ekstasis*, but stick to bodily transport into heaven. And it would be similar to say that justification by faith and freedom from the law are aberrations in Pauline theology because they arose out of the Judaizing (and/or proto-gnostic) controversy as to argue that the Corinthian opponents of Paul pressured him into an uncharacteristically dichotomous statement. The dichotomy is neither uncharacteristic nor necessary as an argument against his opponents. The vision itself – in whatever state Paul experienced it – would have sufficed.

But if the separability of the inner man and the outer man is not clear enough from II Cor 12: 2–3, it surely is in Phil 1: 20–4: 'Christ will be honored in my body, whether by life or by death. For me to live is Christ, and to die is gain. If it is to be life in the flesh, that means fruitful labor for me...My desire is to depart and be with Christ, for that is far better. But to remain in the flesh is more necessary on your account.' At death the inner man departs from the flesh. Not to die is for the inner man to remain housed in flesh. Again, the widespread evidence for anthropological duality, including a bodiless interim state, elsewhere in Pauline writings and in other

---

[1] Whiteley, *The Theology of St Paul*, 38–9. Whiteley vacillates between man as a 'compound' of parts 'closely linked together' and man as a monad; but he stresses the latter.

literature of the period invalidates any claim that the duality here is abnormal. Quite the opposite. It is exactly what we should expect. By the same token there is no necessity to say that in Phil 1: 20–4 the vivid expectation of ultimate fellowship with Christ banishes the intervening period from Paul's mind.[1] In fact, we cannot say that, for Paul writes of absence *from the Philippian Christians*, which could characterize only the intermediate state, not the final state when the saved are united in heavenly bliss. For further discussion we may profit from P. Hoffmann, *Die Toten in Christus*, in its entirety and pp. 286–320 for Phil 1: 20–4 in particular.[2]

Because the expectation of bodiless bliss for the righteous in an interim state was standard for Judaism, it is also unlikely that Paul here expresses the special hope of a martyr to gain individual resurrection immediately at death.[3] Where else – in Paul, other parts of the NT, or Jewish literature of the period – do we find any support for such a view, let alone support comparable in volume to that which favors interpretation in terms of bodiless bliss during an interim prior to resurrection? It is true that Paul contemplates the possibility of his own martyr-

[1] W. D. Stacey, 'Man as a Soul', *ExpT* 72 (1961) 349.

[2] Hoffmann is a much surer guide than K. Hanhart (*The Intermediate State in the New Testament* [Franeker, 1966]), who labors to de-temporalize the intermediate state, with the result that resurrection becomes merely the visible manifestation of the supratemporal. Whatever a modern should think, Hoffman shows (and see our own investigations above) that belief in a bodiless state between death and resurrection was standard for the Judaism of NT times. Thus, in Paul it need not be taken as abandonment of belief in physical resurrection or attributed *immediately* to Hellenistic influence (contra J. Dupont, ΣΥΝ ΧΡΙΣΤΩΙ, *L'union avec le Christ suivant saint Paul* [Paris, 1957]). An exception to the surefootedness of Hoffmann is his accepting the holistic interpretation of OT anthropology (*Die Toten in Christus*, Neutestamentliche Abhandlungen 2/2 [Münster, 1966] 58–80) and consequent opinion that duality came into Judaism from Hellenistic sources prior to the first century A.D. and then from Judaism to Paul (*ibid*. 321–47). In our foregoing consideration of OT anthropology we discovered duality there, too; hence we may strike out Hellenistic thought as the *ultimate* source.

[3] Contra A. Schweitzer, *The Mysticism of Paul the Apostle* (New York, 1931) 135–7; E. Lohmeyer, *Der Brief an die Philipper*, Meyer 9, 12th ed. (Göttingen, 1961) 59–70; H. H. Rex, 'Immortality of the Soul, or Resurrection of the Body, or What?', *Reformed Theological Review* 17 (1958) 75–9. Rex applies this interpretation also to II Cor 5: 1–10.

dom. But he does not take pains to distinguish death by martyrdom from ordinary death and then to make the former, in
contradistinction to the latter, the basis for departing to be
with Christ. If the statement 'For me to live is Christ', might
apply to any true Christian, presumably the statement 'To die
is gain' might also apply to any true Christian, martyred or
not. There is no need for Paul to mention the resurrection in
Philippians 1, for the point of discussion is his fate in the *near*
future, barring occurrence of the Parousia first.

Commentators dispute the passage II Cor 5: 1–10, but (other
questions aside for the moment) it is hard to escape the impression that Paul writes of the present body as physical and
as distinct and separable from the incorporeal self. Above all,
we read the expressions 'at home in the body' (v. 6) and 'away
from the body' (v. 8). In addition, the expressions 'earthly
house' (v. 1), 'tent' (vv. 1 and 4), 'naked' (v. 3), 'unclothed',
'clothed', 'further clothed', and 'mortal' (v. 4) all lead to the
conclusion that Paul writes quite dichotomously here.

E. E. Ellis, building on some ideas of Robinson,[1] tries to
overturn the dichotomous understanding of the passage.[2] The
present tense of *echomen*, he reasons, makes *oikodomē* refer to the
church rather than to a future, individual body at the resurrection (cf. I Cor 3: 9; Eph 2: 21; 4: 12, 16[3]). Both *skēnē* and *oikia*
become figures for the corporate body of the church. The
unclothed state of nakedness then refers to guilt and shame at
the judgement instead of disembodiment during an intermediate
state. Thus the fear of nakedness does not contradict the desire
to be away from the body and at home with the Lord. Since
elsewhere *sōma* can refer to the self in its solidarity with sin

---

[1] *The Body: A Study in Pauline Theology*, SBT 1/5 (London, 1952) 76–83.

[2] Ellis, *Paul and His Recent Interpreters*, 41–8. Cf. Hanhart, *The Intermediate
State*, 126ff., 167ff.; A. Feuillet, 'La demeure céleste et la destinée des
Chrétiens', *RSR* 44 (1956) 360–402.

[3] Ellis' further references to passages which deal with the church under
the related figure of a *naos* do not carry conviction since that term does not
appear in II Corinthians 5. The seemingly impressive parallel, Mark 14: 58,
is undermined not only by the absence of *naos* in II Cor 5: 1, but also by the
noun form of *oikodomē* in II Corinthians against the verbality of *oikodomeō*
in Mark and by the uncertainty of a reference to the church in Mark –
indeed, unlikelihood in view of the association of 'three days' with the
resurrection of the Son of man (Mark 8: 31; 9: 31; 10: 34 and parallels)
and John's interpretation in terms of Jesus' resurrection (John 2: 21).

and death, 'at home in the body' means 'in the solidarities and securities of earthly existence'. To be away from the body and at home with the Lord then refers to the solidarities of the new aeon.[1]

We have seen, however, that elsewhere *sōma* fails to yield the holistic and not-necessarily-physical meaning required for such an interpretation; and the anthropological monism elsewhere in Paul, used here to upset the usual understanding of II Corinthians 5, does not exist. Moreover, it is not surprising that *echomen* should be a futuristic present with reference to the resurrection. Indeed, we should expect it after Paul's predominant use of the futuristic present in the discussion of the resurrection in I Corinthians 15 (see vv. 12 [*bis*], 15, 16, 29, 32, 35 [*bis*], 42, 43 [*bis*], 50 [? *bis*]; cf. Matt 27: 63). In addition, the description of the building/tent/house in II Corinthians 5 closely parallels the description of the resurrected body in I Corinthians 15 with regard to divine origin, the work of the Spirit, incorruptibility and permanence, and heavenly suitability.[2]

Concerning the corporate interpretation of the figures, in Acts 15: 16 the *skēnē* is the Messianic dynasty of David, not the Messianic community as a whole, and in Heb 8: 2 the 'true tent' is the heavenly sanctuary,[3] to say nothing of the fact that Paul uses the slightly different word *skēnos* in II Cor 5: 1. *Oikos* is used corporately for the church, as in I Tim 3: 15; I Pet 2: 5;

---

[1] We should protest the extension of this last idea in a pejorative way, with the result that 'at home in the body...away from the Lord' implies 'dependence on the flesh, and satisfaction with the present order' (Stacey, *The Pauline View of Man*, 183; similarly, J.-F. Collange, *Enigmes de la deuxième épître de Paul aux Corinthiens: Etude exégétique de 2 Cor. 2: 14–7: 4*, NTSMS 18 [Cambridge, 1972] 233–9). Where is any hint of that in the context? Rather, to be away from the Lord and at home in the body is, for Christians, to 'walk by faith'! Ellis' further argument that *oidamen* suggests the lack of novelty in the teaching does not work against the usual interpretation in terms of resurrection, certainly not after Paul's lengthy exposition of that subject to the Corinthians in I Cor 15. And of course *acheiropoiētos* can describe the resurrected body as naturally as it can describe any other reality of the 'new aeon'.

[2] See M. J. Harris, '2 Corinthians 5: 1–10: Watershed in Paul's Eschatology?', *Tyndale Bulletin* 22 (1971) 39–40.

[3] See numerous references in Bauer, *A Greek–English Lexicon*, and *TDNT* s.v.

4: 17; Heb 3: 2–6 (but not Acts 7: 47–8, contra Ellis). However, *oikia*, the word Paul uses in II Cor 5: 1, never represents the church. Both *skēnos* and *oikia*, on the other hand, commonly appear as metaphors for the physical body.[1]

Oikodomē does refer to the church in the passages cited. But Whiteley points out that where *oikodomē* stands for the church, the thought has to do with a building still in the process of construction, i.e., with edification. That is not true of II Cor 5: 1, where edification does not come into view. There *oikodomē* stands in appositional relationship to *oikia*, which by definition cannot refer to the activity of construction. Both words – *oikia* by definition and *oikodomē* by association with *oikia* and by the larger context – refer to the final result of construction.[2]

Thus, *oikodomē* does not here represent the church any more than the other figures do. Phrases such as 'we have', 'from God', 'in heaven', 'our dwelling', 'from heaven', and 'put on' ill suit the church anyway. The church is the dwelling of God, his possession, a community normally viewed in its *earthly* setting. And how does one 'put on' the Messianic community? These phrases better suit the resurrected body, our heavenly dwelling from God to be donned at the last day.

Though nakedness may of course refer to shame, elsewhere the context makes that clear. Nakedness may just as easily refer to bodilessness.[3] We may concede that in the interpretation under scrutiny tension between apprehension over nakedness

---

[1] Whiteley, *The Theology of St Paul*, 256.

[2] See references in A. Oepke, 'γυμνός, γυμνότης, γυμνάζω, γυμνασία', *TDNT* 1 (1964) 774, and esp. the parallel passage I Cor 15:37 ('naked seed') with reference to the death of the present body and reception of a new body at the resurrection. Although I Cor 15: 37 does not have to do with a disembodied spirit, the connection with death and resurrection leads away from the idea of shame in II Cor. 5: 3.

[3] Paul drops the *ep-* in the clause *ei ge kai endysamenoi ou gymnoi heurethēsometha* because he is here stating the certainty of a new body for all Christians ('since indeed' or 'inasmuch as'), including those who have died and for whom therefore the prefix *ep-* would not hold true. He uses *ependyomai* for those Christians who are still alive and therefore can long for a putting on of the new body over the old without dying. Alternatively, the clause refers to Christians who will be found clothed with their mortal bodies at the last day. The situation is different in I Cor 15: 53–4, where Paul cannot use *ependyomai* because the subject is the present earthly body itself; the new body is an *additional* body (therefore *ep-*) only for the 'I', or 'we'.

and preference for absence from the body and presence with the Lord ceases, for nakedness becomes shame rather than absence from the body. That advantage alone, however, hardly outweighs the many considerations which weigh against the interpretation.

The probable solution to the supposed tension is that through the first part of verse 4 Paul expresses confidence that we shall gain heavenly bodies to replace earthly, mortal bodies; but in the further part of verse 4 he explains that we do not on that account morbidly desire death in order to receive a new body. We desire, rather, a new body prior to death. I.e., to desire the new body is not to desire death; it is to desire the arrival of the last day within our lifetime in order that the incorporeal self may put on the new body over the old (*ependyomai*, 'to put on *in addition*'). It is to desire translation rather than death and resurrection. Nevertheless, thinking of the possibility of death before the last day (as he does also in I Cor 15: 51–2), Paul indicates in verses 6–8 that even a disembodied state with the Lord is eminently desirable. Meanwhile, whatever happens first, Christian service forms our main concern (vv. 9–10).

[Note: Some have thought that the failure of Paul to comfort the Thessalonians with the desirability of the bodiless interim state with Christ shows that by the time Paul wrote II Corinthians 5 and Philippians 1 he had undergone Hellenistic influence (see esp. Dupont, ΣΥΝ ΧΡΙΣΤΩΙ). But the reason Paul does not comfort the Thessalonians by recourse to the current bliss of 'the dead in Christ' (I Thes 4: 13–18) is that the Thessalonians are grieving (or are tempted to grieve) over the dead, not for the sake of the dead but for the sake of themselves, the survivors, who wonder whether they will see their deceased loved ones and friends at the Parousia. Present bliss for the departed does not solve that problem; reunion with them at the Parousia does. On the other hand, present bliss for the departed does grant aid and comfort to the living who are concerned over their own possible demise before the Parousia, as in II Cor 5: 6–8 and Phil 1: 20–4. Cf. Hoffmann (*Die Toten in Christus*, 217–18), who argues that in I Thes 4: 14 the phrase *axei syn autō* shows the problem at Thessalonica not to be disbelief in the resurrection (against which Paul would have written *egerei syn autō*), but failure to understand that departed Christians will join living Christians in the triumph of the Parousia. Though he shies from interpreting II Cor 5: 1–10 in terms of an intermediate state, Hoffmann also notes that the two concepts of resurrection at the last day and immediate bliss for the righteous dead stand side by side in Jewish literature. We are therefore not compelled to see any disagreement between I Thessalonians and II Corinthians/ Philippians. In fact, the phrase 'the dead in Christ' in I Thes 4: 16 easily lends itself to the idea of intermediate bliss as expressed in II Corinthians and Philippians. And the passage in II Corinthians is bracketed by references to the resurrection and final judgement (4: 14; 5: 10).

The literature is vast, but for recent expositions similar to the above, see K. Prümm, *Diakonia Pneumatos: Theologie des zweiten Korintherbriefes* (Rome, 1960–67) 1: 262–309, II/1: 168–74, II/2: 659–82; P. E. Hughes, *Paul's Second Epistle to the Corinthians*, NICNT (Grand Rapids, 1962) 153–85. The exposition of Collange (*Enigmes de 2 Corinthiens*, 170–243) in some measure parallels that of Ellis, except that the building which we have from God becomes Christ himself rather than the church, with the result that Paul writes of putting on Christ, equivalent to being at home with the Lord, and divesting oneself of Christ by denial of him, equivalent to being at home in the body as sinful flesh. Most of the foregoing considerations militate against such an exposition. In addition, Paul's desire to please the Lord while he is at home in the body becomes incongruous if being at home in the body stands for conduct according to the flesh (as sin). See the review of Collange's book by P. E. Hughes in *Westminster Theological Journal* 35 (1973) 345–7. C. F. D. Moule has recently propounded the view that Paul shifts from a belief in transformed matter in the resurrected body (I Corinthians 15) to belief in an immortality which takes the place of matter (II Corinthians 5; 'St Paul and Dualism: The Pauline Conception of the Resurrection', *NTS* 12 [1966] 106–23). The appeals to II Apoc Baruch 50: 1 – 51: 10; I Enoch 51: 4, where the risen bodies of the righteous gain a glory like that of the angels and stars, and Matt 22: 30; parallel Luke 20: 35–6, where Jesus says that upon the resurrection there will be no marriage, as in angelic society, do not carry conviction. To become bright is not to become immaterial; and unmarriedness is not equivalent to immateriality. Yet the similarities to angels are stated clearly and solely in terms of brightness and unmarriedness.]

The anthropological duality of II Cor 5: 1–10 stands. Again, it is illegitimate to relegate the passage to the periphery of Pauline theology,[1] as though the duality appeared infrequently or not at all elsewhere. It is equally wrong to think that Paul here flirts with Hellenistic-Gnostic dualism. Bultmann thinks

---

[1] Best, *One Body*, 219.

he does in that the body appears to be a shell for the inner self, even an inappropriate shell since the inner self sighs for a heavenly garment truly appropriate to the self.[1] However, even the heavenly is a garment, a dwelling, house, or building for the self. Therefore, the same figures for the present body do not have a Hellenistic-Gnostic connotation. The sighing derives from the susceptibility of the present body to suffering and death, not from any inappropriateness vis-à-vis the inner self, much less from any evil inherent in its corporeality. Although susceptibility to suffering and death may *be* the inappropriateness of the present body in relation to the inner self according to Gnosticism, in Paul such susceptibility does not stem from the corporeality of the body (as in Gnosticism) but from the fiendish intruder sin. Otherwise Paul would not long for another corporeality.

Stacey notes that in neither II Cor 5: 1–10 nor Phil 1: 20–3 does the word *psychē* appear. Therefore Greek ideas of immortality, if present at all, are radically modified.[2] It is true that for Paul *psychē* does not hold as much significance as it does for Plato. Nevertheless, we ought not to take the verbal difference as an indication of total differentiation between the thinking of Plato and of Paul. Paul may not use *psychē* in writing of the disembodied intermediate state or regard the *psychē* as highly superior to the body, but he does write in these passages about a disembodied state between death and resurrection. Therein lies evidence in favor of his anthropological duality and against a holistic use of *sōma*.

These dichotomous passages are scattered throughout Pauline literature – from the earliest to the latest epistles (wherever the boundary is drawn) – and appear very frequently in Romans and the Corinthian correspondence. The same sort of frequency holds true for the rest of the NT and the Judaistic literature of the era. We conclude, then, that Paul along with most Jews and other early Christians habitually thought of man as a duality of two parts, corporeal and incorporeal, meant to function in unity but distinguishable and capable of separation.

[1] Bultmann, *Theology of the New Testament* 1: 201. W. Schmithals goes so far as to write that here 'to the Gnostics Paul becomes a Gnostic, in order to win the Gnostics' (*Gnosticism in Corinth* [New York, 1971] 271).

[2] Stacey, *The Pauline View of Man*, 125–7.

Into this scheme fits Paul's consistent use of *sōma* for the physical body. Unlike *sarx*, which occasionally stands for the proclivity to sin, *sōma* always carries a physical meaning. And that meaning assumes theological importance only from the context of the discussion in which *sōma* appears, not from any theological freight belonging to the word by itself.[1]

All of this is not to deny that in some passages Paul, and other Biblical writers, may use combinations of anthropological terms in a summarizing rather than carefully analytical fashion. I Thes 5: 23 – 'spirit and soul and body' – provides the outstanding example in Pauline literature. We might think also of the Shema, as quoted in Mark 12: 30: 'heart...soul... mind...strength' (parallel Matt 22: 37; Luke 10: 27). In I Thes 5: 23 the spirit and soul probably stand on one side of man's constitution and the body on the other.[2] Even so, that is not the point, for the emphasis clearly lies on man in his entirety (*holoklēron*). Just as clearly, however, in a veritable host of other passages a certain and frequently emphatic duality pervades the thought.

[1] This is not to say that a word cannot take on such freight with the result that of itself it connotes certain overtones otherwise absent from a passage. It is merely to say that the word *sōma* does not happen to take on such freight. Thus, in classifying five meanings for the Pauline use of *sōma* – flesh, the whole man, the principle of redeemable humanity, the means of resurrection, and the church – with all but the first as Paul's own inventions, Stacey mistakes contexts for definitions (*ibid.* 182). Whatever his excesses, Barr correctly protests against this kind of treatment (*The Semantics of Biblical Language* [London, 1961]).

[2] See Jewett, *Paul's Anthropological Terms*, 175-83, and Kümmel, *Man in the New Testament*, 44–5, for reviews of various possibilities of interpretation. Kümmel's preference for the view that *pneuma* refers to the Holy Spirit accorded to Christians leaves room for *psychē* and *sōma* to be understood dichotomously. Jewett thinks that Paul appropriates the trichotomy of libertinists. This is characteristic of Jewett's thesis that Paul regularly borrows anthropological terms, especially those which are dichotomous, from his opponents. Though that is doubtless true in part, the generally dichotomous anthropology throughout late Judaism and early Christianity reduces the need for supposing that Paul borrowed so much as Jewett thinks. For example, the large number of appearances of *sōma* in the NT outside Pauline and polemical literature shows that Jewett over-emphasizes the polemical thrust in Paul's usage. It is there sometimes, to be sure, but attention should be given to the increase in usage merely because of the Hellenistic culture which prevailed at the time. Still, Jewett's work remains a mine of information and stimulating suggestions.

The Pauline expressions of this duality vary in terminology. We meet no single, set formula, such as a neat and consistently used pairing of *sōma* and *psychē*. 'Inner man', 'spirit', 'soul', 'mind', 'heart' – all do duty for the incorporeal part of man and different functions thereof. 'Outer man', 'flesh', 'body', 'members', 'mouth', 'face', and several metaphors do similar duty for the corporeal part of man. Not only do terms from both categories stand side by side in pairs. That alone could indicate merely two viewpoints on an indivisible entity. But the terms frequently contrast, and sharply, even to the degree of their separation though separation is not desired and the corporeal is not denigrated. For the whole man in the unity of his parts, *anthrōpos* is ready to hand. Context will determine whether personal pronouns refer to the entire person or only to a representative part of him. *Sōma*, however, remains faithful to its solely physical meaning.

PART III

THE THEOLOGY OF
SŌMA AS PHYSICAL BODY

CHAPTER 13

The *Sōma* in Death and Resurrection

There is more than meets the eye in the implications of a consistent use of *sōma* for the physical body. It has theological repercussions in our interpretations of death and resurrection, the being of man, the nature and source of sin and salvation, individuality and corporateness, and the ecclesiastical Body of Christ. We take them in order.

The Sōma *in Death*

With *sōma* as the physical body in distinction from the spirit,[1] death consists neither in cessation of consciousness or of existence (as in un-Biblical materialism) nor in reduction of the substantiality or the functions of the whole man (as in a holistic interpretation of Biblical anthropology). Though these may accompany death, they do not constitute what death is in the first instance. Rather, death consists in the separation of the spirit and the body, which belong together. The body continues to exist for a short while, even though death has occurred, and then the body decays.[2] The spirit continues to exist, and in addition bears consciousness.

The separation of spirit from body affects the spirit as well as the body. In the Biblical perspective, the physical body is just as essential to life which is life indeed as is the spirit. Barring the effects of sin (which touch the spirit, too), the body as such does not shackle the spirit. It provides the spirit with an organ of expression and action, just as the spirit provides the body with animation and direction. By total separation, then, body and spirit die together. The whole man dies.

[1] To avoid confusion, 'spirit' will fairly regularly stand for the incorporeal part of man in the discussions below.

[2] K. Bornhäuser stresses the preservation of the bones of a corpse as the basis for the doctrine of resurrection ('Die Gebeine der Toten', *Beiträge zur Förderung Christlicher Theologie* 26 [1921] 123–78). Except for Matt 23: 27; John 19: 36; and Heb 11: 22, however, the bones of the dead do not figure in the NT at all. And even those exceptions have nothing to do with resurrection.

The Biblical touchstone for truly human life is not consciousness of the spirit, let alone the material being of a physical object such as the body. Rather, man is fully himself in the unity of his body and spirit in order that the body may be animated and the spirit may express itself in obedience to God. Both parts of the human constitution share in the dignity of the divine image. That dignity lies in man's service to God as a representative caretaker over the material creation. For such a task, man needs a physical medium of action as much as an incorporeal source for the conscious willing of action. Neither spirit nor body gains precedence over the other. Each gains in unity with the other. Each loses in separation from the other.[1]

If separation of spirit and body defines death, inaction signals death. But since there are degrees of inaction, we may think of death somewhat elastically. This Biblical way of thinking about death appears frequently in the Psalms (but cf. also II Cor 11: 23: 'in deaths often').[2] The sufferer, still 'alive', conceives of his soul as having gone from his ill body to Sheol. To the degree that his illness has curtailed his activities, he is already dead. His soul has more or less departed. Death becomes complete and humanly irrevocable when the soul departs so far as to reduce activity to nothing and so long as to cancel any hope of reactivation in the immediate future.[3]

[1] For similar understandings of death from the standpoints of philosophical and historical theologies, cf. J. Pieper, 'Tod und Unsterblichkeit', *Pro Veritate*, Festgabe for L. Jaeger and W. Stählin, ed. E. Schlink and H. Volk (Münster–Kassel, 1963) 286–7; O. W. Heick, 'If a Man Die, Shall He Live Again?', *LQ* 17 (1965) 99–110.

[2] Cf. C. Barth, *Die Errettung vom Tode in den individuellen Klage- und Dankliedern des Alten Testaments* (Zollikon–Zürich, 1947). However, Barth does not espouse the anthropological duality set forth here.

[3] This understanding of death may hold implications for moral problems raised in the modern practice of medicine, such as the artificial maintenance of 'vegetable' existence in otherwise hopeless cases.

The Sōma *in Resurrection*

In the nineteenth century, C. Holsten[1] and H. Lüdemann[2] stand out as proponents of the view that *sōma* refers to form and *sarx* to substance. H. H. Wendt[3] and – in the English-speaking world – W. P. Dickson[4] led the opposition to that view. The debate is now somewhat passé.[5] It became quite apparent that a number of factors militate against a neat equation of *sōma* with form and *sarx* with substance:

(1) the influence upon the NT use of *sarx* from the OT use of בשר for flesh organized in the form we know as a (whole) body, in contrast to the Greek view of flesh as the soft part and primary substance of the body;[6]

(2) the emphasis on substance rather than form in several Pauline uses of *sōma*: (a) in the contrast between pommeling the body and beating the air in I Cor 9: 26–7; (b) in the contrast between body and shadow in Col 2: 17; (c) in the contrast between bodily presence and communication by letter in II Cor 10: 10;

(3) the frequent use of *melos* in the plural as a synonym for *sōma* – and 'members' hardly means 'form(s)';

(4) the implication of the exhortation regarding sanctity of the *sōma* (I Cor 7: 34) that *sōma* means substance as well as form;

[1] *Die Bedeutung des Wortes* σάρξ *im Lehrbegriffe des Paulus*, first published in 1855, but reissued with some additions within the volume, *Zum Evangelium des Paulus und des Petrus* (Rostock, 1868). The latter is used here.

[2] *Die Anthropologie des Apostels Paulus und ihre Stellung innerhalb seiner Heilslehre* (Kiel, 1872). See R. Jewett, *Paul's Anthropological Terms* (Leiden, 1971) 49–57, for other proponents and finer shades of interpretation within that school.

[3] *Die Begriffe Fleisch und Geist im biblischen Sprachgebrauch* (Gotha, 1878). Again see Jewett, *Paul's Anthropological Terms*, 57–64.

[4] *St Paul's Use of the Terms Flesh and Spirit* (Glasgow, 1883).

[5] Except perhaps in I Corinthians 15, where some commentators still use the distinction. See, e.g., H. Conzelmann, *Der erste Brief an die Korinther*, Meyer 5, 11th ed. (Göttingen, 1969) 334–5, and below, pp. 165–7. For recent expositions and critiques of the views of Holsten, Lüdemann, and their followers, see O. Kuss, *Der Römerbrief* (Regensburg, 1967) 2: 521–40, as well as Jewett, *Paul's Anthropological Terms*, 49–64.

[6] For *sarx* as body, not just material, Wendt points to Gal 4: 13–14; II Cor 12: 7; Rom 2: 28; I Cor 6: 16 (*Die Begriffe Fleisch und Geist*, 95).

(5) the implication of the similar exhortation regarding sanctification of the *sarx* (II Cor 7: 1) that *sarx* and *sōma* interchange with reference to the body and without distinction as to substance and form;[1]

(6) the same implication from the interchange of *sōma* and *sarx* (and *melē*) elsewhere, as in Romans 6–8 (with the exception of some occurrences of *sarx* where it passes over to practical equation with sin itself) and I Cor 15: 35–44 (where *sōma* and *sarx* interchange for substantival entities but with the distinction that *sarx* may not refer to substantival entities which are other than earthly, whereas *sōma* may refer to both earthly and heavenly substantival entities).

The conclusion is that just as *sarx* usually means the whole body, substance-cum-form without differentiation, so also *sōma* means the body, substance-cum-form without differentiation.

Of course, Holsten and Lüdemann do not mean to say that *sōma* is 'pure' form leading an existence apart from substance; they recognize that *sōma* is form stamped on particular substances. Nevertheless, the distinction they draw distances the use of *sōma* for the *human* body from any necessary connection with the materialism implied in *sarx*. This leads them to interpret the body of resurrection as form stamped on spiritual substance – therefore *pneumatikon sōma* – or *himmlische Lichtsubstanz*. Thus they feel able to satisfy the philosophical idealism of the nineteenth century and escape the scandal of belief in a physical resurrection.[2]

---

[1] See Holsten, *Zum Evangelium*, 386–7, and Lüdemann, *Die Anthropologie*, 144–5, for attempts to overcome the problem, and Wendt, *Die Begriffe Fleisch und Geist*, 110–11, for critique. E. Brandenburger has recently written that '2 Kor 7 1 ist kaum paulinisch' (*Fleisch und Geist*, WMANT 29 [Neukirchen–Vluyn, 1968] 101, n. 1). He wants to interpret Paul in terms of a spiritualizing tendency rather prevalent (so it is claimed) throughout intertestamental literature. Cf. the denial that II Cor 7: 1 is Pauline also by D. Georgi on the ground that Paul would not speak of contamination of the flesh because for him it is already sinful (*Die Gegner des Paulus im 2. Korintherbrief*, WMANT 11 [Neukirchen–Vluyn, 1964] 21–2). But in Paul's usage the 'flesh' is not always or necessarily sinful. Moreover, Georgi overlooks the possibility of a subjective genitive. There may be other reasons for denying that II Cor 7: 1 comes from Paul (cf. above, p. 145, n. 2).

[2] See Holsten's overt comparison of Pauline thought (as understood by Holsten) with the philosophical idealism prevalent in Germany of the nineteenth century (*Zum Evangelium*, 371). For equally overt attempts to

With the exposé of the exegetical weaknesses in the interpretations of Holsten and Lüdemann and with the shift in philosophical mood from idealism to existentialism, R. Bultmann, following the lead of J. Weiss, interpreted *sōma* as designative of the whole human person when used with theological significance and defined that personhood in existentialist categories of self-understanding.[1] Thus the ontological use of *sōma* for organized material substance is relegated to popular parlance and theological insignificance. Where deemed theologically important, *sōma* is treated existentially. The meaning of *sōma* is no more substantival than in the idealistic interpretation of the nineteenth century scholars aforementioned. And the benefit is the same: escape from the scandal of a physical resurrection. For if *sōma* does not of necessity denote substance but basically has to do with self-understanding, the resurrection need not be physical.

[Note. J. Macquarrie penetratingly criticizes Bultmann's emphasis on the cross at the expense of the Incarnation and the resurrection because the cross is easier to accept as an objectively historical event (*An Existentialist Theology* [London, 1955] 181–92). He errs, however, in attributing Bultmann's reticence toward an objectively historical resurrection solely to a hang-over of liberal modernism. Macquarrie fails to see that a consistent existentialism (to which he himself subscribes) undermines the resurrection as an objectively historical event by defining man unsubstantivally with the result that physicalness becomes extrinsic and thus resurrection not necessarily objective. Existentialism may not have anything to say about the possibility of an historically objective resurrection (so Macquarrie), but it does take away the necessity that a resurrection be historically objective. Bultmann has seized on this.

For dematerialization of the resurrection, cf. J. A. T. Robinson, *The Body: A Study in Pauline Theology*, SBT 1/5 (London, 1952) 31–2, who avers that *sōma* fulfils its function 'not by being either material or immaterial'; S. Wibbing, 'Leib', *Theologisches Begriffslexikon zum*

avoid a physical resurrection, see pp. 373ff., 444ff., and Lüdemann, *Die Anthropologie*, 130–1. From the philosophical standpoint the interpretation seems weak, for continuity between the *sōma*, or form, of the flesh and the *sōma*, or form, of the *himmlische Lichtsubstanz* requires an ontological independence of form and substance.

[1] See below, p. 168, and for Bultmann's choice of existentialism see his essay, 'New Testament and Mythology', *Kerygma and Myth*, ed. H. W. Bartsch, revised ed. by R. H. Fuller (New York, 1961) 15–16.

Neuen Testament (Wuppertal-Vohwinkel, 1969) 872, who defines the *sōma* of resurrection as a body 'im Sinne von Ich und Person' rather than a transformed substantival entity; and F. G. Downing, *The Church and Jesus*, SBT 2/10 (London, 1968) 28–30, who, despite admission that for Paul the resurrection is corporeal, contrasts the spirituality of the resurrected body in Pauline literature and the physicalness of the resurrected Christ in Luke–Acts. We might note, however, that writing as a Jew, indeed as an ex-Pharisee, Paul may feel no need to stress the physicalness of the resurrected body. That went without saying and was clearly implied in the very meaning of *sōma*. Because of a keener appreciation of the Greek proclivity to doubt a physical resurrection, Luke may take pains to stress what Paul thinks can hardly be mistaken. There is no necessary contradiction between the two writers. W. Marxsen takes a different tack by arguing that the first disciples deduced corporeal resurrection from the appearances of the risen but incorporeal Christ because they could not conceive of a disembodied soul with enough vitality and substance to make those appearances ('The Resurrection of Jesus as a Historical and Theological Problem', *The Significance of the Message of the Resurrection for Faith in Jesus Christ*, ed. C. F. D. Moule, SBT 2/8 [London, 1968] 15–50). The evidence cited above, pp. 87–156, from the OT, apocrypha, pseudepigrapha, DSS, rabbinical literature, and NT shows late Jewish anthropology to be dichotomous enough for the first disciples to encounter little difficulty with the notion of a disembodied spirit and appearances thereof. Hence, they would feel little or no need to deduce physical resurrection. Of course, an effort to list exhaustively literature in which the resurrection is spiritualized would be unending. Even W. Pannenberg, in whose theology of hope the resurrection figures very prominently, seems to take refuge in an understanding of the resurrection as spiritual and hence understandable only in metaphorical terms (*Jesus – God and Man* [Philadelphia, 1968] 74–88). For an exposition of the way the phrase 'resurrection of the flesh' was intended to combat spiritualization of the resurrection, see W. Bieder, 'Auferstehung des Fleisches oder des Leibes? Eine biblisch-theologische dogmengeschichtliche Studie', *TZ* 1 (1945) 105–20.]

Bultmann makes it plain that dematerialization of the resurrection lies at the heart of his interpreting *sōma* as person rather than physique. 'His [Paul's] hope...expects...the "bodily" resurrection – or rather the transformation of the *soma* from under the power of flesh into a spiritual *soma*, i.e.

a Spirit-ruled *soma*.'[1] Thus Bultmann indicates that resurrection has to do with transformation of the personality rather than with transformation of the physique. This hermeneutical intent becomes clear at the outset of his lengthy discussion of *sōma*. There he immediately takes up the use of *sōma* in connection with the resurrection as expounded by Paul in I Corinthians 15. In particular Bultmann emphasizes the Pauline statements that 'the resurrection body will no longer be a body of flesh (I Cor.xv.50), not a "physical" (ψυχικόν) body or one of "dust" (I Cor.xv.44–9), but a "spiritual" (πνευματικόν) body, a "body of glory" (Phil.iii.21; *cf.* II Cor.iii.18).'[2] He then rightly rejects the older interpretation that the resurrected body is some form stamped on immaterial, spiritual substance.

Bultmann's own understanding may deserve rejection, however. He thinks that in I Cor 15: 35–49 Paul 'lets himself be misled into adopting his opponents' method of argumentation' and consequently uses *sōma* in the sense of 'form' stamped on fleshly or spiritual material, a usage uncharacteristic of him elsewhere and not really intended that way here.[3] But, we may note, a *psychikon sōma* is not a bodily form with soul as its substance; it is a physical body animated by the *psyche* and therefore suited to earthly life. By the same token, a *pneumatikon sōma* is not a bodily form with spirit as its substance;[4] it is a physical

---

[1] Bultmann, *Theology of the New Testament* (New York, 1951) 1: 201. The quotation marks around 'bodily' are those of the translator, Grobel, rather than Bultmann. Nevertheless, they correctly interpret Bultmann's meaning.

[2] *Ibid.* 192.

[3] *Ibid.*; see also Käsemann, *Leib und Leib Christi* (Tübingen, 1933) 118–19, 134ff.

[4] Hence there is no need for W. D. Davies' observation that 'spiritual' would have a slightly physical nuance for Paul as for the rabbis (*Paul and Rabbinic Judaism* [London, 1962] 303–8). We should also reject the reviving of the nineteenth century view that 'glory' is the substance of celestial, spiritual bodies in contrast to the fleshly substance of terrestrial bodies (Brandenburger, *Fleisch und Geist*, 82–5; H. Clavier, 'Brèves remarques sur la notion de σῶμα πνευματικόν', *The Background of the New Testament and Its Eschatology*, ed. W. D. Davies and D. Daube [Cambridge, 1964] 342–62). For terrestrial bodies have 'glory', too (v. 40); hence, 'glory' is not a substance but an attribute. Brandenburger's *religionsgeschichtlich* appeal to a spiritualization of the resurrected body in terms of *pneuma* and *doxa* throughout much of intertestamental literature rests on a doubtful pitting of pneumatic glory against physicality in the relevant texts. See above, p. 89,

body renovated by the Spirit of Christ and therefore suited to heavenly immortality.

For a contrast between embodied (en-formed) material and immaterial substances, such as Bultmann thinks Paul was misled into describing, Paul would have set *sarkikos* rather than *psychikos* opposite *pneumatikos*. Even the term *choikos*, 'earthy, dusty', here stresses mortality due to earthly origin (*ek gēs*) rather than substance as such, for its counterpart *epouranios* ('heavenly') has nothing to do with substance and is defined by the phrase *ex ouranou* ('from heaven'; vv. 47–9). Moreover, these predicates do not modify *sōma*, but *anthrōpos*. The same is true concerning the use of *eikōn* (v. 49), which might otherwise be thought to favor the meaning 'form' for *sōma*.[1] In the statement, 'Flesh and blood cannot inherit the kingdom of God, nor does corruption inherit incorruption' (v. 50), the phrase 'flesh and blood' connotes the present body's weakness and perishability (the parallel is *phthora*),[2] but does not imply immateriality of the resurrected body. On the contrary, *sōma* in and of itself implies materiality.

Sarx and *sōma* alternate in verses 35–40. After the question, 'With what kind of body do they [the dead] come?', Paul writes about the *sōma* of grain, human *sarx*, animal *sarx*, fishy *sarx*, celestial *sōmata*, and terrestrial *sōmata*. The interchange shows that Paul does not here use *sōma* in the sense of 'form'; the alternate term 'flesh' would contradict such a meaning.

n. 2. This is not to deny, of course, that here and there rejection, or loss, of physical resurrection did occur, as in 1QH (see above, pp. 99ff.).

[1] Besides, *eikōn* connotes substantiality as well as form. The same is true of the related terms *morphē*, *schēma*, and cognates. See Phil 3: 20–1, where glorification of the body is in view, and Bultmann, *Theology of the New Testament* 1: 192–3.

[2] See esp. Sir 14: 18; Eph 6: 12; Heb 2: 14; and the rabbinical references in Str–B 1: 730–1; but also Matt 16: 17; Gal 1: 16; Bultmann, *Theology of the New Testament* 1: 233–4; E. Schweizer, 'σάρξ', *TDNT* 7 (1971) 116; J. A. Schep, *The Nature of the Resurrection Body* (Grand Rapids, Mich., 1964) 201–5; C. A. van Peursen, *Body, Soul, Spirit: A Survey of the Body–Mind Problem* (London, 1966) 99, 102; W. Künneth, *The Theology of the Resurrection* (St Louis, 1965) 94; A. Sand, *Der Begriff 'Fleisch' in den paulinischen Hauptbriefen* (Regensburg, 1967) 152–4. Despite suitability to the present thesis, it is doubtful that v. 50*a* refers to those living at the time of the Parousia and v. 50*b* to the deceased (see Conzelmann, *Der erste Brief an die Korinther*, 345–6, against J. Jeremias, ' "Flesh and Blood Cannot Inherit the Kingdom of God" [I Cor. xv. 50]', *NTS* 2 [1955–56] 151–9).

Hence, we would err to think that the meaning 'form' is present because *sōmata* may be composed of different materials.[1] Paul does not write about different *materials* in bodies, but about different *bodies themselves*, just as about different *flesh*. *Sarx* does not carry the Greek meaning 'substance', but the meaning which בשר often has in the OT and which *sarx* frequently carries elsewhere in Pauline literature – viz., 'body',[2] as shown by the interchangeability with *sōma*. In other words, *sōma* does not mean form and *sarx* substance; both terms refer to the physical body.

Nor does the indication of differences in kinds of flesh and bodies open the possibility of an immaterial body. That would be a contradiction in terms. It merely establishes differences in degrees of glory and strength within the realm of equally physical being. Paul avoids 'flesh' in writing about the resurrection of human beings simply because the term would connote weakness, not because he wants to avoid a physical resurrection.[3]

Nevertheless, denying that 'form' was Paul's deeper intention in the use of *sōma*, Bultmann proceeds with his exegetical attempt to establish the meaning of *sōma* as 'person' and his philosophical interpretation of that definition in existentialist categories. That completed, he returns to I Cor 15 to explain that Paul's 'real intention' was not to affirm the resurrection of the *sōma* 'as the phenomenon of the material body', 'somehow or other...a thing of material substance',[4] but the resurrection of the *sōma* 'in the basic sense of that which characterizes human existence', viz., man's 'relationship to himself'. That this is not lucid in I Cor 15 is the unfortunate consequence of the lack of development in Paul's capacity for abstract thinking. Paul fails to distinguish terminologically between

---

[1] E. Best, *One Body in Christ* (London, 1955), 218–19.

[2] See the references cited above, p. 161, n. 6, to which Wendt adds II Cor 4: 10ff.; Phil 1: 22ff.; Col 1: 24; 2: 1, 5; Eph 5: 28–9 in his discussion of I Corinthians 15 (*Die Begriffe Fleisch und Geist*, 102ff.).

[3] Thus the objection to resurrection of the flesh is justified only to the extent that flesh connotes weakness and mortality. It is not justified as an objection to materiality.

[4] To buttress his desubstantializing of *sōma*, Bultmann suggests significance in the fact that Paul fails to call a corpse *sōma*, although that usage is common to the LXX and profane Greek (*Theology of the New Testament* 1: 195). One wonders, however, whether Paul's talk about 'mortal' bodies and about the 'raising' of bodies is essentially different.

sōma in the characteristically Pauline sense of man's person in relationship to himself and *sōma* in the materialistic sense it carries in popular parlance and especially, here, in mythological teaching on the resurrection.[1] Thus dematerializing and existentializing *sōma* entails dematerializing and existentializing the resurrection. On the one hand, the dematerialization allows avoidance of a *sacrificium intellectus*. On the other hand, the existentialization allows correlation of Paulinism with a philosophy which Bultmann thinks is correct as well as currently meaningful. Existentialization is correct in that existentialism is intrinsic rather than extrinsic to Pauline anthropology, and currently meaningful in that existentialism accords with modern ways of thinking about ourselves.[2]

Contrary to all this, however, runs Paul's exceptionless use of *sōma* for a physical body.[3] Had Paul wanted to portray the resurrection in any other fashion than in terms of physical bodies, he would not have used *sōma*. It is to be feared that in both the idealistic and the existentialist treatments of *sōma*, laudable pastoral concern for the limits of modern man's ability to believe has shipwrecked historico-critical exegesis and sacrificed theology to a current, and perhaps past, fashion in philosophy. Put otherwise, the attempt to use current philosophical categories for making the Christian gospel intelligible – an attempt necessary so far as it is possible – has gone so far as to transmute the gospel at this point. The consistent and exclusive use of *sōma* for the physical body in anthropological contexts resists dematerialization of the resurrection, whether by idealism or by existentialism. This is not to pass sweeping judgements on either of these philosophical approaches. But it is to say that the meaning of *sōma* intended by Paul in connection with the resurrection produces a piece of *mōria* as scandalous to twentieth century men as to the ancient Greeks and proto-gnostics (cf. Acts 17: 18, 32; I Cor 1: 23). The scandal is difficult – impossible – to avoid.

Seen in this light, Paul's zeal to defend the future resurrection of the *sōma* is no longer attributable to an anthropological concern, viz., that 'if man were no longer *soma* – if he no

---

[1] *Ibid.* 198.   [2] Cf. Macquarrie, *Existentialist Theology*, 5–26.

[3] A metaphorical use of *sōma* would not constitute an exception, for the metaphor itself would rest on an understanding of *sōma* as physical body.

longer had a relationship to himself – he would no longer be man'.[1] It rather derives from a soteriological concern: denial of a future resurrection of the physical body will work backward to the conclusion that Christ was not raised physically. That in turn, argues Paul, will take away the mainspring of life in the divine economy of salvation: 'if there is no resurrection of the dead, then Christ has not been raised; if Christ has not been raised, then our preaching is in vain and your faith is in vain... by a man has come also the resurrection of the dead...in Christ shall all be made alive' (I Cor 15: 12–28, excerpts from a passage which should be consulted in full). Paul does not orient his soteriology toward inner self-integration, but toward the integration of the incorporeal self and a new corporeality for effectiveness of expression and action in the coming eternal life.[2] Thus Paul uses *sōma* precisely because the physicality of the resurrection is central to his soteriology.

Against a physical understanding, however, E. Güttgemanns asks how the Corinthians could have doubted the resurrection of Christians and not that of Christ as well (if that is the implication of the passage) and why Paul does not argue that denial of the resurrection of Christians logically ends in denial of Christ's resurrection, too.[3] As a matter of fact, Paul does argue that denial of the one logically ends in denial of the other: 'if there is no resurrection of the dead, then Christ has not been raised' [and so on – see our last quotation]. The question concerning *how* the Corinthians could have doubted the one and not the other is exactly the point of Paul's argument. We are forced to say either that Corinthian beliefs and practice (of vicarious baptism) really were inconsistent or that Paul misunderstood them. But since our knowledge of the Corinthians comes only by inference from Paul himself, from the methodological standpoint only as a last resort should we absolve the Corinthians of inconsistency at the expense of charging Paul, who had lived and worked at length among the Corinthians and had received oral information and written

[1] Bultmann, *Theology of the New Testament* 1: 198.
[2] See K. Rahner, 'The Resurrection of the Body', *Theological Investigations*, vol. 11, *Man in the Church* (Baltimore, 1963) 203–16, on the physico-spiritual reality of the resurrection.
[3] E. Güttgemanns, *Der leidende Apostel und sein Herr*, FRLANT 90 (Göttingen, 1966) 56–61.

correspondence from them, with misunderstanding their beliefs.[1] Historically, the Corinthians, only recently converted from paganism, would not be unique in theological inconsistency!

We should not find it too difficult to suppose that the preaching of the resurrection of the savior Christ – the evidence for which Paul reminds the Corinthians both to establish common ground and to keep them from forgetting and denying that, too – had proved convincing to them, but that their Greek or proto-gnostic aversion to bodily resurrection kept them from affirming a future resurrection of the hoi polloi of believers in Christ (and possibly led them to affirm an already accomplished spiritual resurrection by means of the sacraments). Paul does not imply, however, that the Corinthians lacked *any* concept of an afterlife. In fact, his argument that if the dead are not raised, neither is Christ raised, and therefore the dead in Christ have utterly perished with consequent limitation of Christian hope to this life (vv. 12–19, especially 18) opposes a view that bodiless immortality comports with Christian beliefs. Thus Paul shows his awareness that the Corinthians conceived of some sort of afterlife.[2] We may wonder whether they thought of Christ's resurrection in terms of a translation of a hero, body and soul together, into an afterlife, as was commonly believed among Greeks concerning gods, heroes, and specially privileged men but denied to the average man.[3]

[1] See further Hurd, *The Origin of I Corinthians* (New York, 1965) 196–200; J. H. Schütz, 'Apostolic Authority and the Control of Tradition: I Cor. xv', *NTS* 15 (1969) 444; and an excellent survey of the exegetical history of I Cor 15 by J. H. Wilson, 'The Corinthians Who Say There Is No Resurrection', *ZNW* 59 (1968) 90–107.

[2] Schütz's attempt to make the whole of vv. 13–19 a rehearsal of Corinthian argument for an already accomplished resurrection of Christians ('Apostolic Authority', 446–7) is as unlikely as it is unnecessary. Where else do we meet such a lengthy quotation of Paul's opponents in argument? Paul does not waste his papyrus for the purpose of giving them a fair hearing or satisfying our curiosity. And lacking indications to the contrary, the second person plural pronoun looks like Paul's address to the Corinthians rather than their address to him and his companions or to a general audience.

[3] See the material cited in E. Rohde, *Psyche: The Cult of Souls and Belief in Immortality among the Greeks* (New York, 1966) 2: 537–9. Of course, this would logically imply a docetic view of Christ's death, as in later Gnosticism. In that case, Paul might direct the clause 'and that he was buried' (v. 4) and the repeated phrase *ek nekrōn* against such a view. Cf. Wilson, who thinks the Corinthians understood *egeirō* in the sense of ascension rather

Güttgemanns' own view is that Paul writes against Gnostics who spiritualized the resurrection and made their own an accomplished resurrection in union with Christ. Paul does not use *sōma* to materialize the resurrection, but to distinguish between Christ and Christians (against their pneumatic merging in Corinthian Gnosticism) and thus to put a temporal distance between their resurrection and Christ's.[1] The tradition in verses 3–11, including the list of witnesses, then becomes proof that Paul's teaching conforms to general Christian belief rather than evidence for the historicity of Christ's physical resurrection.[2] To buttress this latter point, there comes in the argument of H. Grass that Paul never mentions an empty tomb, although he refers frequently to the resurrection of Christ, because the resurrection of Christ's *sōma* necessarily entailed only the renewing of his *person*.[3] But Güttgemanns goes farther than Grass by arguing that Paul nowhere teaches the bodily resurrection of Christ. Only the resurrection of Christians is somatic.[4]

than resurrection ('The Corinthians', 90–107). The question concerning the suitability of the term '(proto-) gnostic' to Corinthian beliefs is not germane to our discussion. For a caveat against assuming that the Corinthians gnostically put their own spiritual, sacramental resurrection in the present (or past), see R. McL. Wilson, *Gnosis and the New Testament* (Philadelphia, 1968) 52–3, who argues that *anastasis nekrōn ouk estin* (v. 12) reads more naturally as a denial rather than an antedating of the resurrection. On the opposite side, see Schütz, 'Apostolic Authority', 439–57, and J. H. Wilson, 'The Corinthians', 90–107, with a deluge of further references; but Stanley has some highly trenchant criticisms which go even farther than the caveat of R. McL. Wilson (D. M. Stanley, 'Response to James M. Robinson's "Kerygma and History in the New Testament"' in J. P. Hyatt [ed.], *The Bible in Modern Scholarship* [Nashville, 1965] 152–3).

[1] Güttgemanns, *Der leidende Apostel*, 53–94.

[2] *Ibid.* 92. So also K. Barth, *Church Dogmatics* (Edinburgh, 1956) 4/1 : 335; his *Die Auferstehung der Toten*, 2nd ed. (Zollikon–Zürich, 1953) 75–84, and others who follow Barth. On the other hand, Bultmann recognizes the obvious, viz., that Paul regards the list of eyewitnesses as proof of Christ's miraculous resurrection ('New Testament and Mythology', 39). It is difficult to accept the currently fashionable opinion that Paul stresses the death of some of the five hundred witnesses rather than the availability of most of them. Far from being a point of emphasis, the qualification that some have died seems to be added as an afterthought.

[3] H. Grass, *Ostergeschehen und Osterberichte*, 2nd ed. (Göttingen, 1962) 146–73.

[4] Güttgemanns, *Der leidende Apostel*, 247–71, drawing on E. Käsemann, 'On the Topic of Primitive Christian Apocalyptic', *Journal for Theology and the Church* (New York, 1969) 6: 130–3.

Güttgemanns works with a view of *sōma* in which the term indicates relationship to another, especially as the object of another's action and, in this case, as the object of Christ's powerful action. Hence the resurrection of Christ cannot be somatic because he is subject, not object.[1] But the resurrection of Christians is somatic because in it Christ makes them his object by working upon them his power in opening up the future to them. Thus, the resurrection of Christ and that of Christians differ in nature: the former means Christ's active movement into and occupancy of eschatological[2] time; the latter means our deliverance from the power of the past and openness to the power of the future as we are worked upon by Christ through the Spirit. Because of its activeness the former is not somatic; by contrast the latter is somatic in that *sōma* indicates relationship to an outside power as its object.[3]

Where Bultmann dematerializes somatic resurrection in terms of man's relationship to himself within himself, Güttgemanns dematerializes somatic resurrection in terms of man's relation to an outer power as object of its domination – and in so doing denies that Christ's resurrection is somatic. However, the unfalteringly physical meaning of *sōma* resists such an interpretation. Somatic resurrection means physical resurrection, not a vague 'opening up of the future'. Moreover, the physical meaning of *sōma* would admirably suit a Pauline attack on a Greek or proto-gnostic spiritualizing of the resurrection of Christians.

Concerning the claim that for Paul the resurrection of Christ is not somatic, several things may be said. It underestimates the positive and emphatic correlation between the resurrection of Christ and that of Christians, a correlation which runs from verse 12 onward in I Corinthians 15: both are raisings of the dead; Christ is the 'first fruits'; all will be made alive 'in Christ'; and the 'spiritual body' of resurrection is related to the last Adam in such a way that Christians 'will bear the image of the man of heaven' just as they have borne

[1] Cf. C. Hartshorne's view of God as a social being who is supreme (*The Divine Relativity* [New Haven, 1964]).

[2] 'Eschatological' here connotes possibilities of authentic living (Macquarrie, *Existentialist Theology*, 166). What is eschatological, therefore, opens up the future with the result that one is not enslaved to his past.

[3] Güttgemanns, *Der leidende Apostel*, 271–81.

the image of the earthly man. Cf. Rom 8: 29, where because of the same term *eikōn* the phrase 'conformed to the image of his son' perhaps refers to the resurrected body,[1] and Col 1: 18: 'first-born from the dead' (and again Rom 8: 29: 'first-born among many brothers').

Güttgemanns counters that *prōtotokos* need not indicate similarity in kind, indeed, cannot do so in Col 1: 15: 'first-born of all creation'.[2] However, only the indications of Christ's creatorship and lordship in verses 16–17 make us interpret *prōtotokos* in terms of priority to and supremacy over creation. Were it not for those following statements, 'first-born of all creation' would naturally mean 'the first one to be created'. In connection with resurrection, *prōtotokos* lacks any qualifying statements that would lead us away from the normal understanding, 'the first in a series of those to rise from the dead', an understanding which implies a similarity in kind between Christ's resurrection and the somatic resurrection of believers.

Again, Güttgemanns claims that *eikōn* need not indicate similarity of kind, and does not do so in 1 Cor 11: 3, 7, where man is the 'image and glory of God'.[3] To be sure, *eikōn* does not imply identity, but it does indicate similarity. Otherwise, Paul's excusing men from the wearing of a head-covering because of the divine image makes no sense. Man's lordship over woman parallels divine lordship. *Eikōn* expresses the similarity. Likewise, if the resurrection of Christians is bodily, the iconic relationship to the resurrection of Christ implies that his also is bodily.

Güttgemanns thinks to upset all indications of similarity in kind between the resurrection of Christ and the bodily resurrection of Christians by an existentialist interpretation of Rom 8: 9–11.[4] According to that interpretation, Jesus as occupant of eschatological time works his power on Christians (= *sōmata* as objects of communicated power) to deliver them from the power of the past ('flesh') into the power of the future ('Spirit'). Ontically, the Christian as object (*sōma*) remains under the sentence of death, which represents the final outworking of the

---

[1] So, recently, R. Scroggs, *The Last Adam: A Study in Pauline Anthropology* (Philadelphia, 1966) 103–4.

[2] Güttgemanns, *Der leidende Apostel*, 278–9

[3] *Ibid.* [4] *Ibid.* 271–9.

power of the past. But ontologically, the Christian belongs to the future. Thus the resurrection of Christians does not rest causally on that of Christ. The two resurrections are related only in that both have to do with God's opening up the future.

With more attention to death than to resurrection G. Schunack here links hands with Güttgemanns by saying that for Paul physical death is unimportant. Rather, Paul makes death existentially somatic in that it consists in man's way of being under sin, which is a way of being under sin's power. Yet sin, ironically, lacks the power of authentic *Existenz*. Thus existential 'death' occurs in the realm of 'Sprache', specifically, the spoken law of God which condemns sin.[1] We have already seen that as a counterpoise to existential (not physical) death as the power of sin (i.e., the past), Güttgemanns views Jesus' resurrection as occupancy of eschatological time and the resurrection of Christians as their being brought into eschatological time. The latter is somatic because *sōma* indicates the receiving of another's action. Christ's resurrection is not somatic, for he is subject.

We may ask, however, whether even under this interpretation of *sōma* we should not consider the resurrection of Christ somatic in that he became the object of God's powerful action (I Cor 15: 15). But that is largely beside the point. Our main consideration is that the consistently physical meaning of *sōma* rules out a solely functional understanding of *sōma* and the consequent derogation of physical death and resurrection to the merely ontic and unimportantly empirical. The raising of Jesus from the dead and the making alive of Christians' mortal bodies carry substantival meanings.

Under the supposed justification that Paul was only using a way of speaking appropriate to his time,[2] it then becomes very awkward to transmute a futuristic resurrection of bodies at the juncture between this age and the coming age into a *present* 'resurrection' which consists in an opening up of the future.

[1] G. Schunack, *Das hermeneutische Problem des Todes*, Hermeneutische Untersuchungen zur Theologie 7 (Tübingen, 1967) *passim*.

[2] 'Nur die zeitgemässe Redeform' (Güttgemanns, *Der leidende Apostel*, 251), in connection with Christ's resurrection, to which, however, the resurrection of Christians is related.

Although it purports to open the future, such a 'resurrection' already occurs in this lifetime. Against that very denial of future resurrection of the body Paul argues: 'If for this life only we have hoped in Christ, we are of all men most to be pitied' (I Cor 15: 19). Moreover, Paul makes it very clear that Christ's resurrection is at least the mediate cause of the resurrection of believers: 'by a man has come also the resurrection of the dead...in Christ shall all be made alive...Christ the first fruits, then at his coming those who belong to Christ' (I Cor 15: 21–3); 'the last Adam became a life-giving Spirit' (v. 45); 'God...gives us the victory through our Lord Jesus Christ' (v. 57).

Against the dogmatic argument of O. Cullmann and W. C. Robinson, Jnr, that only a bodily resurrection of Christ could conquer sin and death for us, Güttgemanns claims that this line of reasoning would require Christ to have arisen in exactly the same body as the one in which he died.[1] But this is merely to bring up the problem of continuity versus discontinuity which comes forward in any discussion of the resurrection, as it does in Paul's treatment of the resurrection of believers in I Cor 15: 35–58. And there it is as much Güttgemanns' problem as that of anyone else. If believers' victory through Christ over sin and death does not require full identity between the old *sōma* and the new (and Paul flatly denies that it does [v. 37]), then neither should Christ's own victory over sin and death require such identity. This holds true under any interpretation of *sōma*. Thus the dogmatic argument of Cullmann and Robinson that only somatic resurrection on the part of Christ can insure our somatic resurrection remains valid.

Two questions remain in Cullmann's and Robinson's line of reasoning. What is meant by 'somatic'? Our answer (and theirs) is abundantly clear: physical. What is the link of continuity between the old body and the new? The anthropological duality evident in Paul and elsewhere supplies only a partial answer: the human spirit bears the consciousness of continuing personality and thus provides a link between the old body and the new.

[1] *Ibid.* 248–52; O. Cullmann, *Christ and Time*, 3rd ed. (Philadelphia, 1964) 231–42; W. C. Robinson, Jnr, 'The Bodily Resurrection of Christ', *TZ* 13 (1957) 81–110.

Nevertheless, a physical continuity is also needed. If a human spirit – a sort of third party – be the only connection between the mortal and resurrected bodies, the relationship of the two bodies to each other is extrinsic and to that degree unimpressive as a demonstration of Christ's victory over death. Paul does imply, however, a physical continuity within vast contrasts in writing that the body is sown and raised (I Cor 15: 35–44*a*).[1] Not being interested in questions such as those which are posed from the standpoint of modern science, he fails to spell out the how of molecular continuity vis-à-vis the discontinuity of death and dissolution. Bornhäuser makes the bones of the dead the usual physical link between old and new bodies, with the provision that God is able to make up for the lack of bones as a result of some disaster.[2] But neither Paul nor other writers of the NT indicate that the bones play such a role. Exegetically, the scientific questions receive no answer. Beyond exegesis, M. E. Dahl helpfully suggests that the continuous change of cells in the present body without destruction of its identity has some of the same characteristics of continuity-cum-discontinuity seen more radically active in death and resurrection.[3]

To say that for Paul the resurrection of Christ is not somatic also does not pay enough attention to Paul's apparent agreement with the tradition that Christ died and was *buried* and raised. As an ex-Pharisee, Paul could not have used such traditional language without recognizing its intent to portray the raising of a corpse. And in the absence of decisive indications to the contrary, his positive use of the tradition indicates his own acceptance of that view. The same implication concerning

---

[1] See Schep, *Resurrection Body*, 199–200. Against the occasional assertion of complete discontinuity between the old and new bodies in the view of Paul, we may note that his complementary expressions 'it is sown...it is raised' then become nonsensical. He accents differences in characteristics, however, in an attempt to meet the objection, 'How are the dead raised? And with what kind of a body do they come?' (v. 35).

[2] 'Die Gebeine der Toten.'

[3] Dahl, *The Resurrection of the Body*, SBT 1/36 (London, 1962) 194, where the discussion is somewhat muddled. Dahl begins by solving the problem of the relationship between present and resurrected bodies with a definition of *sōma* as the whole personality. But he does not try to evade the physical element in man's personality as a continuing factor. Consequently, the problem of physical continuity and discontinuity remains.

physicalness adheres to his making Christ's resurrection a resurrection 'from' and 'of' the dead. For one who had been a Pharisee, such phraseology could carry only one meaning – physical resurrection. In this light, the failure of Paul to mention an empty tomb is insignificant. He would feel no need to mention it, for it would follow as a matter of course. The only question is that which has to do with the kind of physical body in which the dead will rise. And that question Paul discusses in detail with reference to Christ the last Adam as well as with reference to believers. In view of the argument at hand – whether or not there is a resurrection of the dead – the contention that Paul does not present the list of witnesses to Christ's resurrection as evidence thereof seems singularly weak.

To maintain that Christ's resurrection is not somatic, we would have to dispose of the Pauline reference to the 'glorious body' of Christ in Phil 3: 20–1: 'we await a Savior, the Lord Jesus Christ, who will change our lowly body to be like his glorious body'. This Güttgemanns does, following a lead from E. Lohmeyer,[1] by marshalling evidence that these verses represent a pre-Pauline hymn. There are similarities to the acknowledgedly hymnic quotation in 2: 6–11: there we read *morphē* and *morphēn, hyparchōn, schēma, pan gony kampsē ktl.*, and *kyrios Iēsous Christos*; in 3: 20–1 *symmorphon, hyparchei, metaschēmatisei, tou dynasthai auton kai hypotaxai autō ta panta*, and *kyrion Iēsoun Christon*. To these we might add *etapeinōsen* and *tapeinōseōs*.

The use of *hos* at the head of 3: 21 is typically hymnic (only here we have the good fortune of knowing how the hymn began).[2] Colometric structure appears especially in verse 21. Paul does not elsewhere make the resurrection of Christians the action of Christ. Elsewhere he distinguishes between living and deceased Christians at the Parousia, whereas here we read only

[1] *Der Brief an die Philipper*, Meyer 9, 12th ed. (Göttingen, 1961) 157. J. Becker supports Güttgemanns and cites further literature ('Erwägungen zu Phil. 3, 20–21', *TZ* 27 [1971] 16–29).

[2] We may doubt this, however, for *hos* may have been a conventional way to begin hymns to Christ. Cf. the argument of R. Deichgräber that the hymnic quotation in I Tim 3: 16, which begins with *hos*, is too well-rounded to be considered a fragment (*Gotteshymnus und Christushymnus in der frühen Christenheit*, Studien zur Umwelt des Neuen Testaments 5 [Göttingen, 1967] 133, n. 3).

of living Christians and their transformation in terms reminiscent of Hellenistic mystery religions. Paul himself uses *allassō* of living Christians at the Parousia (I Cor 15: 51–2 *bis*), but here *metaschēmatizō* appears. For Paul the resurrection is a new creation, whereas here we read only of renovation.

Moreover, 'a body of humiliation' disagrees with Paul's view that 'the body of sin' (Rom 6: 6) and 'this body of death' (Rom 7: 24) are no longer the body of a Christian because Christ has conquered sin and death. And the 'mortal body' of which Paul writes in various places is not one of humiliation because its very weakness is paradoxically the epiphany of Christ in power and glory (II Cor 10: 1; Phil 4: 12–13). Phil 3: 20–1 disagrees with this paradox by putting our share in Christ's glory only in the future: temporal dualism replaces the existentialist dialectic of Paul. So goes the argument that in making the resurrection of Christ physical Phil 3: 20–1 does not truly represent Pauline theology.

In criticism we may make several observations concerning vocabulary. The aptness of *politeuma* ('commonwealth') for residents of Philippi, a military colony of resident aliens related to the capital city of Rome,[1] suggests that Paul formulated these verses *ad hoc* rather than quoted them from some hymn. Moreover, it seems strange that there should be two hymns so similar in much of their basic vocabulary as 2: 6–11 and 3: 20–1, and yet so different in the order and applications of their common terms. The order of the common expressions in 3: 20–1 does not follow the order in 2: 6–11. And not a single one of the common terms has the same reference (with the seeming exception of the general thought of subjection to Christ – but here there are no common terms). In addition, each passage has a number of important words missing in the other: *harpagmon, isa theō, ekenōsen, doulou, homoiōmati, thanatou, hyperypsōsen, echarisato* (2: 6–11) and *politeuma, ouranois, apekdechometha, sōma, doxēs, energeian, dynasthai, hypotaxai* (3: 20–1), to take the most important ones. Nevertheless, the mere incidence of several common terms remains striking and calls for explanation.

[1] See the commentaries and A. N. Sherwin-White, *Roman Society and Roman Law in the New Testament*, The Sarum Lectures, 1960–61 (Oxford, 1963) 185.

In 3: 20–1 there is nothing un-Pauline about the use of the word *ouranos*.[1] *Hyparchō* appears in undisputedly Pauline epistles ten times outside of the two passages in question. Although *sōtēr* does not appear in undisputedly Pauline epistles, it does appear in Eph 5: 23 and in the pastorals a number of times. Discounting that, however, *sōzō* appears very frequently in Pauline literature, including a reference to Christ's saving action (Rom 5: 9). Hence an appearance of *sōtēr* should not surprise us. *Apekdechomai* is typically Pauline; elsewhere it appears five times in eschatological connections. The full phrase '(our) Lord Jesus Christ' appears thirty-four times elsewhere in acceptedly Pauline epistles, sixteen times without the possessive pronoun, as in Phil 3: 20, to say nothing about nine appearances in Ephesians, Colossians, and the pastorals and the slightly different order in which *kyrios* comes last in nine places plus five more in the disputed epistles. In fact, 'Lord Jesus Christ' without the possessive occurs close by in Phil 1: 2 and 4: 23.

The relative pronoun *hos* may, but does not necessarily, indicate a hymnic quotation. It often introduces unhymnic material, as in Rom 14: 2, 5; I Cor 6: 5; 7: 37; 10: 13; 11: 21; and Gal 3: 16. *Metaschēmatizō* appears in certainly Pauline composition in I Cor 4: 6; II Cor 11: 13, 14, 15, and *schēma* in I Cor 7: 31. *Sōma* is, of course, common in Pauline literature. *Tapeinōsis* appears only in Phil 3: 21, but cognates appear: *tapeinos* three times, *tapeinoō* three times (excluding Phil 2: 8), and *tapeinophrosynē* once, plus four appearances in Ephesians and Colossians. *Symmorphos* appears in Rom 8: 29. Again cognates are common: *symmorphizomai* in nearby Phil 3: 10, *morphoomai* once, *morphōsis* once (plus an appearance in the pastorals), and *metamorphoomai* twice. In II Cor 3: 18 *metamorphoomai* relates to *doxa* as in Phil 3: 21. *Doxa* appears dozens of times. These include a large number of appearances with

[1] See the concordance. Concerning the vocabulary of these vv., Becker ('Erwägungen') displays remarkable confidence in distinguishing between cognates, singular and plural forms, and between earthly and heavenly, present and future references and the like for the sake of drawing conclusions regarding independence, dependence, and direct quotation in Paul's writing. Whatever validity such distinctions may have, possible influence of traditional formulations (see below) makes unnecessary an assumption that Paul here quotes a hymn.

eschatological reference. In particular, *doxa* relates to the resurrection of the *sōma* in Rom 8: 21–3 and qualifies the raised *sōma* in I Cor 15: 40–4, especially 43–4. We could hardly ask for closer parallels to Phil 3: 21 without demanding complete identity of phraseology.

Energeia appears twice in II Thessalonians and five times in Ephesians and Colossians, usually with *kata*, as in Phil 3: 21. Together, the cognates *energeō*, *energēma*, and *energēs* appear a large number of times (twenty-two, including five in Ephesians and Colossians). *Dynamai* is also very frequent and, as in Phil 3: 21, links with *hypotassō* in Rom 8: 7. *Hypotassō* appears fifteen times in Romans and I Corinthians, plus eight times in Ephesians, Colossians, and Titus. Especially significant are the five appearances of *hypotassō* with *panta* for the subjection of all things to Christ in the discussion of resurrection in I Cor 15: 27–8 (cf. also Eph 1: 22). We could scarcely hope for a more convincing parallel both in wording and in subject matter.

From the standpoint of vocabulary, then, we have little reason to deny the Pauline composition of Phil 3: 20–1, and very much reason to affirm it. On the other hand, the rather striking parallels of several words with 2: 6–11 (though their order and conceptual connections are different) need explanation. We meet the requirements of the data simply but adequately by saying that Paul himself composed 3: 20–1 and in so doing echoed some of the terms which he had quoted in 2: 6–11 from a hymn.

Concerning the further arguments of Güttgemanns, even he admits that the colometric structure in 3: 20–1 might be due to Paul himself and, by implication, that such a structure is not so apparent in verse 20. We need to deny that Paul elsewhere does not make the resurrection of Christians the action of Christ. In context the statement of Paul that 'the last Adam became a life-giving Spirit' (I Cor 15: 45) relates directly to the raising of the bodies of deceased Christians. And in verse 57 God is the ultimate source and Christ the immediate agent of our victory over death: 'But thanks be to God, who gives us the victory through our Lord Jesus Christ.'

The argument that Paul elsewhere distinguishes between the translation of living Christians and the resurrection of deceased Christians at the Parousia, whereas only the translation of living Christians appears in Phil 3: 20–1, also fails to carry conviction. The passage in Philippians is a general statement concerning the glorification of both living and deceased Christians at the Parousia, just as in I Cor 15: 51: 'We shall not all sleep, but we shall all be changed.' I.e., some will die, but all will be changed either by resurrection or by translation. This is plain from the following verses, too, which indicate that both the dead and the living will share in the exchange of mortality for immortality. No reason exists to see in Phil 3: 20–1 an exclusiveness of reference to the living, for 'our body of humiliation' may be either dead or alive at the Parousia, just as in I Cor 15: 51–7.

The difference between *allassō* (I Cor 15: 51–2 *bis*) and *metaschēmatizō* (Phil 3: 21) is insignificant. The double appearance of the former hardly constitutes evidence for a technical usage. And like *metaschēmatizō*, *allassō* also denotes change, or renovation, as shown by the subsequent statements: 'For this perishable nature must put on the imperishable, and this mortal nature must put on immortality [and so on]' (vv. 53–4). Hence the fine distinction between a Pauline doctrine of new creation and an un-Pauline, Hellenistic doctrine of renovation lacks solid basis.

Finally, it goes too far to divorce from Christians 'the body of sin', which will be 'destroyed' (Rom 6: 6), and 'this body of death', from which deliverance is desired (Rom 7: 24). In the tension of living between the times Christians already have and experience such deliverance, but await its full outworking since they still bear the body of sin and death. The same combination of the already and the not-yet holds true for the 'mortal body'. We are already delivered from mortality, yet paradoxically we are still subject to it. For this reason Paul's description of the body as one 'of humiliation' (Phil 3: 21) does not contradict the point that the body in its very weakness is the epiphany of Christ in glorious power. Humiliation and glory – they are part of the paradox, too. And Paul's putting the humiliation in the present and the glory in the future in Phil 3: 21 no more implies a temporal dualism which negates the present existential paradox than his putting the crucifixion of Christians with Christ in the past implies a temporal dualism which negates the present existential paradox that we have to reckon ourselves dead, and the further paradox that Christians who do not survive till the Parousia do in fact die though they have already died and risen with Christ.[1]

We cannot, then, excise from Pauline theology the indication in Phil 3: 20–1 that the resurrection of Christ was just as somatic as that of Christians will be. Rather, those verses say explicitly what we should naturally deduce from I Corinthians 15, Rom 8: 11, and other passages, viz., that the raising of Jesus from the dead was a raising of his physical body. Neither excision of relevant texts nor reinterpretation of *sōma* can lay rightful claim to carry out the ultimate intention of Paul. Quite clearly, that intention included a substantival category: the resurrection of Christ was and the resurrection of Christians will be physical in nature. Anything less than that undercuts Paul's ultimate intention that redeemed man possess physical means of concrete activity for the eternal service and worship of God in a restored creation. Otherwise, God's purpose in the creation – material as it is – would be thwarted. To dematerialize resurrection, by any means, is to emasculate the sovereignty of God in both creative purpose and redemptive grace.

We need to include 'creative purpose' with 'redemptive grace'. It is commonly stated in current literature that in the NT, afterlife does not depend on the nature of man but on the grace of God.[2] That is only partially true. God will restore the broken nature of believers at their resurrection not only because of his grace, but also because the nature of man qua man as a unity of body and spirit represents God's creative purpose.[3] Permanent disruption of body and spirit would con-

---

[1] We might also ask why Paul utilizes a hymn so opposed to his theology as Güttgemanns thinks. But he maintains that Paul took over the hymn with the understanding that the body of the Christian corresponds to the humilation of Christ and therefore is already related to the Lord and thereby to his glory; thus the individual body of Christ in the hymn is extraneous to Paul's point (*Der leidende Apostel*, 246–7). That Paul would bend a source in this way seems doubtful.

[2] See, for example, D. Hill, *Greek Words and Hebrew Meanings*, NTSMS 5 (Cambridge, 1967) 225; Künneth, *The Theology of the Resurrection*, 286–8; D. H. van Daalen, 'The Resurrection of the Body and Justification by Grace', *Studia Evangelica*, ed. F. L. Cross, TU 88 (Berlin, 1964) 3/2: 218–22.

[3] Cf. F. P. Fiorenza and J. B. Metz, 'Der Mensch als Einheit von Leib und Seele', *Mysterium Salutis: Grundriss heilsgeschichtlicher Dogmatik*, vol. 2,

stitute an ultimate defeat of God's will concerning the nature of man. As it is and will be, the divine intent prevails.[1]

Die Heilsgeschichte vor Christus, ed. J. Feiner and M. Löhrer (Cologne, 1965–) 629–30.

[1] To the extent that resurrection is made to rest totally on divine grace, two tendencies arise, one toward resurrection only of the righteous and another toward universal salvation. To the extent that resurrection is seen to derive also from the nature of man by virtue of divine creation, the need for limiting the resurrection and for universalism diminishes, for creative will might allow for damnation of resurrected unbelievers while redemptive will limits itself to believers. In that case, the resurrection to judgement would rest solely on the nature of man by divine creation, and the resurrection to blessedness would rest additionally on redemption by divine grace. Alone, resurrection solely by divine grace requires either that unbelievers not be raised because their lack of faith excludes them from the sphere of grace, or that divine grace draw all men to faith with the result of universal salvation (but see Rom 2: 8–9; 11: 22; Phil 3: 19; I Thes 5: 3; II Thes 1: 6–10; 2: 3, 10–12). The first option defeats creation. The second runs the risk of reducing the stature of man as a creature capable of willing against as well as for God. Such reduction of man's stature does not necessarily enhance God's sovereignty. It tends to reduce God's sovereignty to the mechanical control of objects which cannot truly obey or resist. But since Paul sensed no occasion to discuss a resurrection to damnation (see, however, Acts 24: 15 and G. Vos, *The Pauline Eschatology* [Grand Rapids, 1952] 221), that question lies alongside rather than on the path of our present considerations.

CHAPTER 14

Sōma and the Being of Man

'What is the specific respect in which man is regarded when he is called *soma*?' That is an important question the proper answer to which will give us positive results in building a truly Biblical anthropology. Bultmann answers this, his own question, 'Man is called soma in respect to his being able to make himself the object of his own action or to experience himself as the subject to whom something happens.'[1] He goes on to use phrases such as 'having a relationship to himself', 'to distinguish himself from himself', 'the object of his own conduct' over against himself 'as subject' [of his own conduct] or the object of 'an occurrence that springs from a will other than his own'.

Here it is important to observe the tension between *sōma* as the whole self and *sōma* as the object-'half' as opposed to the subject-'half' of the self.[2] Constitutionally, *sōma* denotes the 'whole' self. Functionally, *sōma* denotes the object-'half' of the self. 'Half' must be put in quotation marks, however, because Bultmann is really putting the 'whole' self as object opposite the 'whole' self as subject. What then does the term 'whole' mean? It, too, must be put in quotation marks. But this only points up the paradox caused by the use of adjectives ('whole' and 'half') proper to substances in dealing with categories which are not substantival, or ontological, but functional – or more specifically, existential. Nevertheless, for a proper evaluation we should pay careful attention to this functional qualification of the adjective 'whole'.

According to Bultmann, *sōma* is the self as the object of perception and action distinguishable at the same time from the subject of perception and action even though that subject be the self. The subject-self – characterized by intentionality, purposefulness, willing, and knowing – may be designated by

[1] Bultmann, *Theology of the New Testament* (New York, 1951) 1 : 195 and *passim* in the following pages.
[2] In the ensuing discussion here, 'subject-self' refers to the self as doer of an action, and 'object-self' to the self as receiver of an action.

several terms with somewhat different nuances: *ho esō anthrōpos, nous, kardia,* but primarily *psychē* and *pneuma*.[1] Interestingly and perhaps significantly, Bultmann describes the subject-self, in contradistinction to the *sōma,* or object-self, as the 'real (*eigentliche*)' self.[2]

All of this, of course, is replete with Heideggerian ways of thinking and speaking.[3] J. Macquarrie has correlated Bultmann's treatment of *sōma* and Heidegger's description of man with particular clarity. Thus, whereas Macquarrie thinks the merit of the work of Kant is that his categories of substance suit the world of nature, the merit of Heidegger is that he recognizes the inappropriateness of substantival categories to human existence and proposes new categories, existentials. In such a scheme, the basic constitution of man – that which makes him man – is his way of being in the world, not spatially but by way of interaction with himself and with forces outside himself. Corporeal and incorporeal substances or any union thereof are extrinsic to the nature of a human being.[4]

Thinking that such philosophical anthropology fits Pauline Biblical anthropology (and Macquarrie agrees), Bultmann utilizes Heideggerian categories and terms to explicate the meaning of *sōma,* not as an organized substance, but as a way of being in the world, more specifically, as being an object to oneself and to outside forces. This meaning develops from man's sensory experiences of himself as a physical body. From that sensory experience evolves Paul's use of *sōma* as the object-self apart from any necessary tangibility.[5]

The idea that *sōma* is the object-self has drawn fire from those who oppose Hebrew to Greek ways of thinking. For example, J. A. T. Robinson accuses Bultmann of Hellenizing Paul's understanding of *sōma* as the 'me' rather than the 'I'. 'Such a way of thinking is essentially un-Hebraic and indeed post-Cartesian.'[6] The charge will not stand up in court, how-

---

[1] Bultmann, *Theology of the New Testament* 1: 202–3, 209. [2] *Ibid.* 203.

[3] See M. Heidegger, *Being and Time* (London, 1962). The particularly relevant discussion begins about p. 71 (45 in the later German editions).

[4] J. Macquarrie, *An Existentialist Theology* (London, 1955) 10–26.

[5] Bultmann, *Theology of the New Testament* 1: 196.

[6] J. A. T. Robinson, *The Body: A Study in Pauline Theology*, SBT 1/5 (London, 1952) 12–13, n. 1; see also E. Schweizer, 'σῶμα κτλ.', *TDNT* 7 (1971) 1066, n. 410.

ever, for Bultmann quite Hebraically and un-Hellenistically regards the object-self as the *whole* self. The self is halved only existentially, not substantivally.[1] Whether the object or subject of a decision, man is 'the one, same, total man in the fulfilment of his existence'.[2] Existentialist analysis may distinguish subject and object, but existential existence overcomes the distinction.[3] Moreover, the inner conflict described in Rom 7: 13–25 validates the notion that Paul could distinguish himself from himself.[4]

Of course, Bultmann has no trouble delineating passages in which *sōma* appears as an object: 'I pommel my body' (I Cor 9: 27); 'if I deliver my body' (I Cor 13: 3); 'Let not sin therefore reign in your mortal bodies...Do not yield your members to sin' (Rom 6: 12–13); 'present your bodies' (Rom 12: 1); 'Christ will be honored in my body' (Phil 1: 20); 'For the wife does not rule over her own body...likewise the husband does not rule over his own body' (I Cor 7: 4).[5] But we have long ago noted that in these and other passages *sōma* bears a specifically and emphatically physical meaning. One does not pommel or burn a body which lacks substance, nor does such

---

[1] Cf. F. P. Fiorenza and J. B. Metz, 'Der Mensch als Einheit von Leib und Seele' in *Mysterium Salutis: Grundriss heilsgeschichtlicher Dogmatik* (Cologne, 1965) 584–636, on the soul as the whole man's subjectivity, and even more appositely, K. Barth: 'Man is wholly and simultaneously both soul and body. But...they are distinguished from each other as subject and object, as operation and work' (*Church Dogmatics* [Edinburgh, 1960] 3/2: 398).

[2] W. Schmithals, *An Introduction to the Theology of Rudolf Bultmann* (Minneapolis, 1968) 60; see also 49–70 for references to Bultmann's less exegetical writings.   [3] *Ibid.* 67–70.

[4] But it does not validate a definition of *sōma* as the object-self (see above, pp. 137–40). Stacey criticizes Bultmann for attributing too much metaphysical speculation to Paul (*The Pauline View of Man* [London, 1956] 191). Doubtless Bultmann would answer that the speculation is simply modern existentialist analysis which reveals an unpremeditated existentialism in Paul's manner of thinking. Grobel tries to justify Bultmann's distinction between the subject-self and the object-self from Job 36: 28*b*: 'Your mind (*hē dianoia*) is not astonished at all these things; neither is your heart estranged (*diallassetai*) from [your] body (*apo sōmatos*).' In the end, however, Grobel recognizes that the v. fails to express the kind of *volitional* estrangement required to support Bultmann's view (K. Grobel, 'Σῶμα as "Self, Person" in the LXX', *Neutestamentliche Studien für Rudolf Bultmann*, BZNW 21 [Berlin, 1954] 58–9).

[5] Bultmann, *Theology of the New Testament* 1: 196.

a body afford the kind of intercourse between husband and wife of which Paul speaks. Since the substantival meaning of *sōma* as physique is absolutely essential to the force of such passages, we may not subtract it in the name of discovering the 'ultimate intention' of Paul. Thus the objectivity of *sōma* is not purely functional. It *is* functional in that it denotes a way of being in the world. But it is more than functional in that it denotes a substantival entity which exists in the concrete world. And without the substantival nature of man's *sōma*, man's way of being in the world ceases. *Vorhandensein* is as necessary to specifically human existence as *Existenz* itself. In other words, we should insist on the substantival meaning of *sōma* as the physical body and, as a lesson learned from existentialist analysis, lay some stress on the functional or operational connotations of *sōma*, which tended to receive less than due attention in the traditional understanding of *sōma* in terms of substance.

II Cor 5: 10 poses a problem for Bultmann's maintenance of *soma* as *consistently* objective (regardless of the substantival and/or functional nature of that objectivity): 'so that each one may receive good or evil, according to what he has done through the body *(hina komisētai hekastos to dia tou sōmatos pros ha epraxen eite agathon eite phaulon)*'. Despite Bultmann's attempt to wrench an objective sense out of *dia tou sōmatos* ('not with his body, but with himself, what he has made of himself'[1]), the grammar of the statement requires *sōma* to be strictly instrumental. Only the actions *(ta...pros ha epraxen)* are the object. Paul does not write about what a man has made *of himself*, as though that were the force of *dia tou sōmatos*, but of those acts a man has performed in the concrete world through the instrumentality of his physical body.

But the instrument is an agent, an actor, with the result that the genitival object of *dia* becomes the intermediate subject of the action. Since *sōma* does not refer to some lifeless instrument separate from the doer, but to a living part of the doer, the phrase *dia tou sōmatos* expresses personal agency in which the body acts as the subject of the doing.[2] This obviously belies a limitation of *sōma* to the status of an object.

[1] *Ibid.* 197.
[2] See Bauer, *A Greek–English Lexicon*, s.v. διά A, III, 2, for a profusion of references in which the genitival object of *dia* is the doer of an action.

A similar implication arises out of Rom 8: 13, where Bultmann admits that *sōma* is 'the implied subject of an action' but explains that the whole expression 'if...you put to death the deeds of the *soma*' indicates that the *sōma* has fallen away from the subject-self into the domination of sin ('the flesh') as an outside power. Hence, *sōma* is the subject of action only in its estrangement from the 'real' subjective self, as also with the 'lusts of the *sōma*' (Rom 6: 12; cf. the 'lust [and passions] of the flesh' in Gal 5: 16–17, 24).[1]

But here an inconsistency appears. In Rom 6: 12 and 8: 13 *sōma* ought not to be the subject of action when it is under the sway of the flesh any more than when it is under the sway of the 'real' subject-self. The power of the flesh should keep *sōma* in its place as object just as much as the power of the 'real' self. As it is, whether dominated by the flesh or by the 'real' self, *sōma* is a doer of action (here in a subjective genitive). That the appeal to the special case of a personality fractured by sin will not explain away uses of *sōma* as subject is shown also by the fact that the body is the instrumental subject of *good* as well as evil deeds in II Cor 5: 10.

So also, 'You have been put to death through the body of Christ' (Rom 7: 4) means that the *sōma* of Christ is the instrumental actor in the putting to death. In II Cor 4: 7 – 5: 10 the outer man, in distress, acts upon (but happily does not overcome with despair) the inner man – to say nothing of the many Biblical passages, especially in the Psalms, where the physical state affects the spirit.

It becomes apparent, then, that *sōma* may be subject as well as object. To insist on an exclusive denotation of the object-self is to squeeze the usage into a Heideggerian schema which fails to do justice to all the exegetical data. And even were it possible to maintain a consistently objective connotation for *sōma*, usage in context demonstrates an emphasis on physicalness that does not accord with the unimportance of substance in Heideggerian objectivity.

The consistently substantival meaning of *sōma*, then, strikes at the heart of the anthropology of Bultmann, which, in turn, is his theology. For that meaning thwarts his primary effort to explicate man solely by means of existentials. However, his

---

[1] Bultmann, *Theology of the New Testament* 1: 197.

effort has rewarded us richly. We shall never again be able to overlook the functional, operational elements in Pauline anthropology, including those in the use of *sōma*. We have learned that they are more than descriptive of man. They are constitutive of man – but not to the exclusion of the substantival. Function must now be related to substance.

Bultmann rejects the substantival character of distinctively human being under the supposition that if the character is substantival, the responsibility of man for his decisions, and thus for the future, is lost to the inexorable flow of natural processes.[1] But a supposition that on the one side substance and on the other side contingency of events and responsibility of decision oppose each other posits an un-Biblical breach between natural objects and personal volition. Bultmann has gained his specific explanation of *sōma* as the 'whole' person only by denigrating the material half of the person and the material world around him. The price is too high, for this is dualism with a vengeance. From the Biblical perspective, the material world, including the physical part of ourselves, does not so much limit our freedom to decide for the future as provide opportunity to carry out our decisions in concrete fashion. Natural processes are not inexorable. They are subject to both divine and human will. The relationship between decision and natural processes is one of interaction and interdependence rather than antithesis.[2]

In reply, Bultmann notes that his own dualism does not denote metaphysical opposition. It is rather a simple phenomenological statement which says nothing about the relationship between nature and history, but only distinguishes the two in order to display the distinctively human characteristic of decision and to emphasize man's responsibility for the future over against irresponsible abandonment to historical or natural conditions.[3] But the desubstantializing of *sōma* belies such a

[1] P. S. Minear makes this point in his article, 'Rudolf Bultmann's Interpretation of New Testament Eschatology', *The Theology of Rudolf Bultmann*, ed. C. W. Kegley (New York, 1966) 68.

[2] The term 'interdependence' comes from Minear, who criticizes Bultmann's dualism of nature and history, or being and existence (*ibid.* 76–82).

[3] 'Reply', *ibid.* 265–8; cf. his "Ist Apokalyptik die Mutter der christlichen Theologie?', *Apophoreta: Festschrift für Ernst Haenchen*, BZNW 30 (Berlin, 1964) 68.

defense here. There really is a metaphysical opposition between *Existenz* and *Vorhandensein*. Otherwise, Bultmann would never have relegated to theological insignificance the physical meaning, which he calls the 'naive popular usage', in creating a special existential meaning for *sōma*.

Of course, the thingness of *sōma* as physical body is not distinctively human. Subhuman creatures have *sōmata*, too. But that does not imply that the physical is theologically unimportant (much less, unnecessary) to specifically human existence. Has Bultmann merely identified the plus in man's being with a responsibility for decision, we should heartily agree. But he has pejoratively subsumed the substantival nature of man's constitution to the existentiality of man's way of being. This unequal and uneasy partnership cannot help but lead to a flight from the material world in which knowable objective events take place. Materiality may not be *distinctively* human; but it is necessarily *important* to human being. Not to think so – whether for idealistic or existentialist reasons – tends toward a turning away from one's own physique as an instrument of concrete action and from the material arena of such action toward a concentration on one's relationship to himself. The consequences are introversion, preoccupation with questions of self-integration and psychological adjustment, and self-centered attempts to gain experiences of ultimate meaning through asceticism, mysticism, and the like. Of course, Bultmann does not himself advocate such practices.[1] But they are logical by-products of an emphasis on *sōma* as man's being in relationship to himself.

Ironically, what begins as an existentialist stress on human responsibility to decide the future ends in withdrawal from the only arena where we can exercise that responsibility – viz., the material world where objective events take place – because of a prior devaluation of the only means by which we can carry out that responsibility – viz., the physical body.[2] Stress on function is certainly apropos, but not at the expense of substance. In the final analysis, substance is as important to

---

[1] See R. Bultmann, *Jesus and the Word* (New York, 1958) 47–8.

[2] Cf. the way in which libertinism and mysticism begin with immersion in sensory experience but rapidly lose meaningful contact with the sensory world.

the retention of function as is function to the significance of substance.

We cannot turn the matter around by saying that to regard *sōma* as a physical prison leads to mysticism and asceticism, which are a 'flight from the uncomfortable tension of a human existence in which a person unavoidably has a relationship to himself'.[1] These are indeed the results of regarding the *sōma* as a physical *prison*. But desubstantializing *sōma* is not the only alternative to that. If the *sōma* is physical but *not* imprisoning – if, rather, it is serviceable to responsible action, then mysticism and asceticism hardly follow. On the contrary, loss of theological significance in the physicality of *sōma* as a substantival means of responsible action in the material world of men and events slides into mysticism and asceticism (or libertinism, we should add) just as surely as does equation of materiality with evil.

That we are not castigating Bultmann unfairly becomes evident from at least two considerations: (1) Bultmann himself lays major stress on *self*-relationship as the meaning of *sōma* and as the core of Pauline anthropological theology, a stress which his own pupils have more than once criticized; (2) the well-recognized flight of Bultmann from the meaningfulness of objective history points up the inevitable tendency of his inward-looking existentialist anthropology, indeed, constitutes a very logical outgrowth from it.

We have already intimated that flight from the materiality of *soma* carries a concomitant flight from the materiality of the worldly environment and consequently from the objectivity of historical events which take place in this arena of the concrete. Bultmann again denies the charge by saying that his existentialist theology, far from repudiating the necessity or relevance of factual history, rather affirms the paradox that a historical event (precisely, Jesus and his history) is at the same time an eschatological occurrence.[2] But this is a defen-

---

[1] Bultmann, *Theology of the New Testament* 1: 199.

[2] Bultmann, 'Reply', 274–5. Cf. chapters 2 and 3 in S. M. Ogden, *Christ without Myth* (New York, 1961), and N. J. Young, *History and Existential Theology* (Philadelphia, 1969) 18–35, 102–31, on Bultmann's attitude toward history and criticisms from right and left. 'The well-recognized flight of Bultmann from the meaningfulness of objective history' refers to his rejection of the 'what' and 'how' of history and retention only of the 'that',

sively grudging affirmation incompatible with the philosophical base of Bultmannian theology, as Bultmann's critics on both left and right have been quick to point out. It is grudging in that Bultmann supplies no philosophical base for the factually historical side of the 'paradox' and in that the purportedly decisive event – Jesus and his history – receives strangely little attention. It is incompatible with the existentialist base of Bultmannian theology in that, as Bultmann himself argues, the grounding of faith in objective history subjects faith to the mercy of historians. That assertion is partially true, but *only* partially since the interplay of philosophy and historiography subjects historians to criticism from philosophers (as well as philosophers to criticism from historians). We may also be tempted to wonder whether the mercy of historians might not equal that of existentialist philosophers. Happily, the alternatives are not so stark. Although Christian faith may not lie fully at the mercy of historians or philosophers, to be a responsible sort of faith it should listen to both (and to others) with discriminating appreciation.

Bultmann's former pupils have tried to soften their teacher's paradox by relating faith to the objective history of Jesus in order that the affirmation of Jesus and his history may carry more conviction. But, although they consequently pay more attention to the history of Jesus, they are not all shifting from an anti-substantival base. This is clear, for example, in Conzelmann's re-echoing the desubstantialized definition of *sōma*:

We have to rid ourselves of the idea of the abstract subject and its works...I achieve my existence in my works. I am the sum of my actions. At every movement I do not consider 'something' – a possible act, a decision, an object – but myself with the alternative of winning myself or losing myself...σῶμα designates the 'I'... the I in so far as it can be grasped by itself and others as the possible object of action through others and through itself. I am σῶμα in so far as I can stand over against myself, govern myself and risk myself. I am σῶμα in so far as I desire...σῶμα is thus the I as a subject

indeed, a severely shrunken amount of 'that'. Even Young, who generally supports Bultmann, admits a deficiency in the minimal interest of Bultmann in the history of Jesus (*ibid.* 120–1). Young wants to make up the deficiency without forsaking the Bultmannian framework. See below that such a correction requires the rehabilitation of substantival categories.

which acts and an object which is acted upon, especially the I as one that acts upon itself.[1]

Although Conzelmann ascribes to *sōma* the notion of the subject-self as well as that of the object-self where his former teacher limits *sōma* to the object-self, he still moves on a purely functional plane so far as the theologically significant use of *sōma* is concerned.

So long, therefore, as those in the Bultmannian tradition fail to shift their philosophical ground, or at least broaden their philosophical base by importation and significant use of substantival categories, their greater attention to Jesus and his history will remain philosophically illegitimate and prove minimally rewarding – both theologically and historiographically. Bultmann's lesser attention is more congruous with the desubstantialization of man and the resultant deobjectivization of history. No attention at all to Jesus and his history would be most congruous, but Bultmann thinks better of faith in Christ than that.

Lest the relationship between the definition of *sōma* and theological attitudes toward history be lost to view, we return to *sōma*, but this time with a look at its consistent reference to the physical body. This usage means that man is substance as well as functional possibility. Since history has to do with man, therefore, it is more than the study of the possible. It is also a study of the factual, the objective.[2]

The antipathy of the desubstantialization and existentialization of *sōma* to the material world, on the one hand, and to the objective events which take place within it, on the other hand,

[1] H. Conzelmann, *An Outline of the Theology of the New Testament* (New York, 1968) 176–7.

[2] Cf. S. Hook, 'Objectivity and Reconstruction in History', *Philosophy and History: A Symposium*, ed. S. Hook (New York, 1963) 250–74, and, indeed, the entire collection of essays for the pros and cons of objective versus existentialist historiography. See also Macquarrie's critique of Bultmann's undervaluation of objective history (*Existentialist Theology*, 159–92). As above, Macquarrie recognizes that Bultmann does not totally repudiate objective history, but recognizes equally that he nearly does so. However, Macquarrie fails to appreciate that his own critique of Bultmann's view of history goes against his acceptance of Bultmannian existentialism, particularly, the Bultmannian desubstantializing of *sōma*. I.e., Macquarrie lacks an anthropological and therefore historical base from which to launch his philosophical critique.

may also be seen in the trajectory of the chronologically successive treatments of *sōma* by Bultmann. Reacting against the idealistic understanding of *sōma* as mere form in an article, 'Die Bedeutung der "dialektischen Theologie" für die neutestamentliche Wissenschaft', *Theologische Blätter* 7 (1928) 57–67, he interprets *sōma* in terms of an I–Thou relationship with God:

Sein [man's somatic] Sein ist nicht natur- oder substanzhaft gedacht, sondern vollzieht sich in seinem Verhalten zu Gottes Anspruch, also in seinem Handeln, sofern dies nicht als ein in der Zeit ablaufender Prozess (wie der Gang einer Maschine) verstanden wird, sondern als entschlossenes und verantwortliches Handeln.

But in the article entitled 'Paulus' in *RGG* 4 (2nd ed. 1930) 1019–45, esp. 1032–4, the emphasis shifts from relationship with God to relationship with others and oneself in a world which is a 'how (Wie)', not a 'what (Was)':

...'Leib' für P. nicht 'Form' bedeutet, sondern den ganzen Menschen bezeichnet, und zwar insofern der Mensch für andere wie für sich selbst Gegenstand der Betrachtung und Objekt eines Tuns sein kann...'Leib' ist der Mensch in seiner Zeitlichkeit und Geschichtlichkeit.

Finally, in his *Theology of the New Testament*, appearing in its German original in 1948, Bultmann almost eliminates God, others, and history in a practically exclusive attention to self-relationship as the meaning of *sōma*.[1] It is important to note that this increasing withdrawal from the outside world of God, men, and events into private individualism naturally and logically follows from the desubstantializing of *sōma*. Or should we say that the desubstantializing of *sōma* is symptomatic of such withdrawal? In either case, the two go together.

At this point we may summarize the verdict of R. Jewett. For Bultmann *sōma* has lost all meaningful association with physicality. Appearances of the term in that sense lack theological significance. This reveals itself in an evasive exegesis of I Cor 6: 12–20, in which Bultmann grudgingly admits rather than interprets *sōma* as the seat of sexual activity.

[1] R. Jewett calls attention to this trajectory in Bultmann's treatment of *sōma* (*Paul's Anthropological Terms* [Leiden, 1971] 209–11).

Straining for evidence that *sōma* means 'you' or 'self', he softens appearances of the physical meaning by speaking of 'nuances' and 'fluctuations'. He can interpret *sōma* only when he thinks it is no longer physical. 'Bultmann has turned σῶμα into its virtual opposite: a symbol for that structure of individual existence which is essentially non-physical.' Although he was right to break from idealism, we should affirm against Bultmann that 'it is man as physical body – man in the physical relationships which σῶμα involves – who is encountered by a Thou in the midst of history, and it is in the bodily relationships that obedience to that Thou is required.'[1]

Thus, the ample exegetical and lexicographical evidence for a consistently physical meaning of *sōma* in Pauline literature (and elsewhere) – evidence with which we began this study – implies not only that the resurrection is physical, but, more broadly, that man cannot anticipate or determine the eternal reality of the future by evading or devaluing the material reality of the present – his own body, the bodies of others, and the objective history constituted by the mass of actions performed bodily in the material world. When concern for openness to the future negates the past in favor of viewing decision as self-relationship, it defeats its own purpose; for such introversion will withdraw from the future as well as the past. Openness to the future depends on respect for the past. Both are rooted in an interdependent combination of the dynamics of function and the substantival nature of entities. And essential among the latter is the *sōma*, man's own materiality as a means of concrete service in a material world.

To say that *sōma* is only an object is to imply that the existential relationships of a man reach their end in himself. Instrumentality, however, implies outgoingness. This, then, is a proper understanding: *sōma* is that part of man's constitution which forms his substantival instrument of performing and receiving actions. Those actions inevitably plunge him into all sorts of relationships to that which and those who are outside and – in a rebound effect – to himself. In other words, man is more than a functional complex of actions and interrelationships. He is a unity of ontological entities, spirit and body, for willing and doing (respectively) in a worldly framework. As

[1] *Ibid.*

performing and receiving actions, *sōma* is functional. But as instrument, *sōma* is also and necessarily substantival.

Upon closer inspection those scriptures which are cited to prove that *sōma* means man as the object of his own action rather indicate that *sōma* means that part of man which is the instrumental performer of his own action. Paul pommels his body not as an end in itself, but as an instrument of 'preaching to others' (I Cor 9: 27). The possible giving up of his body (I Cor 13: 3) falls under the category of Christian witness. Believers are to yield their bodies to God 'as instruments of righteousness' 'to prove what is the will of God, what is good and acceptable and perfect' (Rom 6: 12–23; 12: 1). The honoring of Christ in the body is associated with 'fruitful labor' and martyrdom in Christian service (Phil 1: 20–6; cf. 2: 16–17). And in the ruling of husband and wife over each other's bodies, the *sōma* is not just an object, but an instrument put to the service of the larger marital union.

The use of *sōma* for the instrumental performer of action rather than the object of decision breaks down the belief that Paul zealously defends resurrection of the 'body' in order to retain the authenticity of human existence through incessant decision-making in contrast to the restful contemplation of Hellenistic immortality.[1] Neither the restful contemplation of Hellenistic immortality nor the tension of Heideggerian decision-making marks the eternal state of blessedness. Rather, worshipful service to God through the instrumentality of the resurrected body characterizes that state.

But a man not only generates actions. He also receives them. Here, too, *sōma* is instrumental. It is that part of man through which he first receives actions which originate elsewhere. Synthetically, the entire man is an object. Analytically, his body is the immediate object; his inner man is the ultimate object. Spirit and body are, at the same time, both subjects or both objects, depending on whether the action goes from or comes to the man. But always *sōma* represents the instrumental part of man which expresses the spirit when the man is subject and affects the spirit when the man is object. As the conveyor to and from the spirit, the body will need to be

---

[1] Bultmann, *Theology of the New Testament* 1: 198–9; Schmithals, *Introduction*, 61.

raised for the enjoyment of blessedness as well as for the pursuance of service.[1]

E. Käsemann wishes to give the Bultmannian interpretation of *sōma* a new turn because of its failure to develop the concept of being-with-others (*Mitsein*). According to Käsemann, the meaning of *sōma* deals not so much with relationship to oneself, but with relationship to others – the world around, human beings, cosmic powers, God. *Sōma* means communication. But Bultmann's stress on *sōma* as object carries over to Käsemann's interpretation; for as *sōma* man *receives* communication. Moreover, the nature of this communication is lordship. Man is *sōma*, then, in that he is dominated by outside influences which communicate themselves to him. But to what outside influence? The answer to that question determines the character of a man's existence.[2]

To the extent that Käsemann emphasizes the reference of *sōma* to man as the object of action from the outside and deemphasizes the reference of *sōma* to man as the object of his own action, Käsemann reduces the stress of his former mentor on the activity of faith as decision in favor of accenting the passivity of faith as submission to lordship. Güttgemanns notes, however, that Bultmann and Käsemann do not entirely disagree, because Bultmann, too, sees somatic man as the object

---

[1] Outside the scope of Paul's overt statements, we might say something similar but converse about the fate of the wicked.

[2] E. Käsemann, 'Gottesdienst im Alltag der Welt' in *Judentum, Urchristentum, Kirche: Festschrift für Joachim Jeremias*, ed. W. Eltester, BZNW 26 (Berlin, 1964) 167–8; 'Anliegen und Eigenart der paulinischen Abendmahlslehre', *EvT* 7 (1947/48) 281–2; and 'On the Topic of Primitive Christian Apocalyptic', *Journal for Theology and the Church* 6 (1969) 130–3. Cf. Schunack, *Das hermeneutische Problem des Todes* (Tübingen, 1967) 22–8, esp. 25, n. 117, and K.-A. Bauer, *Leiblichkeit – das Ende aller Werke Gottes: Die Bedeutung der Leiblichkeit des Menschen bei Paulus*, Studien zum Neuen Testament 4 (Gütersloh, 1971) 39–40, where it is suggested that Bultmann has subtly imported idealistic anthropology; Neugebauer, *In Christus* (Göttingen, 1961) 52–3, n. 4; 'Die hermeneutischen Voraussetzungen Rudolf Bultmanns in ihrem Verhältnis zur paulinischen Theologie', *Kerygma und Dogma* 5 (1959) 294, 300–1, where Neugebauer charges that man's withdrawal from God into himself in Bultmannian style is exactly what needs to be broken; Macquarrie, *Existentialist Theology*, 89–100; E. Schweizer, 'Die Leiblichkeit des Menschen: Leben – Tod – Auferstehung', *EvT* 29 (1969) 40–55 = his *Beiträge zur Theologie des Neuen Testaments: Neutestamentliche Aufsätze (1955–1970)* (Zürich, 1970) 165–82.

of domination by outside powers. But for Bultmann they are hostile, with the result that domination from the outside inherently opposes the kind of self-integrated existence which is authentic. In so thinking, Bultmann overlooks that the Christian as *sōma* is dominated by the friendly outside power, Christ. And surely that domination does not oppose authentic existence.[1] But this criticism misrepresents Bultmann, for he clearly indicates that domination by Christ as an outside power integrates the self for authentic existence.[2] Käsemann and Bultmann differ, then, only in emphasis.

Desiring to correct the wrong interpretation of *sōma* in terms of private self-understanding, Käsemann stresses the reference of the term to man's possibilities of communication in and with a world of concrete realities. For this connotation the physical reality of *sōma* becomes crucial: 'the "physical" aspect of earthly existence was of decisive importance for him [Paul] and must certainly not be belittled...for Paul all God's ways with his creation begin and end in corporeality'.[3] Yet for himself Käsemann does not want to believe in a physical resurrection.[4] Therefore, although admitting the strength of Paul's teaching a physical resurrection, he subsumes that doctrine to a supposed deeper intention of Paul, viz., emphasis on the 'communion' of the kingdom in opposition to isolation from nature, society, and history. Thus a mythology concerning the raising of physical bodies at a future last day translates into a present raising up of men as Christians communicative with the world around them. It is easy to sense the tension, if not incoherence, in this treatment. On the one hand communication in a concrete world requires that *sōma* be a 'concrete piece of the world'. On the other hand *sōma* suddenly becomes solely functional in a modern understanding of somatic resurrection. We may question the legitimacy of extracting from Paul a deeper intention which completely omits the future physical resurrection which, it is admitted, lay in the forefront of his

[1] Güttgemanns, *Der leidende Apostel*, 209–10.

[2] Bultmann, *Theology of the New Testament* 1: 196, 199.

[3] E. Käsemann, *Perspectives on Paul* (Philadelphia, 1971) 18, and the following pages for what follows here. Cf. *ibid.* 114–21; and his 'On the Topic of Primitive Christian Apocalyptic', 99–133.

[4] See 'Anliegen und Eigenart', 282.

mind. If that kind of resurrection is left out, perhaps no appeal to Paul should be made.

Like most of those in the Bultmannian tradition, K. Barth limits the function of *sōma* to that of an object:

They [soul and body] are distinguished from each other as subject and object, as operation and work.[1]

In sum, if materialism with its denial of the soul makes man subjectless, spiritualism with its denial of the body makes him objectless.[2]

However, despite his giving pride of place to the functional definition of man as a being-with-God,[3] Barth's concern for concreteness of action keeps him from desubstantializing *sōma*; for apart from the physical body, the soul 'neither has form nor is it active'.[4] Consequently, the body does not victimize the soul. Somatic bounds of spatiality, visibility, and materiality do not imprison the soul, but provide it with 'a significant and ordered economy'.[5]

Barth's making the body 'unequal' to the soul in position and function, then, is both unnecessary and unfortunate.[6] It is unnecessary because in Barth's own exposition the soul and the body are equally interdependent. It is unfortunate because the term 'unequal' along with deliberate subordination of man as a substantival organism to the functional being of man[7] might easily lead to denigration of the body even though Barth affirms that the body shares with the soul in the dignity of the whole man.[8] But though Barth can talk in this manner as would a dichotomist, he thinks of himself as a holist, especially in attacking the notion of an opposition between parts of man's constitution.[9] But what if the parts are not antithetical?

A good deal of our difficulty with Barth lies in the oddity that he works with a substantival-cum-functional view of the body and a purely functional view of the soul. The body consists both in a physical organism and in activity. The soul is only functional. 'Soul is life' – thinking, willing, controlling – and

[1] *Church Dogmatics* 3/2: 398.   [2] *Ibid.* 392.
[3] *Ibid.* 55–324, and esp. the comments on 325.
[4] *Ibid.* 329–31; see also 378–9.   [5] *Ibid.* 351; see generally 350–4.
[6] *Ibid.* 338–40.   [7] *Ibid.* 325.
[8] *Ibid.* 338–40.   [9] *Ibid.* esp. 350, 379–82, 393.

nothing more.[1] Barth might be misunderstood to lapse into statements in which the soul appears as actor rather than action alone. However, he is not saying that the soul thinks, wills, and controls (as though the soul were a substantival subject), but that man *as* soul thinks, wills, and controls.[2] In other words, the soul *is* thinking, willing, and controlling – i.e., living. Since the soul is not substantival, all talk of separation of soul and body is meaningless unless that 'separation' is not meant spatially, but functionally as cessation of the thinking, willing, and controlling which *are* (not, are performed by) the soul.[3]

A functional soul needs a functional body as a counterpart. Barth has provided that in his functional interpretation of the body as service.[4] But his additional emphasis on the materiality of the body has as a logical concomitant a substantival soul (or spirit). Barth has *not* provided that. Both soul and body should receive substantival and existentialist interpretations in combination. As it is, Barth's treatment is incoherent: although the soul as existential life has the body as existential service, the body as a substantival organ lacks a substantival 'organist' since the soul is only the function of living.[5]

We may applaud, therefore, the theocentricity of Barth's functional definition of man as first and foremost a being-with-God as an improvement upon the definitions of man which regard him too individualistically as a being-with-himself and, better but too generally and humanistically, as a being-with-others. And we may commend the emphases on the unity of the body and the soul, on the physicalness of the body, and on the function of the body in service to the soul. We regret, however, that Barth did not carry out his coordination of the substantival and the functional in the matter of the soul as well as in that of the body.

We may sharpen slightly the theocentricity of Barth's functional definition of man – and gain a Biblical, Pauline emphasis at the same time – by saying that man is a being-for-God. *For* God, not simply *with* God, because service for God is the

[1] *Ibid.* 424.
[2] *Ibid.* 394–436.
[3] Cf. *ibid.* 327, 350, 370, 380–2, 393.
[4] *Ibid.* 418–36.
[5] As applied to the soul, of course, the term 'substantival' does not connote physical substance, but carries its philosophical meaning.

telos of fellowship with God rather than vice versa. Had it been the other way round, God would not have needed to create man with a physical body in a material world. Such a creation makes sense only if service for God is primary. Fellowship with God, because he is spiritual and not physical, would have required only bodiless spirits.

Functionally, man as spirit initiates and receives actions, and as body he mediates those actions as they go and come. Substantively, man is a duality – i.e., a proper unity of two parts – of spirit and body.[1] The spirit is that part which bears his consciousness and cognate features. The body is that part through the instrumentality of which man lives in the material and eventful world.[2]

This assessment of Pauline and generally Biblical anthropology harmonizes with the philosophical theory of intercommunication between soul (we may prefer 'spirit') and body. Barth asks how under that theory 'real man' can be on both sides and still be the subject of competitive activity.[3] This objection rests, however, on the false notion that soul and body compete with each other. They do so only with the intrusion of sin. Even then the body is only weak, not sinful *per se*, and the soul may be as sinful as the body is weak. As such, soul and body are not competitive, but mutally supportive. Thus 'real man' has no difficulty in being on both sides. The duality is friendly, not antagonistic.

Without God, as Barth says, the philosophical theory of intercommunication between soul and body is 'ghostly'.[4] But here, the philosophical vice is a theological virtue. Only the creative effort and sustaining power of God bring and hold the corporeal and incorporeal together in active, meaningful

---

[1] On this, see K. Rahner, 'The Unity of Spirit and Matter in the Christian Understanding of Faith', *Theological Investigations*, vi, *Concerning Vatican Council II* (Baltimore, 1969) 153–77, esp. 169. Rahner elsewhere seems to give ground to a spiritualized resurrection by accepting the holistic definition of *sōma* ('Resurrection', *Sacramentum Mundi: An Encyclopedia of Theology* [New York, 1970] 5: 330).

[2] Cf. the admirable way in which Lys holds together substance and function as necessary to each other in his section entitled, 'Existence et Essence' (*Nèphèsh* [Paris, 1959] 29–33). This recognition should have led him away from a monadic view of man.

[3] *Church Dogmatics* 3/2: 428–9.

[4] *Ibid.* 429–30.

relationship.[1] Thus God is an anthropological necessity, and an immediate one at that. He truly possesses the power of life and death. In monadic anthropologies God tends to become an unnecessary encumbrance, or at best only a distant necessity. For to the extent that man is basically just one substance or just one function, he needs nothing from the outside to be himself. This is true of Bultmannian anthropology: *sōma* is the whole man in self-relationship. Why then God? He is anthropologically superfluous.[2]

Even Barth is somewhat exposed to this criticism, for in his definition of man as a being-with-God, God seems to be an assertion rather than a necessity. What in the constitution of man requires God to be there with man? But in that man exists as a unity of two substances, spirit and body, he requires the cohesive force of God for true and full being. Käsemann has seen that there is no way to bind a substantival body and a substantival soul together except by mythological speculation.[3] For mythological speculation, we might prefer God. But the point is the same. A dichotomous distinction within man requires a cohesive force from the outside. And *pace* Käsemann, that is good, for it fuses anthropology and theology. Insofar as theology and anthropology dovetail in this manner, then, our view of man receives confirmation.

In sum, the consistently substantival meaning of the term *sōma* protects the functional element proper to the term. That element consists in the instrumental function of the physical body, a function necessary to human existence. Consequently, *sōma* bars asceticism and mysticism, withdrawal from history and society. Spiritualizing idealism, romanticism, introvertive existentialism – somatic anthropology excludes them.[4] Posi-

---

[1] Hence, the unity of spirit and body is not 'accidental', *pace* Barth, *ibid.* 611.

[2] Cf. Barth's stricture that existentialist anthropology needs no transcendence (*ibid.* 118–21); also K.-A. Bauer, *Leiblichkeit*, 41–2. K. Stalder notes that although God has a relationship to himself, he is not *sōma*, and that although a plant is *sōma*, it does not have a relationship to itself (*Das Werk des Geistes in der Heiligung bei Paulus* [Zürich, 1962] 57–8).

[3] *Leib.* In his more recent writings Käsemann has emphasized the substantival nature of *sōma* as part of the concrete world but still avoids 'mythological speculation' by seeing in the term a holistic reference.

[4] See the trenchant remarks, from a systematic theological standpoint, of P. H. Jørgensen, *Die Bedeutung des Subjekt–Objektverhältnisses für die*

tively, the physicalness of *sōma* affirms life in a material world and our responsibility for it. We do not escape non-Christian materialism by flight, but through sanctification. By assuring the importance of materiality in the future through physical resurrection, *sōma* insures the importance of materiality in the present. Thus theology retains its this-worldly relevance along with its other-worldly hope.

Theologie: Der Theo-onto-logische Konflikt mit der Existenzphilosophie, Theologische Forschung 46 (Hamburg–Bergstedt, 1967) 230–49 ('Die Nähe der Existenzphilosophie zur Mystik'), 289–332 ('Die Nähe der Existenztheologie zur Mystik').

CHAPTER 15

Sōma, Sin, and Salvation

On the one hand, *sōma* consistently refers to a physical entity, and, on the other hand, Paul can designate it 'the body of sin' (Rom 6: 6) and associate it with the 'flesh' in a sinful sense (Rom 8: 4–13). A question naturally arises concerning the relationship between *sōma,* sin, and salvation from sin.

In the nineteenth century C. Holsten[1] and H. Lüdemann,[2] continuing a line of F. C. Baur, propounded the view that under heavy influence from Hellenistic thought Paul saw the physical body as inherently evil and salvation as deliverance from that body.[3] As with the views of those scholars concerning Paul's doctrine of bodily resurrection, it is now commonly agreed that they vastly overestimated Hellenistic influence on Paul, underestimated the force of his Judaistic background, and engaged in minimizing exegesis of the numerous Pauline passages where the physical body appears positively as the temple of the Holy Spirit, an object of sanctification, and an instrument of righteousness – to say nothing of its destined resurrection, already discussed here. Conversely, they over-interpreted those passages where Paul associates the body and sin by transmuting the association into an equation. Paul writes of the body only as the victim of sin, not as the origin of sin. These scholars mistook the influence of nineteenth century idealism *on them* for Hellenistic influence on Paul. Hence, their view is largely and rightfully disregarded nowadays.

But philosophical influence on historico-critical exegesis was not to be denied. (Nor should it be within the bounds of fidelity to the original intent of Paul.) In his existentialist analysis of man as *sōma* – i.e., of man-objectifying-himself –

[1] *Zum Evangelium des Paulus und des Petrus* (Rostock, 1868).
[2] *Die Anthropologie des Apostels Paulus und ihre Stellung innerhalb seiner Heilslehre* (Kiel, 1872).
[3] This line reaches its true end in H. J. Holtzmann, *Lehrbuch der Neutestamentlichen Theologie,* 2nd ed. (Tübingen, 1911) 2: 12ff., 29–30, 42ff. But cf., more recently, J. Klausner, *From Jesus to Paul* (Boston, 1961 reprint) 486–95, 521–2.

Bultmann raises two possibilities which relate to the concept of sin: (1) being at one with oneself, or self-integration; (2) being at odds with oneself, or self-estrangement. Self-integration constitutes authentic existence; self-estrangement constitutes inauthentic existence.[1] Again, Heideggerian forms of thought and expression rise to the surface, since for Heidegger man as being-in-the-world exists in being related to himself, and his existence may be either authentic or inauthentic.[2]

Bultmann goes further. Self-estrangement leads to two additional possibilities: (1) domination by hostile powers outside oneself, with resultant aggravation of self-estrangement; (2) domination by a friendly power outside oneself, with resultant self-reconciliation.[3] Sin becomes self-estrangement – i.e. losing one's grip on oneself – by the choosing of the false securities of the created world (including man himself) which is at one's disposal. Salvation becomes self-control through faith in God despite the insecurity of his not being at one's disposal.[4] In all of this *sōma* plays the key role in its supposed designation of man as his own object in relation to whom he makes choices and as the object whom outside powers dominate when he separates himself from his own best interests.

We may begin our own line of thought by noting that the definition of *sōma* solely as the object-self leads to an over-emphasis on sin as an *outside* power. Though this is an actual consequence of the definition, it is not a necessary consequence, for sin might originate within the subject-self just as well as outside; yet the object-self might still be objective. To a limited extent Bultmann does recognize the inner origin of sin in Pauline thought. Nevertheless, his major point of emphasis, his understanding of Paul's distinctive view, and his assessment of what is relevant to contemporary theology all hinge on the notion of sin as a force pressing in on man from the outside.[5]

---

[1] R. Bultmann, *Theology of the New Testament* (New York, 1951) 1: 195–6.

[2] M. Heidegger, *Being and Time* (London, 1962) *passim*; J. Macquarrie, *An Existentialist Theology* (London, 1955) 40–6.

[3] See also Bultmann, *Theology of the New Testament* 1: 244–5, 254–9.

[4] *Ibid.* 227, 230–46.

[5] Cf. J. Kallas, *The Satanward View* (Philadelphia, 1966), 53–72, for statistical arguments that deliverance from sin as an outside power predominates over forgiveness of sin as inner guilt. Kallas does not pay enough attention to the fact that Paul's two great and lengthy discussions of

To be sure, Paul does write, 'So then it is no longer I that do it ["what I do not want"], but sin which dwells within me ...Now if I do what I do not want, it is no longer I that do it, but sin which dwells within me' (Rom 7: 17, 20). However, although it is 'not I' who sins, but 'sin', it is sin 'which dwells *within me*'. And the 'law of sin' resides *'in my members'* (v. 23). This inwardness of sin might be explained as the invasion of an alien power so fundamentally separate from the person that the person cannot be held accountable. That cannot be so, however, because the 'no condemnation' lies, not in the excusing of man's sin as the product of an alien power, but in the liberation of man from the sinful proclivity *which is his own* (Rom 8: 1–17).

Sin is an outside power only in that it *should* not belong to human nature and in that its force mystifies the 'I'. On the other hand, sin is so wrongfully part and parcel of human nature that man incurs guilt. Man as *victim* of his own wrong-doing needs deliverance by redemptive power. Man as *perpetrator* of his own wrongdoing needs justification on the basis of sacrificial atonement. Bultmann stresses redemptive deliverance from sin as an outside power at the expense of sacrificial atonement for sin as culpable wrongdoing. He desires to avoid the *sacrificium intellectus* of accepting the 'primitive' notion of sacrificial atonement.[1]

In support of the position that release from guilt concerns Paul very little 'whereas the important thing for Paul is release from *sinning*, release from the power of sin', Bultmann assigns the 'forgiveness' of sins in Col 1: 14 and Eph 1: 7 to deutero-Pauline literature. Of course, this will not convince those who on other grounds believe Paul to have authored one or both of these epistles. Bultmann also notes that the beatitude 'Blessed are those whose iniquities are forgiven, and whose sins are covered; blessed is the man against whom the Lord will not reckon his sin' (Rom 4: 7–8) is 'only in the quotation from Ps. 32: 1'. And God's 'passing over former sins' occurs 'only

soteriology in terms of justification – in Galatians and Romans – imply that the human problem is prominently one of guilt. For a balanced account, see G. Delling, 'Der Tod Jesu in der Verkündigung des Paulus', *Apophoreta: Festschrift für Ernst Haenchen*, BZNW 30 (Berlin, 1964) 85–96.

[1] So Bultmann, 'New Testament and Mythology' in H. W. Bartsch (ed.), *Kerygma and Myth* (New York, 1961) 7.

in Rom. 3: 25' and is 'a phrase probably based on a traditional formula.'[1]

On the other hand, we may ask why Paul bothered to quote the Davidic beatitude – especially since it mentions neither righteousness, faith, nor works, the topics under discussion – if he did not regard the problem of juristic guilt (in distinction from enslavement to sin as an outside power) as the nub of justification. We may ask the same kind of question concerning Rom 3: 25. Even though God's passing over former sins might derive from a traditional formula, Paul was under no duress to use, at a crucially pivotal juncture in his argument, a formula the theology of which little exercised him.

Also, it is clearly evident that in the lengthy discussion of human sinfulness beginning at 1: 18 Paul consistently stresses guilt for sin even more than enslavement to sin. Men 'suppress the truth' though they know better; consequently 'they are without excuse' (1: 18–20). 'Although they knew God they did not honor him as God or give thanks to him' (1: 21). God's abandonment of them to evil comes not by the attack of sin from without, but by the choice of evil within. Paul's discussion proceeds in this vein until it reaches a climax in the statements that the law speaks 'so that every mouth may be stopped, and the whole world may be held accountable to God', 'since all have sinned and fall short of the glory of God' (3: 19, 23). Quite apart from snatches derived from traditional formulae, then, Paul himself relates justification to sin as guilt which needs atonement. Besides, it is difficult to relate justification, which at the very least includes the reckoning of righteousness, directly to anything other than sin as guilt. Only through atonement does justification relate to redemption from sin as enslavement. Thus, God put forward Jesus as a *hilastērion* consisting 'in his blood' (or as a *hilastērion* to be received 'through faith in his blood' – 3: 25).[2]

Further statements of Paul confirm an emphasis on the priority of guilt and atonement over enslavement and redemp-

[1] For these statements, see Bultmann, *Theology of the New Testament* 1: 287.
[2] The necessity of treating sin as guilt stands firm whether we take *hilastērion* as expiation or propitiation, whether we interpret justification solely as a reckoning of righteousness, or additionally as a making righteous, or simply as forgiveness.

tion in the doctrine of justification: 'It [faith] will be reckoned [for righteousness] to us who believe in him that raised from the dead Jesus our Lord, *who was put to death for our trespasses* and raised for our justification' (4: 24–5); 'Christ died for the ungodly...while we were yet sinners Christ died for us... we are now justified by his blood' (5: 6–11, excerpts). Cf. the juristic tone of 5: 12–21 and Gal 3: 13, where redemption rests on a juristic solution to the problem of guilt: 'Christ redeemed us from the curse of the law, having become a curse for us – for it is written, "Cursed be every one who hangs on a tree." ' See also II Cor 5: 19, 21: 'God was in Christ reconciling the world to himself, not counting their trespasses against them...For our sake he made him to be sin who knew no sin, so that in him we might become the righteousness of God.' Cf. Gal 1: 4; 2: 20; Rom 8: 3, 32; 14: 15; I Cor 5: 7; 11: 24–5; 15: 3; I Thes 5: 10. The infrequency of the term 'forgiveness' therefore provides inadequate support for a downgrading of sin as guilt which needs atonement.

Not totally overlooking the concept of sin as guilt, Bultmann recognizes that in Paul sin is rebellion against God and guilt toward God.[1] Yet for Bultmann sin as guilt and rebellion relates not so much to divinely established ethical norms as to divinely commanded self-integration. Therefore the mere use of the terms 'guilt' and 'rebellion' does not blunt the edge of the criticism that he utilizes his existentialist interpretation of *sōma* to weaken sin as culpable transgression in the ethical sphere and to promote the concept of sin as existential loss of self-control. And to the degree that sin becomes existential loss of self-control to the neglect of moral perversion issuing in concrete transgressions, 'guilt' becomes less blameworthy.

Hence, man is 'victimized',[2] and the strong meat of Paul's discussion of mankind's involvement in Adam's sin is 'obscure', 'unintelligible', and 'unquestionably' due in large measure to 'the influence of the Gnostic myth'. Moreover, 'mankind is not itself responsible' for the curse. Concerning it, we 'have no right to speak of guilt in the ethical sense'.[3] These remarks veer from the Pauline and traditional concept of guilt. Thus, although death is punishment for sin, 'Paul's thoughts...

---

[1] Bultmann, *Theology of the New Testament* 1: 228, 232–46, 250–3.
[2] *Ibid.* 248.   [3] *Ibid.* 251–2.

lead beyond this traditional juristic conception'[1] into the conception that death is an organic, as opposed to juristic, outcome of sin: sin as the self's division and surrender of itself (*sōma*) to the transitory world with the result that the somatic self increasingly becomes an object among objects to the point of death, which simply completes the procession from the being of a man (*Existenz*) to the being of a thing (*Vorhandensein*).[2] Bultmann sees no harmony between the juristic and organic conceptions of sin and death.[3] It becomes obvious where his preference lies when in his discussion of 'Sin and Death' he devotes one passing paragraph to the juristic view, but seven to the organic view.[4]

Later Bultmann does come to admit the presence of numerous Pauline statements 'which understand Jesus' death in terms of Jewish sacrificial practice – and that also means in terms of the juristic thinking that dominated it – regarding his death as a propitiatory sacrifice by which forgiveness of sins is brought about; which is to say: by which the guilt contracted by sins is canceled'.[5] But making no secret of his dislike for this motif, he passes it off as 'juristic' and 'cultic'. It derives from 'Jewish sacrificial practice', the 'liturgy' and 'tradition' of the early church, and especially the tradition which was 'widespread in Hellenistic Christianity'. 'Paul is in part quoting or paraphrasing the crystallized formulations of this tradition.' However, they do 'not contain Paul's characteristic view'.

The essential thing, then, is that here the categories of cultic–juristic thinking are broken through: *Christ's death* is not merely a sacrifice which cancels the guilt of sin (i.e. the punishment contracted by sinning), but is also *the means of release from the powers of this age: Law, Sin, and Death.*[6]

And so, where Paul puts juristic guilt and atonement ahead of existential enslavement and redemption in a tandem relationship, Bultmann breaks them apart and thrusts aside the juristic in favor of the other as Paul's ultimate intent, which alone provides a handle for contemporary theology. At the core of this

---

[1] *Ibid.* 246; see also 247–8.

[2] *Ibid.* 249. See also Macquarrie, *Existentialist Theology*, 123–4.

[3] Bultmann, *Theology of the New Testament* 1: 249.

[4] *Ibid.* 246–9. The introductory and concluding paragraphs are excluded from the count.   [5] *Ibid.* 295.   [6] *Ibid.* 295–8. Italics are Bultmann's.

interpretation lies *sōma*, supposedly the object-self, man the unfortunate victim, as opposed to the subject-self, man the perverse doer. However, if *sōma* does not delimit man as the object-self alone, but encompasses the substantivally instrumental man as doer as well as receiver, the concepts of guilt and atonement need to be retained. Any downgrading of them will not fairly represent Pauline thought.

Put in a slightly different manner, failure to see *sōma* as in part the instrumental subject of sinful actions originating in the inner man[1] enables Bultmann to minimize human sin as guilt which needs atonement. However, since the body, like the spirit and like the whole man in his duality, is both a subject and an object, both the viewpoints concerning human sinfulness as juristic guilt and as existential enslavement hold true. Where older exegetes may have underplayed enslavement and redemption of the object-self, Bultmann underplays the depravity of the subject-self and the provision of atonement necessary to salvation.

We can see the same tendency to excuse man's sin in the development of Heideggerian anthropology by Macquarrie. He argues that belief in God as Creator overcomes the despair in Heidegger's absolute dualism of facticity (man's imprisonment in the alien being of the world) and possibility (man's responsibility to choose between possibilities). Both aspects have their common ground in God, as indicated in Gen 2: 7: 'then the Lord God formed man of the dust from the ground [= facticity], and breathed into his nostrils the breath of life [= possibility]'.[2] The point is well taken.

Unfortunately, Macquarrie proceeds to existentialize the dust from the ground and the breath of life as ways of being rather than substances. What was gained by appeal to Gen 2: 7 is thus lost by the desubstantialization of man, because the physical world remains basically alien and the physical body basically constrictive. Blame for the frustrations of human existence tends to revert to our 'thrownness' into an alien world and body.

---

[1] This failure comes out very clearly in Bultmann's insistence that in Rom 6: 12 and 8: 13 *sōma* is the object of the outside power of the flesh rather than the instrumental subject which carries out sinful actions initiated by the inner man (*ibid.* 200; see above, p. 188).

[2] Macquarrie, *Existentialist Theology*, 82–9.

Despite affirmation of human responsibility, guilt tends to become the result of limitation instead of perversity: 'Sin is made possible and there is the standing temptation to sin *because he* [man] *is in the world, because his being is constituted* not only by the "inward man" but also *by the "members"* [= body in context].'[1] On the other hand, if we attribute theological importance to the physical nature of the human constitution and the world around as creations of God, man does not become alien to the world. Nor does the world become constrictive to him. Only through human perversity do they become antagonistic to each other. The physical body and the material world remain essentially suitable to human existence, action, and fulfilment.

Concerning the relationship between sin and death, the instrumentality of the physical *sōma* enables us to harmonize the juristic and organic views of sin and death. Death is an inflicted penalty, but it is also a natural outgrowth of sin in that sin as a disobedient withdrawal from service for God reaches its suitable end in the loss of ability to serve God concretely in the world of men and events. That loss consists in the separation of body and spirit at death, a separation which deprives the body of animation and the spirit of means of action.

The illegitimacy of the attempt to limit *sōma* to the existential object-self appears rather surprisingly in an inconsistency of treatment of the inner dividedness depicted in Rom 7: 14–25. In one place Bultmann explains the passage in terms of a split between the subject-self and the *sōma*, the object-self.[2] In another place he correctly discerns that the split has to do with two selves which are *both* subjects: since both selves are 'opposed to each other in regard to "willing", then it is apparent that the subject-self, the true self of a man, is inwardly split'.[3] Exactly so. The trouble with the sinner is not that his object-self has split off from his subject-self, but that his subject-self is split between wanting the good and doing the bad. And the

---

[1] *Ibid.* 88 (italics supplied). Cf. Macquarrie's statement that 'man is discontinuous in his being with nature' (*ibid.* 98). Such a statement is possible only by dematerializing *sōma*. Of course, man is more than 'nature', but he is hardly discontinuous with nature. Otherwise, we have true reason to despair.

[2] Bultmann, *Theology of the New Testament* 1: 200–1.   [3] *Ibid.* 245.

difference between wanting and doing does not derive from the difference between spirit and body[1] – whether considered substantivally or functionally. Rather, the whole man is divided. Both spirit and body together want the good but do the bad. The *sōma* as object-self is not the key, for it, too, is subject – instrumentally so – just as the spirit is also object – terminally so. In sin as in righteousness both spirit and body are both subject and object, substantivally and functionally. The difference between them lies in their respective ultimacy and instrumentality.

Where is God in the conception of sin as alienation of the somatic self? He is behind the broken commandment to live authentically, i.e., integratedly with the somatic self. But that commandment has little if anything to do with the ethical character of God himself. At least Bultmann fails to relate self-integration to the ethical character of God. And it would seem that by definition self-integration tends to shut out God from an inner relationship to sin. For one could be alienated from his self without the entrance of another party into the picture.

Therefore, despite statements concerning man's placement before God in the responsibility of decision, God seems to be an unnecessary adjunct to the concept of sin as self-alienation. We cannot merely tack God on as the prohibitor of self-alienation. *Why* does he prohibit self-alienation? If the reason lies within his ethical character, then the basic nature of sin consists in ethical alienation of the whole man, spirit and body together, from God rather than in existential alienation of a somatic object-self from a subject-self. Then existential separation within the human being becomes consequent upon ethical separation from God instead of requisite to it. In other words, ethical separation from God is primary to a proper concept of sin; existential separation within man's being is secondary.

With reference to this secondary separation, the dividing line within man's being does not run between the subject-self and the object-self, but throughout each, with the result that subjective man, spirit and body, wants to *do* the good and does the evil, and objective man, spirit and body, wants to *receive* the good and receives the evil. In the name of *sōma*, Bultmann

---

[1] This remains true even though the needs and desires of the body become a bridgehead for sin, as in Romans 7 and elsewhere.

exalts existential separation within man's being at the expense of ethical separation from God and by that much makes God extrinsic to the nature of sin. But if *sōma* receives its proper interpretation as the physical instrument by which man performs and receives actions, the way is open to see sin, vis-à-vis the ethical character of God, as moral perversity of the spirit expressed by the body in acts of rebellion against God – as opposed to moral virtue of the spirit expressed by the body in acts of service for God.

Without saying so explicitly, we have just been discussing sin as guilt. But a proper understanding of *sōma* also affects the way we look at sin as slave-service. If *sōma* is not the existential object-self, alienation from the self and consequent enslavement to hostile powers do not follow. On the contrary, in this aspect sin is first and foremost slave-service *to oneself* – quite the opposite of alienation from oneself – over against slave-service to God, which is true freedom in its being the carrying out of God's intent for man. (We may regard freedom as fulfilment of divine creative intent and thus of divinely created potential.)

Ironically, this self-service, which is sin, sounds very much like that which Bultmann sees as the true calling of man: man 'is a being to whom what matters and should matter is his "life"', his self...Man [is] called to selfhood'.[1] This call to selfhood can be distinguished from self-service only by making the pursuit of selfhood secondary, i.e., a means of glorifying God. But Bultmann's anthropological theology prohibits such a move, nor does Bultmann make it. Self-service and the pursuit of selfhood remain indistinguishable and proper goals.

Not self-service, therefore, but self-reliance is wrong to Bultmann.[2] Anthropology has here devoured theology. Service to self *is* sinful, and truly enslaves. Service for God is good, and truly liberates. The outside powers which are hostile come in only as they are put to the service of the self; i.e., they are 'used' by the self for the self and become objects of worship and terror only in so far as they are needed for selfish ends.

Thus, in the matter of sin, the basic hostility arises not between malevolent powers and the self, but between an ethical God and the self. In service for God with spirit and body, man might have experienced freedom. But in service for self with

---

[1] Bultmann, *Theology of the New Testament* 1: 246.   [2] *Ibid.* 239–46.

spirit and body, man experiences thralldom, primarily to his own lusts and secondarily to outside powers which promise satisfaction of those lusts. God overcomes the hostility arising from ethical rebellion by providing atonement. He likewise overcomes the thralldom arising from self-service by providing his Spirit. The resurrection of Christ forms the link between the atonement and the gift of the Spirit. It is the bodily resurrection of Christ which assures the adequacy of the atonement on the one hand and enables the transmission of the Spirit on the other hand. Hence, salvation consists in reconciliation to God *before* (but not to the exclusion of) reconciliation to one's self.

We have seen that God is not essential to the Bultmannian view of sin. It is not surprising, then, that neither is he essential to the Bultmannian view of salvation. If salvation is the counterpart to sin and sin is separation of the object-self from one's own control, salvation ought to consist in the gaining of self-control. So in his treatment of faith Bultmann puts primary emphasis on obedience instead of trust.[1] All of this runs toward salvation by self-reliant attempts to take one's self in tow, something akin to Heidegger's salvation by conscience, i.e., by the call of the authentic self to the fallen self.[2] At least this would be the logical outcome. But, of course, the Pauline attack upon self-reliance and the Lutheranism of Bultmann prevent his traveling that route. Yet we may still ask with C. W. Kegley whether, if Heidegger's analysis of human existence is accurate, talk of faith, revelation, and grace may be unnecessary, irrelevant, obscurantist, or all three: 'Is not Bultmann's characteristically evangelical emphasis on faith, grace, and the revelation in Jesus Christ a kind of unnecessary encumbrance?'[3]

---

[1] *Ibid.* 314–17, 322–4.

[2] Heidegger, *Being and Time*, 312–48; cf. Macquarrie, *Existentialist Theology*, 128–31, 138–9, 141–53.

[3] *'Preface'*, *The Theology of Rudolf Bultmann*, ed. C. W. Kegley (New York, 1966) xv–xvi. Cf. Neugebauer's lengthy criticism that Bultmann double-talks in accepting the Pauline emphasis on divine action in salvation, especially predestination, while pressing an existentialist emphasis on human decision. This criticism does not simply drag out the old problem of reconciling divine sovereignty and human responsibility, but questions whether Bultmann too facilely skirts the problem by eliminating divine sovereignty without knowing he has done so ('Die hermeneutischen Voraussetzungen Rudolf Bultmanns', *Kerygma und Dogma* 5 [1959] 300–2).

To avoid salvation by self-reliant attempts to reconcile the subject-self and the object-self, appeal may be made to the sinner's inability on account of domination by hostile outside powers. We would then be bound to say that were it not for those outside powers man could reconcile himself to himself without the help of God. In that case, the divine action in saving men is demanded only by the hostility of outside powers. By itself, human sinfulness would require only human action. But this conclusion runs counter to the Pauline view that because of his own depravity even more than because of domination by outside powers, man cannot save himself. Such an un-Pauline conclusion concerning salvation is avoidable only by reinstituting the view that sin is ethical separation from God through human depravity rather than existential separation of the subject-self and the object-self through domination by outside powers.

On the other hand, Bultmann sees bad theology lurking as a danger within the 'original naive' meaning of *sōma* as the physical body. It is that man misunderstands 'his relationship to himself as that between his self and a totally foreign being, a "not-I". In such misunderstanding...the "double" to which the self is bound is regarded to be the material body. That is the understanding of the self that is found in (Gnostic) dualism, according to which man's self is imprisoned in the body...And this dualism's attitude in practical life is mysticism and asceticism...' Thus, Bultmann warns that to give theological significance to the physical, as opposed to the existential, meaning of *sōma* plunges us into the error of Gnostic-like dualism.[1]

However, that error does not consist in regarding the physical *sōma* as theologically significant, but in regarding its theological significance as negative (the body is inferior, foreign, sinful *per se*) through lack of a proper doctrine of creation. Theological significance might run in the opposite direction, too, and in this case ought to do so because of the doctrine of creation. In other words, the real error in Hellenistic thought does not lie in the distinction between body and soul. It lies in an unnecessary denigration of the body, which leads to its being regarded as unessential and undesirable.

---

[1] Bultmann, *Theology of the New Testament* 1: 199.

Dualism provides, not the source of this denigration, but only its occasion. The source is the problem of evil and its conquest: why does man have so many wrong passions and how is he to master them? The Hellenistic answer – allowed by the lack of a doctrine of creation – is to locate evil in the body, place the immediate (if not ultimate) blame on physical needs and desires,[1] deny or satisfy those needs and desires (asceticism and libertinism, respectively) in order to free the soul for higher pursuits, and wait for the demise of the body as unessential for any future existence there might be. Thus the problem of human evil is facilely 'solved' by placing that evil in a part of the human make-up which is unessential to human being. For the libertine this opens a way of salvation by escape from moral responsibility. For the ascetic it demands salvation by self-abnegation. The Pauline answer is to locate evil throughout the whole man, willing spirit and acting body alike, provide forgiving grace for human guilt through Christ's atonement and overcoming power through the Spirit, demand sanctified service for God from the whole man, both intentional spirit and instrumental body, and look forward to the glory of the resurrection/translation.

[1] This general statement needs qualification. Plato was capable of locating evil in the soul as well as the body (*Phaedrus* 246–57; *Respublica* 439–41). Nevertheless, he more strongly emphasizes the body as the source of the soul's infections and impediments (*Phaedo* 64–8; cf. *Timaeus* 86). And in Hellenistic times popular thought put heavy responsibility for evil upon the body. See D. R. G. Owen, *Body and Soul* (Philadelphia, 1956) 52–62, for the church fathers' railing against non-Christians for their facilely blaming sin on the physical body.

CHAPTER 16

Sōma, Individuality, and Solidarity

Sōma carries weighty implications concerning the old problem of the one and the many. We have seen that Bultmann's existentialist interpretation of *sōma* as the object-self leads into a private individualism. At the other end of the spectrum we find J. A. T. Robinson. In the name of Hebraic thought, he inveighs against the notion of individualism in the term *sōma* and presses for solidarity as the keynote. In going from Bultmann to Robinson, then, we pass from somatic individualism to somatic socialism. Finally we shall find a middle way which does justice to the merits of both viewpoints.

Robinson begins by claiming that the Hebrews did not, as the Greeks did, think of the body as the boundary of individuation which marks off and isolates one man from another. A man's person does not stop at his fingertips. This is shown, it is reasoned, by the fact that the Hebrews did not even have a word for the body. Rather, the word which they did use – 'flesh' (בשר) – indicates that which binds a man together 'in the bundle of life with all men and nature, so that he could never make his unique answer to God as an isolated individual, apart from his relation to his neighbor. The *basar* [later called "non-individuating 'flesh'"] continued, even in the age of greater religious individualism, to represent the fact that personality is essentially social.'[1] In other words, the Hebrews did not think in terms of bodies of individuals, but in terms of the flesh which mankind as a whole shares. Where individuality came into view, its locus did not appear at the point of difference between two bodies, but at the point of the individual responsibility of each man to God (Jer 31: 29–30; Ezekiel 18; Deut 24: 16).

At the same time, the Hebrews thought of the flesh in very physical terms – *psycho*physical, to be sure, but definitely physical. In fact, it is the common share in the materiality of being

[1] J. A. T. Robinson, *The Body: A Study in Pauline Theology*, SBT 1/5 (London, 1952) 15; see also 21.

217   8-2

flesh which 'ties men up with each other, rather than what separates them as individuals'.[1] Not only is physical individuality lost to the common materiality of all mankind; it is also lost to the common materiality of 'nature', or 'the rest of creation'.[2]

Since Paul frequently uses *sōma* where an OT writer would use בשר and interchanges *sōma* and the Greek equivalent for בשר, viz., *sarx*, it is evident at least initially that for Paul *sōma* indicates solidarity rather than individuality. Now, 'flesh' denotes man in his weakness and consequent subjection to the powers of sin and death. Because of its synonymy, *sōma* can do the same. But it is not *bound* to do so. The body may be weak and subject to sin and death. On the other hand, it may be strong through the Spirit and in the might of resurrection. Thus, 'while σάρξ stands for man, in the solidarity of creation, in his distance from God, σῶμα stands for man, in the solidarity of creation, as made for God'.[3]

However, the very foundation of the foregoing argument – viz., the claimed connotation of solidarity rather than individuality in the Hebraic use of 'flesh' – is weak. In our discussion of anthropological duality in the OT we noted that the Hebrews did possess the concept of the human body, living as well as dead. For that concept they used (among other words) גויה and, above all, בשר. We further noted that in a large number of passages בשר denotes the human body as an individual organism, and can be taken in no other way. Consequently, even though the Pauline use of *sōma* may derive from the Hebraic use of בשר, the latter use does not necessarily favor solidarity or militate against individuation. At that point the question remains open precisely because בשר may connote solidarity or individuation with equal ease. Therefore, the same goes for *sōma* – and *sarx*, we might add, for both Greek words appear in the LXX for בשר.

[1] *Ibid.* 29.

[2] *Ibid.* 15 and 30, respectively; cf. Schlatter's similar but scattered statements as rehearsed by K.-A. Bauer, *Leiblichkeit – das Ende aller Werke Gottes* (Gütersloh, 1971) 13–30.

[3] Robinson, *The Body*, 31; see also 29–33; E. Schweizer, 'σῶμα κτλ.', *TDNT* 7 (1971) 1062–6. Stacey praises Robinson's 'great contribution' and 'discovery' that 'in a true Hebrew fashion, there is a sense of corporateness behind every use of σῶμα in Paul' (Stacey, *The Pauline View of Man* [London, 1956] 188).

We may go further than that. It is well recognized that in non-Semitic Greek *sōma* is associated with *horismos* as denoting the physical boundary of the individual. But did the Hebrew use of בשר turn the corresponding use of *sōma* in Semitic Greek (here, specifically Pauline Greek) from individuation to solidarity? In the LXX the appearances of *sōma* for בשר ought to provide a clue. They do. In every instance where *sōma* stands for בשר, the meaning of the Hebrew word is not flesh as shared substance, but flesh as the body of an individual.[1] We come to the conclusion that in Semitic Greek *sōma* did not lose its individuating force, for בשר *may* individuate and always *does* where the translators of the LXX put *sōma* for it.

It therefore over-interprets II Cor 5: 6 to say that an expression such as ' "at home in the body"...means "in the solidarities and securities of earthly existence" '.[2] 'In the body' bears no necessary relationship to solidarities and securities. The phrase simply denotes the dwelling of the soul, or spirit, in the body, in contrast to their separation at death. It similarly over-interprets Heb 13: 3, 'Remember those who are in prison, as though in prison with them; and those who are ill-treated, since you also are in the body', to comment, 'The body is that which joins all people, irrespective of individual differences, in life's bundle together.'[3] The author of Hebrews does not have in mind a kind of ontological unity of mankind, but the simple thought that as individuals we all have bodies and therefore can, and should, sympathize with those who are physically oppressed. To have something in common is not tantamount to being corporate.

In Paul's writings, the commonness of our having bodies – plural – never becomes the basis for unity. Rather, Paul uses *sōma* in the *singular* for the idea of unity. The singularity of *sōma*

---

[1] The vast majority of references have to do with Levitical washings of the body (Lev 14: 9; 15: 11, 13, 16, 21, 27; 16: 4, 24, 26, 28; 17: 16; 22: 6; Num 19: 7–8). Closely related is the shaving of the body (Num 8: 7). Still in the same frame of reference is the matter of 'issues' from, or in, the body (Lev 15: 2–3, 19). Then there are the cutting of the body for the dead (Lev 19: 28), the clothing of the body (Lev 6: 10 [3]; III Kgs 20 [21]: 27), the covering of Job's body with the corruption of worms (Job 7: 5), the appearance of the body after the special diet of Daniel and his three friends (Dan 1: 15), and the scales on the body of Leviathan (Job 41: 14 [15]).

[2] Robinson, *The Body*, 29. [3] *Ibid.*

in its connection with the motif of unity supports, then, the individualism of the body. Of course, bodies may *become* united, as in sexual intercourse. And within itself a single, individual body does represent the solidarity of parts in a working whole. But bodies qua bodies do not symbolize solidarity.

Robinson continues his critique of individuation and his argument for solidarity by writing that 'Paul can use the plural σώματα as a substitute for the reflexive pronoun (Rom. 1. 24; 8. 11; 12. 1; I Cor. 6. 15; Eph. 5. 28), but never does he do it to stress individuation.'[1] We have already seen that *sōmata* does not merely substitute for the reflexive pronoun in these passages, but in context stresses the physical side of man's constitution. But what of the claim that the plural *sōmata* does not stress individuation? Actually, it is not a question of stress, but whether the plural form individuates at all, with or without stress. Individuation to any degree will work against the idea of solidarity as opposed to individuation. And no one can maintain solidarity with total consistency, for in connection with the Body of Christ the plural *sōmata* shows that Body to be regarded 'sometimes from the point of view of the individuals composing it'.[2]

Be that as it may, in all the passages cited, Paul might easily have used the singular, and surely would have done so were he holding in view solidarity instead of individuation. The very meaning of 'the dishonoring of their bodies among themselves' (Rom 1: 24) indicates illicit interplay among individuals rather than a solidarity which blurs distinctions among them. Cf. the plural 'their hearts' in the same verse. This is not to deny that Paul could use a collective singular. He does elsewhere, as in the expressions 'their senseless heart' (v. 21), 'the redemption of our body' (8: 23), 'your [plural] body' (I Cor 6: 19–20), and 'our lowly body' (Phil 3: 21). It is to deny, however, that the collective singular cancels out individuation. The individuating plurals stand against such a conclusion.[3]

---

[1] *Ibid.*   [2] *Ibid.* 79, n. 1.

[3] Robinson argues against individuation from the collective singular in Rom 8: 23 and Phil 3: 21, but admits that the argument is not strong because of Paul's similar alternation between the singular and plural of 'heart'. Apparently the alternation is only stylistic. Nevertheless an appeal is made to the rarity in the OT of נֶפֶשׁ in the plural (*ibid.* 29–30). But against the appeal, why the frequency of the plural form of *kardia* in

So also the statements 'he...will give life to your mortal bodies' (Rom 8: 11), 'present your bodies' (Rom 12: 1), 'your bodies are members of Christ' (I Cor 6: 15), and 'husbands should love their wives as their own bodies' (Eph 5: 28) direct attention to Christians as individuals – individuals in the glorious destiny of their resurrection and in the responsibility to carry out through their bodily actions the principles of Christian conduct. In the last passage a good deal of emphasis falls upon individuation, as seen in verse 33: 'let each one of you (*hymeis hoi kath' hena hekastos*) love his wife as himself'. Here we may appropriately note that it is the very cohesiveness of the body within itself and as the tangible concentration of an individual's personality which suits *sōma* to its use for the Church as the Body of Christ in distinction from the unbelieving world.

M. E. Dahl notes that verses in I Corinthians 15 give some trouble to an exclusive stress on solidarity in *sōma*. The statements 'Not all flesh is the same flesh, but there is one kind for man, another for animals, another for birds, and another for fish. There are celestial bodies and there are terrestrial bodies; but the glory of the celestial is one, and the glory of the terrestrial is another' (vv. 39–41) – these statements show that *sarx* and *sōma* may differentiate rather than bind together.[1] D. E. H. Whiteley further argues that under Robinson's view the statement, 'It is sown a natural body, it is raised a spiritual body' (v. 44), must awkwardly be divided between references to individual death and to collective resurrection.[2]

C. A. van Peursen has noted that primitive men do not differentiate themselves from the mythico-social world precisely because they have not discovered the individuating function of their own bodies. Consequently, they have not discovered the spiritual dimensions of the inner personality. Religion becomes ceremonial and sacramental.[3] We may fear that an exclusive emphasis on solidarity in the Pauline use of *sōma* would constitute a retrogressive step toward primitive anthropological and religious views. It is not entirely illogical

Pauline literature and the rarity of *kardia* as a *collective* singular? See the concordance.

[1] Cf. M. E. Dahl, *The Resurrection of the Body*, SBT 1/36 (London, 1962) 32.

[2] D. E. H. Whiteley, *The Theology of St Paul* (Philadelphia, 1964) 196–7.

[3] C. A. van Peursen, *Body, Soul, Spirit* (London, 1966) 80–6.

that huge stress on sacramentalism and the 'crudity' of a 'materialism' which is 'almost impossible to exaggerate' in Paul's doctrine of the Church as Christ's Body should follow such an emphasis,[1] and that prayer should be thought meaningless as converse between an individual and God.[2]

Picking up the theme of solidarity, R. Tannehill cites the use of *sōma* for sexual relationships (Rom 1: 24; cf. 4: 19; I Cor 6: 12–20; 7: 4). *Sōma* then refers to the self which joins to what is outside itself and becomes a part of a larger unity.[3] But here lies the key to the question of somatic individuality versus somatic socialism. The physical body does indeed enable man to interact, even to unite, with entities outside himself. But at the loss of his individuality? No, *sōma* stands at the frontier between individuality and contact with other entities. As the 'outer man' it is both the boundary of the concrete being of the individual and his means of touching the material realities around him. Thus *sōma* protects individual identity and enables social interaction at the same time. Where Bultmann introverts the term, Robinson extroverts it. Neither one has observed its position on the frontier between individuality and solidarity rather than within one territory or the other. Better yet, *sōma* straddles the boundary.

Just as *sōma* is both substantival and functional, it is also both individualistic and social. Its sociality does not detract from its individuality. And its individuality is not introvertive. 'The lesser totality exists, then, in dynamic relation to the greater without losing its distinctive individuality.'[4] *Sōma* does double duty. In its substantiality *sōma* prevents the privatism of flight from the material world of men and events. In its individuation it also prevents capitulation to the facelessness of collectivization in the modern as well as ancient world.

---

[1] Robinson, *The Body*, 51.
[2] J. A. T. Robinson, *Honest to God* (Philadelphia, 1963) 19–20.
[3] Tannehill, *Dying and Rising with Christ*, BZNW 32 (Berlin, 1967) 70–4.
[4] Dahl, *The Resurrection of the Body*, 62.

CHAPTER 17

Sōma and the Church as the
Body of Christ

Robinson's stress on solidarity as the leading motif in *sōma* leads into the Pauline concept of the Church as the Body of Christ. That concept warrants a whole book. Here we can afford to touch only those aspects which relate most directly to the anthropological use of *sōma*. Yet it is necessary to do at least that much because a distinction between the anthropological and ecclesiastical uses of *sōma* is commonly denied nowadays. Once again, by applying what we have learned concerning the use of *sōma* to current opinions, we shall increase our understanding of the Body of Christ.

As might be expected, the private individualism of Bultmann deeply affects his interpretation of the Church as Christ's Body. He does recognize the communal element, but plays it down as secondary. The main point is not that Christians constitute the Body, but that Christ constitutes the Body. Therefore the Body was there as a cosmic entity before Christians came into being and remains there now above them. The 'Body of Christ' indicates, then, primarily the supramundane, transcendental origin of the Church.[1]

A chief difficulty here lies in the failure of Paul to stress, or even to mention, the temporal priority of the Body of Christ over Christians, or its transcendence above the earthly Church. In fact, Paul's comments point the other way. For all we can see, the Body of Christ has no existence apart from the historical Church on earth. Bultmann appeals to I Cor 12: 12–13: 'For just as the body is one and has many members, and all the members of the body, though many, are one body, so it is with Christ. For by one Spirit we were all baptized into one body.' However, these verses themselves contain a refutation of the temporal priority and transcendence of Christ's Body. For Paul here indicates that the Body has many members. Without them it would not be a body. Yet those members are

---

[1] R. Bultmann, *Theology of the New Testament* (New York, 1951) 1: 310–11.

Christians, as the following verses set out in great detail and as verse 27 categorically states: 'Now you (emphatic *hymeis*) are the body of Christ and individually members of it.' Ergo, Christ is the Body only insofar as he has members, viz., Christians united to him through the operation of the Spirit. There is no supramundane body.

Other statements confirm that conclusion: 'For as in one body we have many members, and all the members do not have the same function, so *we*, though many, *are one body in Christ*, and individually members one of another' (Rom 12: 4–5); 'He is the head of *the body, the church*' (Col 1: 18); 'I complete what is lacking in Christ's afflictions for the sake of *his body, that is, the church*' (Col 1: 24); 'he...has made him the head over all things for *the church, which is his body*' (Eph 1: 22–3). Believing Jews and Gentiles make up the 'one body' in Eph 2: 16. The 'one body' in Eph 4: 4 relates to forbearance among Christians as they seek 'to maintain the unity of the Spirit in the bond of peace', and also to the one hope of their calling. The 'body of Christ' in verse 12 consists of 'the saints', the 'we all', the 'whole body' which derives its unity and growth from Christ (vv. 11–16). The same thought appears in Col 2: 19. And in Eph 5: 23, 30 'his [Christ's] body' is again 'the church', which is constituted by the 'members of his body'. Although some of these passages might be discounted as deutero-Pauline, at the very least the indubitably Pauline passages make plain the constitution of the Body of Christ by the Church, with the result that without the Church there is no Body of Christ.[1]

Not only do Paul's statements just quoted fail to establish any supramundane pre-existence of the Body of Christ. They also stress the communal nature of the Body. Paul goes to great lengths in drawing out the equality in unity and the harmony in diverse ministries of all those who make up the Body. Macquarrie criticizes Bultmann quite rightly, then, for excessive individualism in his concept of the Church and for under-interpretation in saying that the unity of the Church has to do

---

[1] The lone exception is the human body of Christ. But what Bultmann needs is a supramundane, not a mundane, body. We shall consider attempted equations of the human and the ecclesiastical bodies of Christ below.

merely with believers' common disinterest in worldly differences – as though nihilists, non-Christian existentialists, and Buddhists might also qualify for membership.[1]

Surprisingly, Bultmann does not press into service his existentialist interpretation of *sōma* as the object-self for his explication of Christ's Body. He could have made an overt appeal to the introvertive understanding of *sōma* in defense of his slighting the communal nature of the Body of Christ. And the flight from the material and historical into the object-self might have provided a base for the concept of Christ's Body as supramundane. Nevertheless, Bultmann lays none of his somatic anthropology under contribution to his somatic ecclesiology. On the other hand, even though *sōma* may be purely metaphorical in the phrase, 'the Body of Christ', the physicality of *sōma* tends away from the supramundane. And the connotation of involvement in the world of nature, events, and other men tends away from the pre- or suprahistorical as well as from excessive individualism.

E. Käsemann illustrates the difficulty, perhaps the impossibility, of reversing the fairly obvious error of privatism in an exposition of Christ's Body without forsaking the transcendental interpretation. He changes the existentialist interpretation of *sōma* from relationship to one's object-self to relationship with others. *Sōma* becomes the possibility of communication – particularly the possibility of becoming the object of communication from God or from the Power of Evil. But the definition of *sōma* remains functional in opposition to substantival. Then, following Bultmann's lead, Käsemann traces the Body of Christ to the supramundane Ur-Anthropos of Gnostic mythology. Thus Christ's Body is, initially, a transcendent aeon, or sphere.[2] But if *sōma* in the phrase 'the Body of Christ' indicates communication with God, how can that Body exist, Gnostic-like, prior to the present historical existence of those believers who are the objects of that communication? Communication implies historical existence and thereby contradicts the view that Christ's Body is transcendentally prehistorical and supramundane. Moreover, the physicality of the Body and the materialism of the sacraments by which believers enter the

---

[1] J. Macquarrie, *An Existentialist Theology* (London, 1955) 219–20.
[2] E. Käsemann, *Leib und Leib Christi* (Tübingen, 1933) 50ff.

Body, according to Käsemann's interpretation of Paul,[1] are far too mundane to agree with an exclusively functional interpretation of *sōma* or a Gnostic background in the Ur-Anthropos, who was a *spiritual* light-being.[2]

At the opposite pole E. Schweizer proposes that Christ's Body implies substantival subjectivity in the form of activity in the concrete world. From this, he proceeds to interpret that Body as a missionary body, i.e., as an extension of the incarnation through evangelistic activity.[3] However, where Paul uses the phrase, 'the Body of Christ', he discusses the *inner* structure and workings of the body in the interrelationship of its various organs and limbs. Paul nowhere relates the Body of Christ to outward activities in relationship to others. Thus the cohesiveness and harmonious function of a single physical body, considered by itself, provides Paul with a model for the Church in the interrelationships of its own members. Missionary activity in an extension of the incarnation lies outside the purview.

We gain a closer approach to Robinson's well-known understanding of Christ's Body through the view of L. Cerfaux. Both scholars emphasize the physicality of the Body of Christ and the literalness of the sacramental means by which union with that body is attained. However, where Robinson (we shall see) stresses the wholeness of Christians and Christ in their solidarity as one Body, Cerfaux stresses the individuality of Christ's physical body, to which Christians are united. (We should carefully observe that although Cerfaux individualizes, he does not do so on an existentialist base.) Following F. de Visscher,[4]

---

[1] *Ibid.* 125–6, 161–2, 174ff.

[2] See further R. Jewett, *Paul's Anthropological Terms* (Leiden, 1971) 216–19. C. Colpe and H.-M. Schenke have undermined a presupposition necessary to Käsemann's (and H. Schlier's) view, viz., the uniting of the Gott '*Mensch*' and the *Allgott-Vorstellung* in pre-Christian times (Colpe, *Die religionsgeschichtliche Schule*, FRLANT N.S. 60 [Göttingen, 1961]; Schenke, *Der Gott '*Mensch*' in der Gnosis* [Göttingen, 1962]; cf. Jewett, *Paul's Anthropological Terms*, 230–7.

[3] E. Schweizer, *The Church as the Body of Christ* (Richmond, Va., 1964) 23–40; 'The Church as the Missionary Body of Christ', *NTS* 8 (1961) 5; and 'σῶμα κτλ.', *TDNT* 7 (1971) 1074–80. Though Schweizer maintains the theological significance of the substantiality of *sōma*, he includes the whole person within its reference.

[4] *Les édits d'Auguste découverts à Cyrène* (Louvain, 1940) 91. The pre-Pauline phrase which de Visscher tries to show does *not* refer to a collec-

Cerfaux argues that outside the NT and before the time of Paul, *sōma* could refer to a unity, or a whole, but not to a collectivity. Therefore, the Body of Christ cannot be a collective, social Body. It must refer to the physical body of the risen Christ, with which the believer is brought into real, though mystical, identification through baptism and the Eucharist.[1]

Whether or not by the time of Paul the term 'body' had been used for a collectivity, or better, a collective but single *organism*,[2] is still open to debate.[3] Yet it would be wrong to make the outcome of that debate crucial. Someone had to be the first to use 'body' in such a way, and if Paul was the first – so be it. That should occasion neither surprise nor excessive admiration, since others in the Greco-Roman world were about to make a similar use independently.

tivity appears in an edict of Augustus found in Cyrene and reads, *leitourgein ...tō tōn Hellēnōn sōmati*. Viewed in context, the phrase refers to carrying out of liturgical responsibilities by the Greeks *themselves* – i.e., by their own physical action – rather than by proxy. Cf. the contrasts between one's body and one's reputation, financial records, and the like noted above, pp. 13–14.

[1] L. Cerfaux, *The Church in the Theology of St Paul* (New York, 1959) 262–86, with support from J. Havet, 'La doctrine paulinienne du "Corps du Christ": Essai de mise au point', *Littérature et théologie pauliniennes* (Paris, 1960) 184–216, and J. Reuss, 'Die Kirche als "Leib Christi" und die Herkunft dieser Vorstellung bei dem Apostel Paulus', *BZ* N.S. 2 (1958) 103–27. Similar in most respects is R. Schnackenburg, *The Church in the New Testament* (New York, 1965) 165–76.

[2] J. A. T. Robinson dislikes collectivity and favors wholeness, or solidarity (*The Body* [London, 1952] 49–83). J. de Fraine remarks, however, that 'it seems difficult to disassociate a "whole" from a "collectivity"; a whole, even if the emphasis is on the unity, necessarily implies parts that are associated and united in a collectivity' (*Adam and the Family of Man* [Staten Island, 1965] 250 1). De Visscher himself admits that a collectivity may be viewed as a unity, a *sōma*, so that an expression such as *sōma tēs poleōs* is quite regular (*Les édits d'Auguste*, 91, n. 2).

[3] Robinson, *The Body*, 49, 1, 59, n 1; T. W. Manson, 'A Parallel to a N.T. Use of σῶμα', *JTS* 37 (1936) 385; G. C. Richards, 'Parallels to a N.T. Use of σῶμα', *JTS* 38 (1937) 165; W. L. Knox, 'Parallels to the NT use of σῶμα', *JTS* 39 (1938) 243–6; Best, *One Body* (London, 1955) 221–5; Meuzelaar, *Der Leib des Messias* (Assen, 1961) 149–68; Wikenhauser, *Die Kirche* (Münster, 1940) 130–43; A. Oepke, *Das Neue Gottesvolk* (Gütersloh, 1950) 225; De Fraine, *Adam*, 251–2; Cerfaux, *Christ in the Theology of St Paul*, 350–3; R. I. Hick, 'Aesop and the Organic Analogy: The Body Political and the Body Ecclesiastical', *JBR* 31 (1963) 29–35; Jewett, *Paul's Anthropological Terms*, 227ff.

But whether or not Paul was the first to use 'body' for a collective but single organism, a better reading of Paul will bring into view a distinction between the physical body of Christ and the ecclesiastical Body of Christ. Paul himself knows the distinction in writing, on the one hand, about Christ's 'glorious body' (Phil 3: 21; cf. I Cor 15: 42–9) and, on the other hand, about the larger Body whose feet, hands, ears, eyes, and other members consist of believers (I Corinthians 12). Moreover, to equate the present physical body of Christ with believers wreaks havoc with the temporal distinction Paul carefully makes between the pastness of Christ's resurrection and the futurity of believers' resurrection (see esp. I Cor 15: 20–8; cf. II Tim 2: 17–18). On the other side, not to equate believers with a body of Christ, merely to attach them sacramentally and mystically, would fail to do justice to Paul's statements (previously quoted) that the Church *is* the Body of Christ and that individual believers make up the specific organs and limbs.

If equation and non-equation of believers with Christ's body are both wrong, a distinction between two bodies of Christ has to be drawn – an individual body, distinct from believers, in which he arose, ascended, and lives on high, and an ecclesiastical Body, consisting of believers, in which he dwells on earth through his Spirit. In one sense the ecclesiastical Body is just as physical as the individual body of Christ, not because it consists in the individual body of Christ but because it consists of believers whose bodies (as well as spirits) belong to Christ (I Cor 6: 15, 19–20). In a larger sense, however, the ecclesiastical Body is metaphorical in that the equation of one member with the eye of the Body, another member with the ear, and so on can be understood (but is easily understood) only in a figurative way. Cerfaux unwittingly acknowledges this in writing that the identification is 'mystical' and 'spiritual' as well as 'real'. The terms 'mystical' and 'spiritual' tend to take back what the term 'real' offers; but they fail to cover up the difficulty in carrying through the 'real' with consistent literalness to the end. We might just as well have the courage to say 'metaphorical'.

The same criticisms apply to the view of A. Schweitzer that the elect come into corporeal union with the risen Christ.[1]

[1] *The Mysticism of Paul the Apostle* (New York, 1931) 117–18, 127–8.

R. Jewett thinks the view is generally rejected only because it seems strange to modern man.[1] However, Jewett himself criticizes Schweitzer for making believers into supernatural men and for failure to see that Paul always puts the resurrection of believers' bodies in the future. But Schweitzer has seen that a fully corporeal Body of Christ, in the ecclesiastical sense, forces him to this. That it does not agree with Paul's distinctions between believers and Christ, as Jewett has seen, simply means that we should modify the idea of a fully corporeal Body of Christ – from the exegetical standpoint, not just from the standpoint of strangeness to modern man.

Of course, the physical bodies of believers help make up the reality to which the metaphor 'Body of Christ' points, simply because physical bodies form part of the constitution of believers and therefore belong to Christ. That is enough to explain Paul's strictures against the physical sins of intercourse with a prostitute (I Cor 6: 12–20), submission to circumcision after baptism (Gal 5: 2–6), and participation in pagan banquets (I Cor 10: 1–22). There is no need for recourse to union between the physical body of Christ and the physical bodies of believers – an idea that would put the physical resurrection of believers in the past and contradictorily equate their present lowly bodies with Christ's glorious body.

Going further, however, Robinson attempts to carry through a corporeal identification between the physical bodies of Christ and of believers with full consistency, with denial of any distinction between the risen and ascended body of Christ and his Body which is the Church, and (contrary to Schweitzer) with avoidance of all that smacks of mysticism.[2] He wants to bring together 'what is usually differentiated as the glorified, the mystical and the eucharistic body of Christ, along with the Christian's hope of the resurrection and renewal of his own body'.

[1] Jewett, *Paul's Anthropological Terms*, 215.
[2] In his third and longest chapter, 'The Body of the Resurrection', *The Body*, 49–83; cf. P. Benoit, *Exégèse et Théologie* (Paris, 1961) 2: 107–62; R. P. Shedd, *Man in Community* (London, 1958) 159–65; C. Spicq, *Dieu et l'homme selon le Nouveau Testament*, Lectio Divina 29 (Paris, 1961) 170–3; E. Percy, *Der Leib Christi* (Lund, 1942) 11–15; J. Kallas, *The Satanward View* (Philadelphia, 1966) 92–114. Percy correctly denies that in I Corinthians and Romans the relationship of Christ to his Body is that of a soul to its body.

Christians 'are in literal fact the risen organism of Christ's person in all its concrete reality...It is almost impossible to exaggerate the materialism and crudity of Paul's doctrine of the Church as literally now the resurrection *body* of Christ...its unity is that of a single physical entity: disunion is dismemberment. For it is in fact no other than the glorified body of the risen and ascended Christ...It is to be noted how uncompromisingly physical is the language in which Paul depicts Christians as going to compose the resurrection body of Christ', so uncompromisingly physical that even the statement, 'But he who is united to the Lord becomes one *spirit* with him' (I Cor 6: 17), refers to *physical* union. Moreover, 'there is no real line between the body of His [Christ's] resurrection and the flesh-bodies of those who are risen with him; for they are members of it'. Almost inevitably, this line runs to the conclusion that the resurrection of believers as well as their death is a present reality from the time of baptism, with the result that the *inner* man, now being renewed (II Cor 4: 16), is man as *sōma*! All of this rests on the notion that Paul thought Hebraically of the *sōma* as a unifying rather than individuating principle.

However, we have already seen that in Hebraic thought 'flesh (בשר)' may either generalize or individuate. By itself the term is neutral. The context is determinative. On the other hand, in the LXX *sōma* appears for בשר only where the Hebrew word is used individuatingly. So the foundation for an exposition of the Body of Christ in terms of physical solidarity crumbles away.

In addition, where Paul makes the body serve for the idea of solidarity-cum-diversity, he puts *sōma* in the singular and refers to the solidarity-cum-diversity of its *parts* rather than to the solidarity-cum-diversity of various bodies. In other words, only alone, as a single entity and within itself, does a body symbolize solidarity-cum-diversity. Yet the Body of Christ consists of people who have, and are, many bodies which are individually entire in themselves. It becomes evident, therefore, that the Body of Christ encompasses their bodies not as a single physical organism as though an individual's small but entire physical body composes a literal hand or foot of a larger physical body, but as a figurative Body of which their individual physical bodies are, figuratively, parts.

Of course, Robinson does not wish to fall into the absurdity of requiring that the literal hands and feet and ears and eyes of the Body of Christ be the literal bodies of believers. These straits result in the surprising statement that Paul's use of the human body for Christ's body is an 'analogy' which is not a 'metaphor'![1] Is not a metaphor one kind of analogy? Beyond his distinctions between an analogy and a metaphor, Robinson contents himself to say that in I Corinthians 12 Paul shows that the Body of Christ is one body despite the multiplicity of its members. We read no discussion of the dilemma that either the physical bodies of believers are the literal hands and feet and other parts of the physical Body of Christ, or the being hands and feet and other parts is figurative with the result that the entire Body is also figurative.

This is not to deny an equation between Christ and his Body, but only to deny that the equation is of a physical sort. We do not establish an equation by noting that Paul says, 'You are the Body *of* Christ' (I Cor 12: 27), rather than, 'You are a body *in* Christ', or by noting that Paul never writes of 'a body of Christians' but always of 'the Body of Christ'. Other things being equal, the genitive *Christou* just might be taken as possessive rather than explicative.[2] Other things are not equal, however, for an equation of some sort is clear from I Cor 6: 15, 'your bodies are members of *Christ* [not, the Body of Christ]', and 12: 12–13, 'For just as the body is one and has many members, and all the members of the body, though many, are one body, so it is with Christ [not: the Body of Christ].'

Christ is the Body; yet Christians, the many members, are the body, too. A good parallel appears in Galatians 3, where Paul makes the offspring of Abraham both Christ and Christians: ' "And to your [Abraham's] offspring", which is Christ...you are Abraham's offspring' (vv. 16 and 29). Here the language of procreation is definitely physical, just as physical as the language of *sōma*. Yet Paul makes membership in Abraham's offspring a matter of faith alone. That member-

[1] Robinson, *The Body*, 51.
[2] So Mcuzclaar, *Der Leib des Messias*, 6. II. Schlier does the same in I Corinthians and Romans, but sees an explicative genitive in Colossians and Ephesians (*Christus und die Kirche im Epheserbrief*, Beiträge zur historischen Theologie 6 [Tübingen, 1930] 41–2).

ship does not derive from any physical relationship, despite the illegitimate interpolation by Robinson in his quotation of Gal 3: 27: 'you...have put on (the body of) Christ'.[1] The erasure of the distinction between male and female (v. 28) also establishes the non-physical character of the union with Christ which qualifies one as Abraham's offspring. Such erasure has not physically taken place. But at another level – in Christ – it has taken place. And for Paul the Body of Christ is ethical rather than physical. Paul rarely speaks of it in soteriological passages, and never at length. Only in parenetic passages, where being a member of the Body has to do with working relationships among Christians, does Paul develop the theme.[2] Therefore the physical language concerning Abraham's offspring and the Body of Christ figuratively portrays reality of a kind different from the physical.

The statement, 'your bodies are members of Christ' (I Cor 6: 15) thus means that union with Christ includes the physical bodies of believers along with the rest of their constitution. But although membership in the Body involves the physical simply because the body is integral to the whole person, the physical does not define the essential nature of that membership. Similarly, the equation between Christ and the one body with many members (I Cor 12: 12) means that Christians and Christ are one, not with an implication that the union is physical but only with an illustration drawn from the physical realm.

Insistence that physicality defines the very nature of membership in Christ's Body runs into a variety of impossibilities. We have previously noted the impossibility of reconciling the realistic view with the futurity of the death and resurrection, or translation, of Christians. For physical fusion of their mortal bodies with the physical body of the risen Christ, over whom death has no more power, should automatically immortalize their present bodies and thereby put their resurrection in the past. The mere facts that Christians die, and did so in Paul's

---

[1] Robinson, *The Body*, 79.

[2] Best, *One Body*, 16; E. Schweizer, 'σῶμα κτλ.', 1067, 1069, 1073. Schweizer may overstate his argument by denying that Paul *ever* speaks of the Body of Christ in a soteriological passage. But Schweizer doubtless discounts exceptions in Colossians and Ephesians as deutero-Pauline.

time, and that Paul carefully assigns the resurrection of Christ to the past but that of Christians to the future refutes the notion.

Nevertheless, Robinson writes that our present physical bodies die and yet are being transformed, i.e., resurrected, from the time of baptism onward. He calls this a 'paradox', which 'follows directly from the fact that the resurrection body of Christ is the body of His death, bearing the imprint of the nails'.[1] But for Christ physical resurrection chronologically followed physical death. We can hardly make the physical death and the physical resurrection of Christians simultaneous; for if we do, the parallel with Christ falls to the ground and the 'paradox' becomes a genuine contradiction.

For Paul the physical resurrection of Christians follows their physical death, as in the case of Christ. Present anticipation of the resurrection has to do only with the inner man, or spirit; the present body remains bound to mortality. Paul could hardly put it more clearly than he does in II Cor 4: 7–18. Robinson quotes the reference to renewal of the inner man in that passage as though it has to do with current and gradual resurrection of the body — and fails to quote that part which contrasts the decay of the outer man.[2] Here we are not concerned, however, with a mistaken view of the resurrection in Paul so much as with the necessity of that mistaken view to an understanding of the Body of Christ in a literalistic, physical fashion. If we cannot accept the pastness of the physical resurrection of believers, we cannot accept the physicality of Christ's ecclesiastical Body.

As substance, the present *sōma* of believers is destined to die because of sin. Functionally, however, the present *sōma* of believers is their being-for-God, their activity of service to the Lord in the concrete world of men and events. Hence, although the futurity of physical death and resurrection rules out identification with Christ's physical body, the present tense of activity for God entails involvement of the believer's present physical body. Functionally, the present body serves God; substantivally, it is dying. Final redemption will resolve the tension between the doom of the present body and its function for God. Through resurrection, the substantiality of the body will catch up with its function. Until then the tension remains. Hence, the unity of

---

[1] Robinson, *The Body*, 73–83. [2] *Ibid.* 81.

the larger Body of Christ is not substantival; i.e., it is not physical.

There is the further impossibility of maintaining physical literalism to the end in the sexual nature of Paul's language concerning the union of Christians with Christ in one Body (Rom 7: 4; I Cor 6: 12–20 – with the use of *kollaomai*, and the quotation of Gen 2: 24; II Cor 11: 2; Eph 5: 21–33). Robinson calls attention to this as an indication of the intimacy of the union between Christ and the Church.[1] But suddenly it is a 'metaphor'. Why? Obviously because even to suggest marital relationship of a physical sort between Christ and the Church would be utterly ridiculous (if not blasphemous) and certainly beyond the intent of Paul. But if we take the sexuality of the language as figurative, ought we not to take the physicality of the language in the same way? Yes, indeed, since the sexuality and physicality are bound up with each other in Paul's discussion.[2]

We read of 'other, equally physical, metaphors' and of an 'image'. They are Paul's travail over the Galatians until the embryonic Christ is formed in them (Gal 4: 19), the growing up of believers into the full stature of Christ (Eph 4: 13), and (in connection with God and the Holy Spirit) the picture of the Church as a building or temple.[3] There are also the spatial 'metaphor' of being in Christ and his being in believers and the 'metaphor' of being planted together with Christ (Rom 6: 5).[4] We might add the grafting of Gentile believers into the olive tree (Rom 11: 17–24).

But what justifies our treating such expressions as metaphors and images while insisting that the Body of Christ is literal? Paul never makes the Church *like* the Body of Christ but writes that the Church *is* his Body. But failure to use simile does not decide against the use of metaphor.[5] As a matter of fact, Paul

---

[1] *Ibid.* 52–3.

[2] Taking the view of A. Schweitzer and Robinson, Kallas writes that Christ has two bodies, his own in heaven and the Church on earth, just as a married couple are two, yet really one (*The Satanward View*, 99–100). But in the case of a married couple, each has a complete body with organs and limbs, whereas in the literalistic view of Christ's ecclesiastical Body, believers form Christ's *own* body, part by part à la I Corinthians 12, not a separate body physically united to Christ's own body.

[3] Robinson, *The Body*, 64–5.   [4] *Ibid.* 61–2.

[5] Contra *ibid.* 51; Cerfaux, *Christ in the Theology of St Paul*, 350–3.

does not write that believers are *as it were* in Christ, or that they are *like* wild olive branches or plants or a building or temple, or that he the apostle is *similar to* a mother in travail. Yet all parties treat these spatial, horticultural, structural, and familial expressions as metaphors – apparently for the sensible reason that they do not make good literal sense. But we have not seen that the Church as Christ's physical Body makes good literal sense.

Recognizing the impossibility of its making good literal sense, Robinson rather emphasizes the extreme violence and crudity of the literal sense. So also Schweitzer writes that 'the obscurity [of any differentiation between the individual and corporate bodies of Christ] was intended by Paul'.[1] Thus a virtue is made out of a necessity. But failure to explain the nature of the purported union between the physical bodies of Christians and Christ betrays embarrassment over the fact that the ecclesiastical Body of Christ makes no better literal sense than other physical expressions in the same category and therefore deserves no more literal interpretation than they do.

In addition, affirmation that Paul always draws an equation, never a comparison, with the body overlooks the leading statement in his longest discussion of the motif: 'For *just as (kathaper)* the body is one and has many members, and all the members of the body, though many, are one body, so *(houtōs)* it is with Christ' (I Cor 12: 12). Also overlooked is Rom 12: 4–5: 'For as *(kathaper)* in one body we have many members, and all the members do not have the same function, so *(houtōs)* we, though many, are one body in Christ, and individually members one of another'. The following verses in I Corinthians 12 show that 'Christ *(ho Christos)*' is the corporate rather than solely individual Christ. This is apparent also in the parallel in Rom 12: 4–5, where 'we...the many' follows *houtōs* and thereby confirms our understanding of *ho Christos* after *houtōs* in I Cor 12: 12 as a reference to the larger Christ. The combination *kathaper... houtōs* shows that other statements which equate the Body of Christ with the Church – such as the statement later on in the same passage in I Corinthians, 'Now you are the body of Christ and individually members of it' (12: 27) – are to be taken metaphorically. A realistic interpretation violates this clear

---

[1] A. Schweitzer, *Mysticism*, 118, quoted by Robinson, *The Body*, 47.

indication of a comparison. It would be nonsensical for Paul to *compare* Christ, or his Body, with a human physical body when he, or it, *is* a human physical body. (Only by making the Body of Christ non-human, while still physical, could the nonsense be avoided.) But it does make sense for Paul to compare a non-physical body – the total Christ, i.e., Christ plus those in him by faith – with a physical body.[1]

Not even an appeal to the sacraments of baptism and the Lord's supper (cf. esp. I Cor 10: 16) helps to explain a union between the physical bodies of Christ and believers, for to avoid magic, transubstantiation, and the like Robinson writes of these as 'quasi-physical'.[2] But '*quasi*-physical' is a long way from the '*uncompromisingly* physical' with which the interpretation starts.[3] If sacramental relationships are only seemingly physical, they fail to fill the vacuum left by the meaninglessness of literal union with the physical body of Christ and by the incoherence of treating one expression literally and others, closely related, metaphorically for the very reason that literally taken they become ridiculous.

It is not enough just to assert a physical union with Christ's body. We need an explanation for the means by which the believer purportedly experiences such union with a body which long ago expired, rose to life, and now dwells in heaven. (If the body is literal, presumably these expressions

---

[1] Jewett distinguishes a realistic Body *of* Christ in I Corinthians 12 and a metaphorical Body *in* Christ in Romans 12, and suggests that Paul forsook realism in the later epistle because of Gnostic misuse of such realism (*Paul's Anthropological Terms*, 302–4). But the slight change in expression hardly suffices to constitute a polemical correction (cf. P. Minear, *Images of the Church in the New Testament* [Philadelphia, 1960] 194). It would be strange for Paul to use the expression supposedly open to Gnostic misuse in the epistle where he is thought to be more concerned to oppose Gnosticism. Actually, the phrase 'in Christ' could also be taken realistically. But the recurrent Greek expression *kathaper...houtōs* establishes the figurative nature of the Body in both passages. Jewett also argues that Paul began dictating I Cor 12: 12 with the intention of producing a metaphor ('For just as...') but switched in mid-sentence to realism ('...so also is *Christ*' rather than 'so the congregation is a unified body despite the variety of its members' [*Paul's Anthropological Terms*, 271–3]). But we have already seen that *ho Christos*, like 'the offspring of Abraham', includes believers. And the following verses in I Corinthians 12 explicate Paul's statement in a fashion which is both metaphorical and inclusive of believers in the *ho Christos* who is the Body.   [2] Robinson, *The Body*, 53–4, cf. 46–8.   [3] *Ibid.* 52.

are, too). *How* is the Church brought into physical assimilation with the same structure of flesh, blood, and bones that died on the Cross and the same organism which rose and ascended still bearing the scars of crucifixion? Even if baptism were more than 'quasi-physical', it would still fail to supply an answer. For in what way is *Christ's* body involved in the waters with which a Christian's body is baptized? With reference to the Lord's Supper, old-fashioned transubstantiation would pose a possible solution. But it is precisely the literalism of such transubstantiation which makes the doctrine problematic. In other words, we can hardly solve the difficulty in conceiving of literal union with Christ's physical body by appeal to transubstantiation or to any other chemical brand of sacramentalism, for they pose the very same difficulty. One obscurity does not explain another.

To be sure, we may point to the statements of Paul that some desecrators of the Lord's table have fallen ill and died (I Cor 11. 17–32) and to his letting vicarious baptism for the dead go unchallenged (I Cor 15: 29) as indicative of some chemical magic in his view of the sacraments. But even under the most magical understanding of baptism for the dead, nothing in it suggests union with the physical body of Christ. It is therefore irrelevant to our question.

Concerning physical punishment for failure to 'discern the body', whether we understand 'the body' as individual or corporate or both, the question is whether the elements supply the means of punishment, a poison of mortality, or whether illness and death simply provide a poetic justice for gluttony. The latter option seems better. In the case of the immoral man of I Corinthians 5, the illicit sexual act is not the means of the possible destruction of his flesh. The physical nature of the punishment merely suits the physical nature of the offense. The same holds true in ch. 11, where Paul lays stress on the manner of participation in the Lord's supper, not on the nature of the elements as such. In the tradition which he utilizes, the cup is not even identified with Christ's blood. Moreover, it is hard to think that Paul holds to the other side of the 'chemical' view – viz., that worthy partakers will never fall sick or die – for the sheer fact that many good Christians do become ill and die rules out the possibility. The physical ailments of Paul himself, particularly his thorn in the flesh, preclude our thinking that he teaches a physical potency for life and death in the elements of the Lord's Supper as such. Only if Paul classes himself among desecrators of the Lord's Table can we think that.[1]

In further support of physical identification with Christ's body through sacramental means, appeal is made to I Cor 10: 17, according to Rawlinson's translation: 'Because there is one loaf, we, that are many, are one body, for we all partake of one loaf.'[2] The appeal fails, though, because Paul seems unconcerned to equate the 'one body' with 'the body of Christ' which complements 'the blood of Christ' in the preceding verse. This is Paul's golden opportunity to equate the 'one body' of believers with the physical body of Christ just mentioned. He does not. On the contrary, when he comes to a fuller delineation of his thought, far from making an equation, he draws a comparison: 'For just as (*kathaper*) the body is one... so (*houtōs*) it is with Christ' (12:12; also Rom 12: 4–5). The extension of the simile in ch. 12 shows that Paul intended his statement in ch. 10 to be taken as a metaphor. We conclude this: through their participation in the Lord's Supper believers show that they are like a single physical body, not that through their participation they are Christ's physical body.

We have already noted a major defect in the view according to which corporeal relationship with a believer sanctifies an unbelieving spouse and children (I Cor 7: 12–16), viz., the implication in verse 16 that the sanctification falls short of salvation.[3] Nevertheless, that view is used to argue for 'realistic' union with Christ in one Body. One proponent of the view reverses his field by denying, on the basis of I Cor 6: 17 ('one spirit with him'), that the union is *crassly* physical.[4] In what way *is* it physical, then? From the standpoint of *sōma*, we may also note that Paul nowhere in the passage associates the sanctification of the unbelieving spouse and children with

[1] Cf. G. W. H. Lampe, 'Church Discipline' in W. R. Farmer et al. (eds.), *Christian History and Interpretation* (Cambridge, 1967) 347, against Cullmann in both his *The Early Church* (Philadelphia, 1956) 171–3, and 'Immortality of the Soul or Resurrection of the Dead?', *Immortality and Resurrection*, ed. K. Stendahl (New York, 1965) 34–5.   [2] Robinson, *The Body*, 56.

[3] See above, pp. 67–8.

[4] Proudfoot, 'Imitation or Realistic Participation?', *Int* 17 (1963) 146.

somatic union. Coitus between husband and wife does not come into the discussion. Neither does physical generation of children. Paul speaks only of homelife. Even otherwise, familial relationships hardly establish or illustrate a relationship in which the Church *is*, not merely is united with, the Body of Christ.

Robinson draws a further exegetical argument from the parallel between Col 1: 21–2, 'And you...he has now reconciled in his body of flesh by his death', and Eph 2: 15–16, 'that he...might reconcile us both to God in one body through the cross'. 'His body of flesh' parallels 'us...in one body'. Thus the physical body of Christ and the body constituted by believers are one and the same.[1] But part of the sentence in Eph 2: 15–16 which Robinson omits to quote contains a reference to Christ's crucified 'flesh' as the means by which 'one new man', i.e., 'one body' consisting of both Jewish and Gentile believers, might come into being. Within the sentence as a whole, then, Christ's 'flesh', which died on a cross, is distinguishable from the 'Body' which is the recently created Church, the 'one new man'. In his second and more extended quotation of Eph 2: 12–16, Robinson again omits the damaging reference to Christ's 'flesh'.[2] In all probability Paul shifts his terminology from the 'flesh' which was crucified to the 'Body' which is the 'one new man' in order to distinguish what Robinson wants to equate, the physique of Christ and the Church.

To Robinson, Rom 7: 4 'could stand as a summary of the whole of Pauline theology':[3] 'you have died to the law through the body of Christ, so that you may belong to another, to him who has been raised from the dead in order that we may bear fruit for God'. The verse receives interpretation in terms of 'the Christian's participation in the resurrection body of the Lord'. Ensuing discussion shows that the term 'participation' means physical identification.

As a proof text, however, the verse is wanting. Nothing in the immediate context or in the entire preceding part of Romans (and Paul had not previously instructed the Roman Christians by letter or word of mouth) suggests that the 'body' of Christ includes more than that individual body in which he died and rose. In ch. 6 Paul writes of union with Christ in his

---

[1] Robinson, *The Body*, 47.   [2] *Ibid.* 48, n. 1.   [3] *Ibid.* 49; cf. 47, 52.

death, burial, and resurrection. But although our body comes into view (v. 6), Christ's does not. In other words, Paul fails to ground union with Christ on physical identification with his body. Thus in 7: 4 the body of Christ is the instrument through the death of which the believer gains freedom from the law. Yet although it is irresistibly tempting for Robinson to explain how this happens by enlarging the concept of Christ's body while retaining its physicality, Paul simply does not here engage in such enlargement. Instead, he uses *sōma* with reference to the death (but not the resurrection) of Christ because of the frequent and long-standing use of *sōma* for a corpse. And, as Jewett points out, Paul wants to leave room for Christ as the living *new* master; to have written the phrase 'through the death of Christ' might have led to an allegorical interpretation of his marital analogy in which Christ would be the dead *old* master.[1]

If Rom 7: 4 summarizes Paul's somatic theology for Robinson, Acts 9: 4–5; 22: 7–8; 26: 14–15 supplies its fountainhead: ' "Saul, Saul, why do you persecute me?...I am Jesus (of Nazareth – 22: 8) whom you are persecuting." '[2] But if the words Paul heard on the road to Damascus are the source for the concept of the Church as Christ's Body, why does that concept not appear very early in Pauline literature?[3] Maybe the deduction was slow in coming. Even so, it is a long step from persecution of Christ in Christians to a sacramental literalism in which Christians *are* the physical body of Christ. (We should keep in mind that what Robinson wants and needs is not a union with the physical body of Christ like the union of two bodies in coitus, but a fusion so complete that only a single body is discernible, Christ's.) If the dominical saying 'He who receives you receives me' (Matt 10: 40; cf. 18: 5; Mark 9: 37; Luke 9: 48; 10: 16; John 13: 20) does not imply fusion with Christ's physical body – and who would dare to say that the parallel clause 'He who receives me receives him who sent me' (cf. also John 5: 23; 12: 44–5; 14: 9–11) implies a physical fusion between Christ and the Father? – then neither do the words to Paul on the Damascus road need to imply the kind of sacramental literalism which is drawn out of them.

---

[1] Jewett, *Paul's Anthropological Terms*, 300. [2] Robinson, *The Body*, 57–8.
[3] D. E. H. Whiteley, *The Theology of St Paul* (Philadelphia, 1964) 192.

We conclude that sacramentalism fails to produce an exegetically valid rationale for a physical fusion of the individual and corporate bodies of Christ. The more physical the anthropological use of *sōma*, the more figurative its ecclesiastical use because the usage for an individual physique makes literalistic nonsense of a corporate physique – nonsense not merely to modern ways of thinking but also within the framework of Pauline thought other factors considered.

In denying literalism, we admittedly have not solved the problem of the true nature of union with Christ. We have only seen that it is not basically physical even though it carries implications for the conduct of life in the body. Perhaps part of the very point of the Pauline metaphors – spatial, horticultural, structural, familial, and somatic – is that they stand for a reality understandable but incomprehensible. If so, the attempt to exhaust its meaning is doomed from the start.

Robinson caps his treatment of the Body of Christ with a discussion of its implications for the doctrine of the resurrection.[1] We have already noted the un-Pauline way in which he is forced to antedate physical resurrection to baptism. He tempers this somewhat by gradualizing physical resurrection, with the result that it extends from the past into the present and future. But then we have the contradiction that the same physical body is both dying and rising, concurrently. What interests us here, however, is the way in which Robinson enables himself by this means to avoid clear affirmation of a definite physical resurrection in the future. Instead, we read about a future laying bare of the new corporeity which already exists.

Idealistic commentators have escaped the scandal of physical resurrection by Hellenizing *sōma* as form. Bultmann and his followers do the same by a combination of dematerializing and functionalizing *sōma* where it is deemed to carry theological significance. Is Robinson also trying to escape the scandal of physical resurrection, but by the tour de force of literalizing the corporate Body of Christ and limiting the resurrection to the formation, growth, and final revelation of that Body? His demythologizing of futuristic resurrection in the book *In the End God*[2] strongly suggests an affirmative answer to the ques-

---

[1] Robinson, *The Body*, 73–83.
[2] Religious Perspectives 20 (New York, 1968) 95–109.

tion. The scandal remains, however, for to accomplish the feat there must be retention of a no less scandalous physicalness of Christ's resurrection and employment of an equally scandalous brand of sacramentalism.

Robinson sees the danger that his exposition of the resurrection in terms of the corporate Body of Christ already existent combined with his denial of individuation in *sōma* tends to erode the hope of an individual afterlife. As a stopgap for individual afterlife he offers everyone's call of God 'to a unique and eternal relationship with Himself', 'each man's gift from God (I Cor. 7. 7, 17) and each man's inalienable responsibility to Him (I Cor. 3. 13–15; 2 Cor. 5. 10; Rom. 14. 12)'.[1] To that we may agree, except that in I Cor 7: 7, 17 Paul writes only of *this* life. Moreover, Paul wants physical as well as individual afterlife, relates the two, and ties them up in the same bundle with individual responsibility. His discussion of the resurrection in II Cor 4: 16 – 5: 10 closes with the words: 'For we must all appear before the judgment seat of Christ, so that each one may receive good or evil, according to what he has done in the body.' Resurrection, individuation, and responsibility – all three appear without violating the solidarity of the 'we all'. It is un-Pauline to separate bodily individuation from individual responsibility and future resurrection.

The detachment of *sōma* from individuation and its attachment to a physically and corporately conceived 'Body of the Resurrection' finally leads to universalism:

The mass of human existence, for all its sin, its destructiveness, its determinisms, is still σῶμα: it is made for God...it has been... redeemed in Christ. The Church is at once the witness to the world of its true nature and the pledge and instrument of its destiny... So Paul sees the redemption of the body...as the hope ultimately, not only of all men, but of 'the creation itself' (Rom. 8. 21)...then the Body of Christ will stand forth, not, as it is now, a world within a world, but as the one solidarity...where...'Christ is all, and in all' (Col. 3. 10f.).[2]

[1] Robinson, *The Body*, 78–9.
[2] *Ibid.* 82–3; and his *In the End God*, 119–33. So also M. E. Dahl, *The Resurrection of the Body*, SBT 1/36 (London, 1962) 76. We might observe that a materialistic and socialistic concept of Christ's Body could easily join up with a revived, or revised, social gospel and a concept of sin as estrangement from others. Cf. Robinson, *Honest to God* (Philadelphia, 1963),

However much we might wish for universalism, it is another weight too heavy for *sōma* to bear. *Sōma* does not necessarily represent the physical oneness of all men and the entire creation in a salvific destiny. It may rather represent an individuation which at the judgement will separate between those who have done good and those who have done evil (II Cor 5: 10). The corporate use is limited to believers. Whether or not all will become members of that Body through faith depends on factors other than the use of *sōma*.

We now step back to look at the whole picture. Robinson might have lessened the scandals of bodily resurrection and sacramentalism by appealing to the definition of *sōma* as the whole person rather than the physique alone. This is what Bultmann does in defining *sōma* as the whole person, releasing the human personality from any necessary connection with physicality, and tying it down, instead, to *Existenz*. Since *sōma* obviously refers to physicality in numerous passages, however, Bultmann has to distinguish between popular and theological meanings of *sōma* and assign physicality to the popular meaning and personality to the theological meaning.

By contrast, Robinson is too Biblical and Pauline to relegate the physicality of *sōma* to a theological limbo. Recognizing the importance of physicality, he takes the definition of *sōma* as the whole person in an opposite direction. Instead of releasing personality – i.e., distinctively human *Existenz* – from physicality, he limits it to physicality.[1] Where Bultmann makes personality vault beyond substantiality (his existentialism here has roots in German idealism), Robinson makes substantiality confine personality (his literalism has roots in British empiricism). Robinson thereby frees himself from the necessity to distinguish between an insignificant popular meaning of *sōma* and a significant theological meaning. But on the debit side, concurrent insistence on physicality and on holism in *sōma* leads him to materialize the corporate Body of Christ, and consequently to sacramentalize union with Christ in a fashion admittedly crude and to antedate physical resurrection.

the last four chs.; and his *On Being the Church in the World* (Philadelphia, 1960) *passim*.

[1] 'Physicality' is to be understood here in the broad sense of psychophysicality.

The insistence of Robinson on the physicality of *sōma* is right. His limitation of the human personality to *sōma* as a result of adopting the holistic definition of *sōma* is wrong. The insistence of Bultmann that the human personality goes beyond physicality is right. His demotion of physicality to theological insignificance by use of the larger, holistic definition of *sōma* is wrong. Paul fully personalizes *sōma* as a necessary part of the human constitution and of authentic existence. However, he neither dematerializes *sōma* in theological usage nor makes it comprehend the total person. To do either would lay upon the term a burden heavier than it can bear. Rather, without having to do double duty for the spirit, *sōma* gains theological significance as the physical body, man's means of concrete service for God.

SELECT BIBLIOGRAPHY

Ahern, B. M. 'The Christian's Union with the Body of Christ in Cor, Gal, and Rom', *CBQ* 23 (1961) 199–209.

Barr, J. *The Semantics of Biblical Language*. London: Oxford U.P., 1961.

Barth, C. *Die Errettung vom Tode in den individuellen Klage- und Dankliedern des Alten Testaments*. Zollikon–Zürich: Evangelischer Verlag, 1947.

Barth, K. *Church Dogmatics* 3/2, 4/1. Edinburgh: Clark, 1956, 1960.

Barth, K. *Die Auferstehung der Toten*. 2nd ed. Zollikon–Zürich: Evangelischer Verlag, 1953.

Batey, R. 'The μία σάρξ Union of Christ and the Church', *NTS* 13 (1967) 270–81.

Bauer, K.-A. *Leiblichkeit – das Ende aller Werke Gottes. Die Bedeutung der Leiblichkeit des Menschen bei Paulus*. Studien zum Neuen Testament 4. Gütersloh: Mohn, 1971.

Becker, J. 'Erwägungen zu Phil. 3, 20–21', *TZ* 27 (1971) 16–29.

Best, E. *One Body in Christ*. London: SPCK, 1955.

Bieder, W. 'Auferstehung des Fleisches oder des Leibes? Eine biblisch-theologische dogmengeschichtliche Studie', *TZ* 1 (1945) 105–20.

Bornhäuser, K. 'Die Gebeine der Toten. Ein Beitrag zum Verständnis der Anschauungen von der Totenauferstehung zur Zeit des Neuen Testaments', *Beiträge zur Förderung Christlicher Theologie* 26 (1921) 123–78.

Brandenburger, E. *Fleisch und Geist*. WMANT 29. Neukirchen–Vluyn: Neukirchener Verlag, 1968.

Bultmann, R. 'Die Bedeutung der "dialektischen Theologie" für die neutestamentliche Wissenschaft', *Theologische Blätter* 7 (1928) 57–67.

Bultmann, R. 'Paulus', *RGG* 4 (2nd ed. 1930) 1019–45.

Bultmann, R. *Theology of the New Testament*, vol. 1. New York: Scribner, 1951.

Cambier, J. 'La Chair et l'Esprit en I Cor. v. 5', *NTS* 15 (1969) 221–32.

Cerfaux, L. *The Church in the Theology of St Paul*. New York: Herder, 1959.

Select Bibliography

Charles, R. H. *Eschatology*. New York: Schocken, 1963.
Clavier, H. 'Brèves remarques sur la notion de σῶμα πνευματικόν' in W. D. Davies and D. Daube (eds.), *The Background of the New Testament and Its Eschatology. In Honour of Charles Harold Dodd*, 342–62. Cambridge University Press, 1964.
Collange, J.-F. *Enigmes de la Deuxième Epître de Paul aux Corinthiens. Etude exégétique de 2 Cor. 2: 14–7: 4*. NTSMS 18. Cambridge University Press, 1972.
Colpe, C. *Die religionsgeschichtliche Schule*. FRLANT N.S. 60. Göttingen: Vandenhoeck & Ruprecht, 1961.
Conzelmann, H. *An Outline of the Theology of the New Testament*. New York: Harper & Row, 1968.
Cullmann, O. 'Immortality of the Soul or Resurrection of the Dead?' in K. Stendahl (ed.), *Immortality and Resurrection*, 9–53. New York: Macmillan, 1965.
Daalen, D. H. van. 'The Resurrection of the Body and Justification by Grace' in F. L. Cross (ed.), *Studia Evangelica* 3/2 (TU 88), 218–22. Berlin: Akademie Verlag, 1964.
Dahl, M. E. *The Resurrection of the Body*. SBT 1/36. London: SCM, 1962.
Dautzenberg, G. *Sein Leben bewahren*. Ψυχή *in den Herrenworten der Evangelien*. München: Kösel, 1966.
Dhorme, P. *L'emploi métaphorique des noms de parties du corps en hébreu et accidien*. Paris, 1923.
Dickson, W. P. *St Paul's Use of the Terms Flesh and Spirit*. Glasgow: Maclehose, 1883.
Dupont, J. ΣΥΝ ΧΡΙΣΤΩΙ. *L'union avec le Christ suivant saint Paul*. Paris: Desclée, 1957.
Eichrodt, W. *Theology of the Old Testament*, vol. 2. The Old Testament Library. Philadelphia: Westminster, 1967.
Ellis, E. E. *Paul and His Recent Interpreters*. Grand Rapids: Eerdmans, 1961.
Evans, C. F. *Resurrection and the New Testament*. SBT 2/12. London: SCM, 1970.
Feuillet, A. 'La demeure céleste et la destinée des Chrétiens', *RSR* 44 (1956) 360–402.
Fiorenza, F. P., and Metz, J. B. 'Der Mensch als Einheit von Leib und Seele' in *Mysterium Salutis: Grundriss heilsgeschictlicher Dogmatik*, 584–636. Vol. 2 of J. Feiner and M. Löhrer (eds.), *Die Heilsgeschichte vor Christus*. Cologne: Benziger, 1965.
Flusser, D. 'The Dualism of Flesh and Spirit in the Dead Sea Scrolls', *Tarbiz* 27 (1958) 158–65.
Fraine, J. de. *Adam and the Family of Man*. Staten Island: Alba, 1965.

Grass, H. *Ostergeschehen und Osterberichte*. 2nd ed. Göttingen: Vandenhoeck & Ruprecht, 1962.

Grobel, K. 'Σῶμα as "Self, Person" in the LXX', *Neutestamentliche Studien für Rudolf Bultmann*, 52–9. BZNW 21. Berlin: Töpelmann, 1954.

Güttgemanns, E. *Der leidende Apostel und sein Herr*. FRLANT 90. Göttingen: Vandenhoeck & Ruprecht, 1966.

Hanhart, K. *The Intermediate State in the New Testament*. Franeker: Wever, 1966.

Harris, M. J. '2 Corinthians 5: 1–10: Watershed in Paul's Eschatology?', *Tyndale Bulletin* 22 (1971) 32–57.

Havet, J. 'La doctrine paulinienne du "Corps du Christ". Essai de mise au point', *Littérature et théologie pauliniennes*, 184–216. Paris: Desclée de Brouwer, 1960.

Heick, O. W. 'If a Man Die, Shall He Live Again?', *LQ* 17 (1965) 99–110.

Héring, J. 'Entre la mort et la résurrection', *RHPR* 40 (1960) 338–48.

Hick, R. I. 'Aesop and the Organic Analogy: The Body Political and the Body Ecclesiastical', *JBR* 31 (1963) 29–35.

Hirzel, R. 'Die Person: Begriff und Name derselben im Altertum', *Sitzungsberichte der Bayerischen Akademie der Wissenschaften der philosophisch-philologischen und historischen Klasse* 10 (1914) 1–54.

Hoffmann, P. *Die Toten in Christus*. Neutestamentliche Abhandlungen 2/2. Münster: Aschendorff, 1966.

Holsten, C. *Zum Evangelium des Paulus und des Petrus*. Rostock: Stiller, 1868.

Holtzmann, H. J. *Lehrbuch der Neutestamentlichen Theologie*, vol. 2. 2nd ed. Tubingen: Mohr, 1911.

Hughes, P. E. '[Review of] J. F. Collange, *Enigmes de la Deuxième Epître de Paul aux Corinthiens. Etude Exégétique de 2 Cor. 2: 14–7: 4*', *Westminster Theological Journal* 35 (1973) 345–7.

Jaeger, W. 'The Greek Ideas of Immortality' in K. Stendahl (ed.), *Immortality and Resurrection*, 97–114. New York: Macmillan, 1965.

Jeremias, J. ' "Flesh and Blood Cannot Inherit the Kingdom of God" [I Cor. xv. 50]', *NTS* 2 (1955/56) 151–9.

Jewett, R. *Paul's Anthropological Terms*. Arbeiten zur Geschichte des antiken Judentums und des Urchristentums 10. Leiden: Brill, 1971.

Johnson, A. R. *The One and the Many in the Israelite Conception of God*. Cardiff: University of Wales, 1961.

Johnson, A. R. *The Vitality of the Individual in the Thought of Ancient Israel*. 2nd ed. Cardiff: University of Wales, 1964.

Käsemann, E. 'Gottesdienst im Alltag der Welt (zu Rm 12)' in
W. Eltester (ed.), *Judentum, Urchristentum, Kirche. Festschrift für
Joachim Jeremias*, 165–71. 2nd ed. BZNW 26. Berlin: Töpelmann,
1964.

Käsemann, E. *Leib und Leib Christi*. Beiträge zur historischen
Theologie 9. Tübingen: Mohr, 1933.

Käsemann, E. *Perspectives on Paul*. Philadelphia:
Fortress, 1971.

Kempthorne, R. 'Incest and the Body of Christ: A Study of I Corinthians vi. 12–20', *NTS* 14 (1968) 568–74.

Knox, W. L. 'Parallels to the NT Use of σῶμα', *JTS* 39
(1938) 243–6.

Kuhn, K. G. 'New Light on Temptation, Sin, and Flesh in the
New Testament', in K. Stendahl (ed.), *The Scrolls and the
New Testament*, 94–113. New York: Harper, 1957.

Kümmel, W. G. *Man in the New Testament*. 2nd ed. London:
Epworth, 1963.

Kümmel, W. G. *Römer 7 und die Bekehrung des Paulus*. Untersuchungen
zum Neuen Testament 17. Leipzig: Hinrichs, 1929.

Lampe, G. W. H. 'Church Discipline and the Interpretation
of the Epistles to the Corinthians' in W. R. Farmer,
C. F. D. Moule, and R. R. Niebuhr (eds.), *Christian History
and Interpretation. Studies Presented to John Knox*, 337–61.
Cambridge University Press, 1967.

Leaney, A. R. C. 'The Doctrine of Man in 1 Corinthians', *SJT* 15
(1962) 394–9.

Léon-Dufour, X. 'Corps' in X. Léon-Dufour et al. (eds.),
Vocabulaire de Théologie Biblique, 162. Paris: Cerf, 1962.

Lüdemann, H. *Die Anthropologie des Apostels Paulus und ihre Stellung
innerhalb seiner Heilslehre*. Kiel: University, 1872.

Lys, D. *Nèphèsh*. Etudes d'histoire et de philosophie religieuses 50.
Paris: University of France, 1959.

Macquarrie, J. *An Existentialist Theology*. London: SCM, 1955.

Manson, T. W. 'A Parallel to a N.T. Use of σῶμα', *JTS* 37
(1936) 385.

Marshall, I. H. 'Uncomfortable Words. VI. "Fear him who
can destroy both soul and body in hell" [Mt 10 28 R.S.V.]',
ExpT 81 (1970) 276–80.

Martin-Achard, R. *From Death to Life*. Edinburgh:
Oliver & Boyd, 1960.

Marxsen, W. 'The Resurrection of Jesus as a Historical and
Theological Problem' in C. F. D. Moule (ed.),
*The Significance of the Message of the Resurrection for Faith in
Jesus Christ*, 15–50. SBT 2/8. London: SCM, 1968.

Meuzelaar, J. J. *Der Leib des Messias*. Van Gorcum's theologische Bibliothek 35. Assen: Van Gorcum, 1961.

Meyer, R. *Hellenistisches in der rabbinischen Anthropologie*. BWANT 4/2. Stuttgart: Kohlhammer, 1937.

Minear, P. S. *Images of the Church in the New Testament*. Philadelphia: Westminster, 1960.

Moule, C. F. D. 'St Paul and Dualism: The Pauline Conception of the Resurrection', *NTS* 12 (1966) 106–23.

Murphy, R. E. 'Bśr in the Qumran Literature and Sarks in the Epistle to the Romans', *Sacra Pagina* 2 (1959) 60–76.

Murtonen, A. *The Living Soul*. StudOr 23/1. Helsinki, 1958.

Mussner, F. *Christus das All und die Kirche*. Trier: Paulinus, 1955.

Neugebauer, F. 'Die hermeneutischen Voraussetzungen Rudolf Bultmanns in ihrem Verhältnis zur paulinischen Theologie', *Kerygma und Dogma* 5 (1959) 289–305.

Nickelsburg, G. W. E., Jnr. *Resurrection, Immortality, and Eternal Life in Intertestamental Judaism*. Harvard Theological Studies 26. Cambridge, Mass.: Harvard University Press, 1972.

Nikolainen, A. T. *Der Auferstehungsglauben in der Bibel und ihrer Umwelt*. Annales Academiae Scientiarum Fennicae XLIX, 3. Helsinkl: Finnische Literaturgesellschaft, 1944.

Onians, R. B. *The Origins of European Thought About the Body, the Mind, the Soul, the World, Time, and Fate*. 2nd ed. Cambridge University Press, 1954.

Owen, D. R. G. *Body and Soul*. Philadelphia: Westminster, 1956.

Pedersen, J. *Israel: Its Life and Culture I–II*. London: Oxford U.P., 1926.

Peel, M. L. 'Gnostic Eschatology and the New Testament', *NovT* 12 (1970) 141–65.

Percy, E. *Der Leib Christi*. Lunds Universitets Årsskrift, N.F. sect. 1, vol. 38, no. 1. Lund: Gleerup, 1942.

Peursen, C. A. van. *Body, Soul, Spirit: A Survey of the Body–Mind Problem*. London: Oxford U.P., 1966.

Pieper, J. 'Tod und Unsterblichkeit' in E. Schlink and H. Volk (eds.), *Pro Veritate. Festgabe für L. Jaeger und W. Stählin*, 274–93. Münster–Kassel: Aschendorff/Staude, 1963.

Ploeg, J. van der. 'The Belief in Immortality in the Writings of Qumran', *BO* 18 (1961) 118–24.

Proudfoot, C. M. 'Imitation or Realistic Participation?', *Int* 17 (1963) 140–60.

Reicke, B. 'Body and Soul in the New Testament', *ST* 19 (1965) 200–12.

Reuss, J. 'Die Kirche als "Leib Christi" und die Herkunft dieser Vorstellung bei dem Apostel Paulus', *BZ* N.S. 2 (1958) 103–27.

Rex, H. H. 'Immortality of the Soul, or Resurrection of the Body, or What?', *Reformed Theological Review* 17 (1958) 73–82.

Richards, G. C. 'Parallels to a N.T. Use of σῶμα', *JTS* 38 (1937) 165.

Robinson, H. W. *The Christian Doctrine of Man*. 2nd ed. Edinburgh: T. & T. Clark, 1913.

Robinson, H. W. 'Hebrew Psychology' in A. S. Peake (ed.), *The People and the Book*, 353–82. Oxford: Clarendon, 1925.

Robinson, H. W. 'Hebrew Psychology in Relation to Pauline Anthropology' in *Mansfield College Essays*, 265–86. London: Hodder & Stoughton, 1909.

Robinson, J. A. T. *The Body. A Study in Pauline Theology*. SBT 1/5. London: SCM, 1952.

Robinson, W. C., Jnr. 'The Bodily Resurrection of Christ', *TZ* 13 (1957) 81–101.

Rohde, E. *Psyche: The Cult of Souls and Belief in Immortality among the Greeks*. 2 vols. New York: Harper & Row, 1966.

Rosa, G. de. 'Immortalità dell'anima e rivelazione cristiana', *Divinitas* 4 (1960) 81–101.

Sand, A. *Der Begriff 'Fleisch' in den paulinischen Hauptbriefen*. Biblische Untersuchungen 2. Regensburg: Pustet, 1967.

Sander, O. 'Leib–Seele-Dualismus im Alten Testament?', *ZAW* 77 (1965) 329–32.

Schenke, H.-M. *Der Gott 'Mensch' in der Gnosis*. Göttingen: Vandenhoeck & Ruprecht, 1962.

Schep, J. A. *The Nature of the Resurrection Body*. Grand Rapids, Mich.: Eerdmans, 1964.

Schlier, H. *Christus und die Kirche im Epheserbrief*. Beiträge zur historischen Theologie 6. Tübingen: Mohr, 1930.

Schmid, J. 'Anthropologie, Biblische A.' in J. Höfer and K. Rahner (eds.), *Lexikon für Theologie und Kirche* 1, 604–15. 2nd ed. Freiburg: Herder, 1957.

Schmid, J. 'Der Begriff der Seele im Neuen Testament' in J. Ratzinger and H. Fries (eds.), *Einsicht und Glaube. Festschrift für G. Söhngen*, 128–47. 2nd ed. Freiburg: Herder, 1962.

Schmidt, T. *Der Leib Christi*. Leipzig: Deichert'sche, 1919.

Schnackenburg, R. *Man Before God: Toward a Theology of Man*. New York: Kenedy, 1966.

Schubert, K. 'Das Problem der Auferstehungshoffnung in den Qumrântexten und in der frührabbinischen Literatur', *Wissenschaftliche Zeitschrift der Königlichen Universität in München* 56 (1960) 154–67.

Schubert, K. 'Die Entwicklung der Auferstehungslehre von der nachexilischen bis zur frührabbinischen Zeit', *BZ* 6 (1962) 177–214.

Schunack, G. *Das hermeneutische Problem des Todes.*
Hermeneutische Untersuchungen zur Theologie 7. Tübingen:
Mohr, 1967.
Schütz, J. H. 'Apostolic Authority and the Control of Tradition:
I Cor. xv', *NTS* 15 (1969) 439–57.
Schweitzer, A. *The Mysticism of Paul the Apostle.* New York:
Holt, 1931.
Schweizer, E. 'Die Leiblichkeit des Menschen: Leben–Tod–
Auferstehung', *EvT* 29 (1969) 40–55.
Schweizer, E. 'πνεῦμα, πνευματικός', *TDNT* 6 (1968) 332–455.
Schweizer, E. 'σάρξ', *TDNT* 7 (1971) 98–151.
Schweizer, E. 'σῶμα κτλ.', *TDNT* 7 (1971) 1024–94.
Schweizer, E. *The Church as the Body of Christ.* Richmond:
Knox, 1964.
Schweizer, E. 'The Church as the Missionary Body of Christ',
NTS 8 (1961) 1–11.
Scroggs, R. *The Last Adam: A Study in Pauline Anthropology.*
Philadelphia: Fortress, 1966.
Sevenster, J. N. 'Die Anthropologie des Neuen Testaments'
in C. J. Bleeker (ed.), *Anthropologie Religieuse*, 166–77.
Studies in the History of Religions (Supplements to *Numen*) 2.
Leiden: Brill, 1955.
Shedd, R. P. *Man in Community.* London: Epworth, 1958.
Smith, C. R. *The Bible Doctrine of Man.* London: Epworth, 1951.
Soiron, T. *Die Kirche als Leib Christi.* Düsseldorf: Patmos, 1951.
Spicq, C. *Dieu et l'homme selon le Nouveau Testament.*
Lectio Divina 29. Paris: Cerf, 1961.
Stacey, W. D. 'Man as a Soul', *ExpT* 72 (1961) 349f.
Stacey, W. D. 'St Paul and the "Soul"', *ExpT* 66 (1955) 274–7.
Stacey, W. D. *The Pauline View of Man.* London: Macmillan, 1956.
Sutcliffe, E. F. *The Old Testament and the Future Life.*
The Bellarmine Series 8. London: Burns Oates &
Washbourne, 1946.
Torge, P. *Seelenglaube und Unsterblichkeit im Alten Testament.*
Leipzig: Hinrichs, 1909.
Tresmontant, C. *A Study of Hebrew Thought.* New York: Desclée,
1960.
Tromp, N. J. *Primitive Conceptions of Death and the Nether World in
the Old Testament.* BibOr 21. Rome: Biblical Institute Press, 1969.
Visscher, F. de. *Les édits d'Auguste découverts à Cyrène.* Louvain:
Bibliothèque de l'Université, 1940.
Vos, G. *The Pauline Eschatology.* Grand Rapids: Eerdmans, 1952.
Wendt, H. H. *Die Begriffe Fleisch und Geist im biblischen Sprachge-
brauch.* Gotha: Perthes, 1878.

Wibbing, S. 'Leib' in *Theologisches Begriffslexikon zum Neuen Testament*, 869–73. Wuppertal–Vohwinkel: Brockhaus, 1969.

Wikenhauser, A. *Die Kirche als der mystische Leib Christi nach dem Apostel Paulus.* 2nd ed. Münster, Westphalia: Aschendorff, 1940.

Wilson, J. H. 'The Corinthians Who Say There Is No Resurrection', *ZNW* 59 (1968) 90–107.

Wolfson, H. A. 'Immortality and Resurrection in the Philosophy of the Church Fathers' in K. Stendahl (ed.), *Immortality and Resurrection*, 54–96. New York: Macmillan, 1965.

Young, N. J. *History and Existential Theology.* Philadelphia: Westminster, 1969.

INDEX OF PASSAGES CITED

PAPYRI AND INSCRIPTIONS

APOCRYPHA AND PSEUDEPIGRAPHA

DEAD SEA SCROLLS AND RELATED TEXTS

Index of Passages

NEW TESTAMENT

PATRISTIC LITERATURE

INDEX OF AUTHORS